ABOUT THIS PUBLICATION

FOR SERVICE ASSISTANCE

Customer Service:
1.704.898.0770

North Carolina General Statues is published by The Muliti-Media Group of Greater Charlotte in Charlotte, North Carolina. Copyright 2015 by the Multi-Media Group of Greater Charlotte. This book or parts thereof may not be reproduced in any form, stored in a retrieval system, or transmitted in any form by any means—electronic, mechanical, photocopy, recording or otherwise—without prior written permission of the publisher, except as provided by United States of America copyright law.

The records required by U.S. Code 2257(a) through (c) and the pertinent regulations 28 C.F.R. Cli. 1, Part 75 with respect to this publication and all materials associated with such records are maintained by The Multi-Media Group of Greater Charlotte, Publisher and available for review by Attorney General.

www.visionbooks.org

Copyright © 2015 by MMGGC
All rights reserved!

TID: 5072103
ISBN (10) digit: 1502990334
ISBN (13) digit: 978-1502990334

123-4-56789-01239-Paperback
123-4-56789-01239-Hardback

First Edition

090520140547

Printed in the United States of America

2015 EDITION

# North Carolina Criminal Law And Procedure-Pamphlet # 64

## Printed In conjunction with the Administration of the Courts

North Carolina Criminal Law and Procedure
Pamphlet Reference Guide

| Chapters | Pamphlet |
|---|---|
| Chapter 1 Civil Procedure | 1 |
| Chapter 1 Civil Procedure (Continue) | 2 |
| Chapter 1A Rules of Civil Procedure | 2 |
| Chapter 1B Contribution. | 2 |
| Chapter 1C Enforcement of Judgments. | 2 |
| Chapter 1D Punitive Damages. | 2 |
| Chapter 1E Eastern Band of Cherokee Indians. | 2 |
| Chapter 1F North Carolina Uniform Interstate Depositions and Discovery Act. | 2 |
| Chapter 2 - Clerk of Superior Court [Repealed and Transferred.] | 3 |
| Chapter 3 - Commissioners of Affidavits and Deeds [Repealed.] | 3 |
| Chapter 4 - Common Law | 3 |
| Chapter 5 - Contempt [Repealed.] | 3 |
| Chapter 5A - Contempt | 3 |
| Chapter 6 - Liability for Court Costs | 3 |
| Chapter 7 - Courts [Repealed and Transferred.] | 3 |
| Chapter 7A – Judicial Department | 3 |
| Chapter 7A – Continuation (Judicial Department) | 4 |
| Chapter 7A – Continuation (Judicial Department) | 5 |
| Chapter 7B - Juvenile Code | 5 |
| Chapter 8 - Evidence | 6 |
| Chapter 8A - Interpreters for Deaf Persons [Recodified.] | 6 |
| Chapter 8B - Interpreters for Deaf Persons | 6 |
| Chapter 8C - Evidence Code | 6 |
| Chapter 9 - Jurors | 6 |
| Chapter 10 - Notaries [Repealed.] | 6 |
| Chapter 10A - Notaries [Recodified.] | 6 |
| Chapter 10B - Notaries | 6 |
| Chapter 11 - Oaths | 6 |
| Chapter 12 - Statutory Construction | 6 |
| Chapter 13 - Citizenship Restored | 6 |
| Chapter 14 - Criminal Law | 7 |
| Chapter 14 –Criminal Law (Continuation) | 8 |
| Chapter 15 - Criminal Procedure | 9 |
| Chapter 15A - Criminal Procedure Act (Continuation) | 10 |
| Chapter 15A - Criminal Procedure Act (Continuation) | 11 |
| Chapter 15B - Victims Compensation | 11 |
| Chapter 15C - Address Confidentiality Program | 11 |
| Chapter 16 - Gaming Contracts and Futures | 11 |
| Chapter 17 - Habeas Corpus | 11 |

| | |
|---|---|
| Chapter 17A - Law-Enforcement Officers [Recodified.] | 11 |
| Chapter 17B - North Carolina Criminal Justice Education and Training System [Recodified.] Chapter 17C - North Carolina Criminal Justice Education and Training Standards Commission | 11<br>11 |
| Chapter 17D - North Carolina Justice Academy | 11 |
| Chapter 17E - North Carolina Sheriffs' Education and Training Standards Commission | 11 |
| Chapter 18 - Regulation of Intoxicating Liquors [Repealed.] | 12 |
| Chapter 18A - Regulation of Intoxicating Liquors [Repealed.] | 12 |
| Chapter 18B - Regulation of Alcoholic Beverages | 12 |
| Chapter 18C - North Carolina State Lottery | 12 |
| Chapter 19 - Offenses against Public Morals | 12 |
| Chapter 19A - Protection of Animals | 12 |
| Chapter 20 - Motor Vehicles | 13 |
| Chapter 20 - Motor Vehicles (Continuation) | 14 |
| Chapter 20 - Motor Vehicles (Continuation) | 15 |
| Chapter 20 - Motor Vehicles (Continuation) | 16 |
| Chapter 21 - Bills of Lading | 17 |
| Chapter 22 - Contracts Requiring Writing | 17 |
| Chapter 22A - Signatures | 17 |
| Chapter 22B - Contracts Against Public Policy | 17 |
| Chapter 22C - Payments to Subcontractors | 17 |
| Chapter 23 - Debtor and Creditor | 17 |
| Chapter 24 – Interest | 17 |
| Chapter 25 – Uniform Commercial Code | 18 |
| Chapter 25 – Uniform Commercial Code (Continuation) | 19 |
| Chapter 25A – Retail Installment Sales Act | 20 |
| Chapter 25B - Credit | 20 |
| Chapter 25C - Sales of Artwork | 20 |
| Chapter 26 - Suretyship | 20 |
| Chapter 27 - Warehouse Receipts [Repealed.] | 20 |
| Chapter 28 - Administration [Repealed.] | 20 |
| Chapter 28A - Administration of Decedents' Estates | 20 |
| Chapter 28B - Estates of Absentees in Military Service | 20 |
| Chapter 28C - Estates of Missing Persons | 20 |
| Chapter 29 - Intestate Succession | 21 |
| Chapter 30 - Surviving Spouses | 21 |
| Chapter 31 - Wills | 21 |
| Chapter 31A - Acts Barring Property Rights | 21 |
| Chapter 31B - Renunciation of Property and Renunciation of Fiduciary Powers Act | 21 |
| Chapter 31C - Uniform Disposition of Community Property Rights at Death Act | 21 |
| Chapter 32 - Fiduciaries | 21 |
| Chapter 32A - Powers of Attorney | 21 |
| Chapter 33 - Guardian and Ward [Repealed and Recodified.] | 21 |

| | |
|---|---|
| Chapter 33A - North Carolina Uniform Transfers to Minors Act | 21 |
| Chapter 33B - North Carolina Uniform Custodial Trust Act | 21 |
| Chapter 34 - Veterans' Guardianship Act | 22 |
| Chapter 35 - Sterilization Procedures | 22 |
| Chapter 35A - Incompetency and Guardianship | 22 |
| Chapter 36 - Trusts and Trustees [Repealed.] | 22 |
| Chapter 36A - Trusts and Trustees | 22 |
| Chapter 36B - Uniform Management of Institutional Funds Act [Repealed.] | 22 |
| Chapter 36C - North Carolina Uniform Trust Code | 22 |
| Chapter 36D - North Carolina Community Third Party Trusts, Pooled Trusts | 23 |
| Chapter 36E - Uniform Prudent Management of Institutional Funds Act | 23 |
| Chapter 37 - Allocation of Principal and Income [Repealed.] | 23 |
| Chapter 37A - Uniform Principal and Income Act | 23 |
| Chapter 38 - Boundaries | 23 |
| Chapter 38A - Landowner Liability | 23 |
| Chapter 39 - Conveyances | 23 |
| Chapter 39A - Transfer Fee Covenants Prohibited | 23 |
| Chapter 40 - Eminent Domain [Repealed.] | 23 |
| Chapter 40A - Eminent Domain | 23 |
| Chapter 41 - Estates | 23 |
| Chapter 41A - State Fair Housing Act | 23 |
| Chapter 42 - Landlord and Tenant | 23 |
| Chapter 42A - Vacation Rental Act | 23 |
| Chapter 43 - Land Registration | 23 |
| Chapter 44 - Liens | 24 |
| Chapter 44A - Statutory Liens and Charges | 24 |
| Chapter 45 - Mortgages and Deeds of Trust | 24 |
| Chapter 45A - Good Funds Settlement Act | 24 |
| Chapter 46 - Partition | 24 |
| Chapter 47 - Probate and Registration | 25 |
| Chapter 47A - Unit Ownership | 25 |
| Chapter 47B - Real Property Marketable Title Act | 25 |
| Chapter 47C - North Carolina Condominium Act | 25 |
| Chapter 47D - Notice of Settlement Act [Expired.] | 25 |
| Chapter 47E - Residential Property Disclosure Act | 25 |
| Chapter 47F - North Carolina Planned Community Act | 25 |
| Chapter 47G - Option to Purchase Contracts | 25 |
| Chapter 47H - Contracts for Deed | 25 |
| Chapter 48 - Adoptions + | 26 |
| Chapter 48A - Minors | 26 |
| Chapter 49 - Bastardy | 26 |
| Chapter 49A - Rights of Children | 26 |
| Chapter 50 - Divorce and Alimony | 26 |
| Chapter 50A - Uniform Child-Custody Jurisdiction and | |

| | |
|---|---|
| Enforcement Act | 26 |
| Chapter 50B - Domestic Violence | 26 |
| Chapter 50C - Civil No-Contact Orders | 26 |
| Chapter 51 - Marriage | 26 |
| Chapter 52 - Powers and Liabilities of Married Persons | 27 |
| Chapter 52A - Uniform Reciprocal Enforcement of Support Act [Repealed.] | 27 |
| Chapter 52B - Uniform Premarital Agreement Act | 27 |
| Chapter 52C - Uniform Interstate Family Support Act | 27 |
| Chapter 53 - Banks | 27 |
| Chapter 53A - Business Development Corporations and North Carolina Capital Resource Corporations | 28 |
| Chapter 53B - Financial Privacy Act | 28 |
| Chapter 54 - Cooperative Organizations | 28 |
| Chapter 54A - Capital Stock Savings and Loan Associations [Repealed.] | 28 |
| Chapter 54B - Savings and Loan Associations | 29 |
| Chapter 54C - Savings Banks | 29 |
| Chapter 55 - North Carolina Business Corporation Act | 30 |
| Chapter 55A - North Carolina Nonprofit Corporation Act | 31 |
| Chapter 55B - Professional Corporation Act | 31 |
| Chapter 55C - Foreign Trade Zones | 31 |
| Chapter 55D - Filings, Names, and Registered Agents for Corporations, Nonprofit Corporations, and Partnerships | 31 |
| Chapter 56 - Electric, Telegraph and Power Companies [Repealed.] | 31 |
| Chapter 57 - Hospital, Medical and Dental Service Corporations [Recodified.] | 31 |
| Chapter 57A - Health Maintenance Organization Act [Recodified.] | 31 |
| Chapter 57B - Health Maintenance Organization Act [Recodified.] | 31 |
| Chapter 57C - North Carolina Limited Liability Company Act. | 31 |
| Chapter 58 - Insurance. | 32 |
| Chapter 58 - Insurance (Continuation) | 33 |
| Chapter 58 - Insurance (Continuation) | 34 |
| Chapter 58 - Insurance (Continuation) | 35 |
| Chapter 58 - Insurance (Continuation) | 36 |
| Chapter 58 - Insurance (Continuation) | 37 |
| Chapter 58 - Insurance (Continuation) | 38 |
| Chapter 58A - North Carolina Health Insurance Trust Commission [Recodified.] | 38 |
| Chapter 59 - Partnership. | 39 |
| Chapter 59B - Uniform Unincorporated Nonprofit Association Act. | 39 |
| Chapter 60 - Railroads and Other Carriers [Repealed and Transferred.] | 39 |
| Chapter 61 - Religious Societies | 39 |
| Chapter 62 - Public Utilities | 39 |

| | |
|---|---|
| Chapter 62 - Public Utilities (Continuation) | 40 |
| Chapter 62A - Public Safety Telephone Service And Wireless Telephone Service | 40 |
| Chapter 63 - Aeronautics | 40 |
| Chapter 63A - North Carolina Global TransPark Authority | 40 |
| Chapter 64 - Aliens | 40 |
| Chapter 65 – Cemeteries | 40 |
| Chapter 66 - Commerce and Business | 41 |
| Chapter 67 - Dogs | 41 |
| Chapter 68 - Fences and Stock Law | 41 |
| Chapter 69 - Fire Protection | 41 |
| Chapter 70 - Indian Antiquities, Archaeological Resources and Unmarked Human Skeletal Remains Protection | 42 |
| Chapter 71 - Indians [Repealed.] | 42 |
| Chapter 71A - Indians | 42 |
| Chapter 72 - Inns, Hotels and Restaurants | 42 |
| Chapter 73 - Mills | 42 |
| Chapter 74 - Mines and Quarries | 42 |
| Chapter 74A - Company Police [Repealed.] | 42 |
| Chapter 74B - Private Protective Services Act [Repealed.] | 42 |
| Chapter 74C - Private Protective Services | 42 |
| Chapter 74D - Alarm Systems | 42 |
| Chapter 74E - Company Police Act | 42 |
| Chapter 74F - Locksmith Licensing Act | 42 |
| Chapter 74G - Campus Police Act | 42 |
| Chapter 75 - Monopolies, Trusts and Consumer Protection | 42 |
| Chapter 75A - Boating and Water Safety | 43 |
| Chapter 75B - Discrimination in Business | 43 |
| Chapter 75C - Motion Picture Fair Competition Act | 43 |
| Chapter 75D - Racketeer Influenced and Corrupt Organizations | 43 |
| Chapter 75E - Unlawful Activities in Connection With Certain Corporate Transactions | 43 |
| Chapter 76 - Navigation | 43 |
| Chapter 76A - Navigation and Pilotage Commissions | 43 |
| Chapter 77 - Rivers, Creeks, and Coastal Waters | 43 |
| Chapter 78 - Securities Law [Repealed.] | 43 |
| Chapter 78A - North Carolina Securities Act | 43 |
| Chapter 78B - Tender Offer Disclosure Act [Repealed.] | 43 |
| Chapter 78C - Investment Advisers | 43 |
| Chapter 78D - Commodities Act | 43 |
| Chapter 79 - Strays [Repealed.] | 43 |
| Chapter 80 - Trademarks, Brands, etc. | 44 |
| Chapter 81 - Weights and Measures [Recodified.] | 44 |
| Chapter 81A - Weights and Measures Act of 1975. | 44 |
| Chapter 82 - Wrecks [Repealed.] | 44 |
| Chapter 83 - Architects [Recodified.] | 44 |

| | |
|---|---|
| Chapter 83A - Architects | 44 |
| Chapter 84 - Attorneys-at-Law | 44 |
| Chapter 84A - Foreign Legal Consultants | 44 |
| Chapter 85 - Auctions and Auctioneers [Repealed.] | 44 |
| Chapter 85A - Bail Bondsmen and Runners [Recodified.] | 44 |
| Chapter 85B - Auctions and Auctioneers | 44 |
| Chapter 85C - Bail Bondsmen and Runners [Recodified.] | 44 |
| Chapter 86 - Barbers [Recodified.] | 44 |
| Chapter 86A - Barbers | 44 |
| Chapter 87 - Contractors | 44 |
| Chapter 88 - Cosmetic Art [Repealed.] | 44 |
| Chapter 88A - Electrolysis Practice Act | 44 |
| Chapter 88B - Cosmetic Art | 45 |
| Chapter 89 - Engineering and Land Surveying [Recodified.] | 45 |
| Chapter 89A - Landscape Architects | 45 |
| Chapter 89B - Foresters | 45 |
| Chapter 89C - Engineering and Land Surveying | 45 |
| Chapter 89D - Landscape Contractors | 45 |
| Chapter 89E - Geologists Licensing Act | 45 |
| Chapter 89F - North Carolina Soil Scientist Licensing Act | 45 |
| Chapter 89G - Irrigation Contractors | 45 |
| Chapter 90 - Medicine and Allied Occupations | 45 |
| Chapter 90 - Medicine and Allied Occupations (Continuation) | 46 |
| Chapter 90 - Medicine and Allied Occupations (Continuation) | 47 |
| Chapter 90 - Medicine and Allied Occupations (Continuation) | 48 |
| Chapter 90A - Sanitarians and Water and Wastewater Treatment Facility Operators | 48 |
| Chapter 90B - Social Worker Certification and Licensure Act | 48 |
| Chapter 90C - North Carolina Recreational Therapy Licensure Act | 48 |
| Chapter 90D - Interpreters and Transliterators | 48 |
| Chapter 91 - Pawnbrokers [Repealed.] | 48 |
| Chapter 91A - Pawnbrokers Modernization Act of 1989 | 48 |
| Chapter 92 - Photographers [Deleted.] | 48 |
| Chapter 93 - Certified Public Accountants | 48 |
| Chapter 93A - Real Estate License Law | 49 |
| Chapter 93B - Occupational Licensing Boards | 49 |
| Chapter 93C - Watchmakers [Repealed.] | 49 |
| Chapter 93D - North Carolina State Hearing Aid Dealers and Fitters Board. | 49 |
| Chapter 93E - North Carolina Appraisers Act | 49 |
| Chapter 94 - Apprenticeship | 49 |
| Chapter 95 - Department of Labor and Labor Regulations | 49 |
| Chapter 95 - Department of Labor and Labor Regulations (Continuation) | 50 |
| Chapter 96 - Employment Security | 50 |
| Chapter 97 - Workers' Compensation Act | 50 |
| Chapter 97 - Workers' Compensation Act (Continuation) | 51 |

| | |
|---|---|
| Chapter 98 - Burnt and Lost Records | 51 |
| Chapter 99 - Libel and Slander | 51 |
| Chapter 99A - Civil Remedies for Criminal Actions | 51 |
| Chapter 99B - Products Liability | 51 |
| Chapter 99C - Actions Relating to Winter Sports Safety and Accidents | 51 |
| Chapter 99D - Civil Rights | 51 |
| Chapter 99E - Special Liability Provisions | 51 |
| Chapter 100 - Monuments, Memorials and Parks | 51 |
| Chapter 101 - Names of Persons | 51 |
| Chapter 102 - Official Survey Base | 51 |
| Chapter 103 - Sundays, Holidays and Special Days | 51 |
| Chapter 104 - United States Lands | 51 |
| Chapter 104A - Degrees of Kinship | 51 |
| Chapter 104B - Hurricanes or Other Acts of Nature | 51 |
| Chapter 104C - Atomic Energy, Radioactivity and Ionizing Radiation [Repealed and Recodified.] | 51 |
| Chapter 104D - Southern States Energy Compact | 51 |
| Chapter 104E - North Carolina Radiation Protection Act | 51 |
| Chapter 104F - Southeast Interstate Low-Level Radioactive Waste Management Compact [Repealed] | 51 |
| Chapter 104G - North Carolina Low-Level Radioactive Waste Management Authority Act of 1987 [Repealed] | 51 |
| Chapter 105 - Taxation | 51 |
| Chapter 105 - Taxation (Continuation) | 52 |
| Chapter 105 - Taxation (Continuation) | 53 |
| Chapter 105 - Taxation (Continuation) | 54 |
| Chapter 105A - Setoff Debt Collection Act | 55 |
| Chapter 105B - Defaulted Student Loan Recovery Act | 55 |
| Chapter 106 - Agriculture | 55 |
| Chapter 106 - Agriculture (Continue) | 56 |
| Chapter 106 - Agriculture (Continue) | 57 |
| Chapter 107 - Agricultural Development Districts [Repealed.] | 57 |
| Chapter 108 - Social Services [Repealed and Recodified.] | 57 |
| Chapter 108A - Social Services | 57 |
| Chapter 108B - Community Action Programs | 58 |
| Chapter 108C Medicaid and Health Choice Provider Requirements. | 58 |
| Chapter 108D Medicaid Managed Care for Behavioral Health Services. | 58 |
| Chapter 109 - Bonds [Recodified.] | 58 |
| Chapter 110 - Child Welfare | 58 |
| Chapter 111 - Aid to the Blind | 58 |
| Chapter 112 - Confederate Homes and Pensions [Repealed.] | 58 |
| Chapter 113 - Conservation and Development | 58 |
| Chapter 113 - Conservation and Development (Continuation) | 59 |

| | |
|---|---|
| Chapter 113A - Pollution Control and Environment | 59 |
| Chapter 113A - Pollution Control and Environment (Continuation) | 60 |
| Chapter 113B - North Carolina Energy Policy Act of 1975 | 60 |
| Chapter 114 - Department of Justice | 60 |
| Chapter 115 - Elementary and Secondary Education [Repealed.] | 60 |
| Chapter 115A - Community Colleges, Technical Institutes, and Industrial Education Centers [Repealed.] | 60 |
| Chapter 115B - Tuition and Fee Waivers | 60 |
| Chapter 115C - Elementary and Secondary Education | 60 |
| Chapter 115C - Elementary and Secondary Education (Continuation) | 61 |
| Chapter 115C - Elementary and Secondary Education (Continuation) | 62 |
| Chapter 115C - Elementary and Secondary Education (Continuation) | 63 |
| Chapter 115D - Community Colleges | 63 |
| Chapter 115E - Private Educational Facilities Finance Act [Recodified] | 63 |
| Chapter 116 - Higher Education | 63 |
| Chapter 116 - Higher Education (Continuation) | 64 |
| Chapter 116A - Escheats and Abandoned Property [Repealed.] | 64 |
| Chapter 116B - Escheats and Abandoned Property | 64 |
| Chapter 116C - Continuum of Education Programs | 64 |
| Chapter 116D - Higher Education Bonds | 64 |
| Chapter 116E - Education Longitudinal Data System | 64 |
| Chapter 117 - Electrification | 64 |
| Chapter 118 - Firemen's and Rescue Squad Workers' Relief and Pension Funds [Recodified.] | 64 |
| Chapter 118A - Firemen's Death Benefit Act [Repealed.] | 64 |
| Chapter 118B - Members of a Rescue Squad Death Benefit Act [Repealed.] | 64 |
| Chapter 119 - Gasoline and Oil Inspection and Regulation | 64 |
| Chapter 120 - General Assembly | 65 |
| Chapter 120 - General Assembly (Continuation) | 66 |
| Chapter 120 - General Assembly (Continuation) | 67 |
| Chapter 120C - Lobbying | 67 |
| Chapter 121 - Archives and History | 67 |
| Chapter 122 - Hospitals for the Mentally Disordered [Repealed.] | 67 |
| Chapter 122A - North Carolina Housing Finance Agency | 67 |
| Chapter 122B - North Carolina Agricultural Facilities Finance Act [Repealed.] | 67 |
| Chapter 122C - Mental Health, Developmental Disabilities, and Substance Abuse Act of 1985 | 67 |
| Chapter 122C - Mental Health, Developmental Disabilities, and Substance Abuse Act of 1985 (Continuation) | 68 |

| | |
|---|---|
| Chapter 122D - North Carolina Agricultural Finance Act | 68 |
| Chapter 122E - North Carolina Housing Trust and Oil Overcharge Act | 68 |
| Chapter 123 - Impeachment | 69 |
| Chapter 123A - Industrial Development [Repealed.] | 69 |
| Chapter 124 - Internal Improvements | 69 |
| Chapter 125 - Libraries | 69 |
| Chapter 126 - State Personnel System | 69 |
| Chapter 127 - Militia [Repealed.] | 69 |
| Chapter 127A - Militia | 69 |
| Chapter 127B - Military Affairs | 69 |
| Chapter 127C - Advisory Commission on Military Affairs | 69 |
| Chapter 128 - Offices and Public Officers | 69 |
| Chapter 128 - Offices and Public Officers (Continuation) | 70 |
| Chapter 129 - Public Buildings and Grounds | 70 |
| Chapter 130 - Public Health [Repealed.] | 70 |
| Chapter 130A - Public Health | 70 |
| Chapter 130A - Public Health (Continuation) | 71 |
| Chapter 130A - Public Health (Continuation) | 72 |
| Chapter 130B - Hazardous Waste Management Commission [Repealed.] | 72 |
| Chapter 131 - Public Hospitals [Repealed.] | 72 |
| Chapter 131A - Health Care Facilities Finance Act | 72 |
| Chapter 131B - Licensing of Ambulatory Surgical Facilities [Repealed.] | 72 |
| Chapter 131C - Charitable Solicitation Licensure Act [Repealed.] | 72 |
| Chapter 131D - Inspection and Licensing of Facilities | 72 |
| Chapter 131E - Health Care Facilities and Services | 72 |
| Chapter 131E - Health Care Facilities and Services (Continuation) | 73 |
| Chapter 131F - Solicitation of Contributions | 73 |
| Chapter 132 - Public Records | 73 |
| Chapter 133 - Public Works | 74 |
| Chapter 134 - Youth Development [Recodified.] | 74 |
| Chapter 134A - Youth Services [Repealed.] | 74 |
| Chapter 135 - Retirement System for Teachers and State Employees; Social Security; Health Insurance Program for Children | 74 |
| Chapter 135 - Retirement System for Teachers and State Employees; Social Security; Health Insurance Program for Children | 75 |
| Chapter 136 - Transportation | 75 |
| Chapter 136 - Transportation (Continuation) | 76 |
| Chapter 137 - Rural Rehabilitation [Repealed.] | 76 |
| Chapter 138 - Salaries, Fees and Allowances | 76 |
| Chapter 138A - State Government Ethics Act | 76 |

| | |
|---|---|
| Chapter 139 - Soil and Water Conservation Districts | 76 |
| Chapter 140 - State Art Museum; Symphony and Art Societies | 76 |
| Chapter 140A - State Awards System | 76 |
| Chapter 141 - State Boundaries | 76 |
| Chapter 142 - State Debt | 76 |
| Chapter 143 - State Departments, Institutions, and Commissions | 77 |
| Chapter 143 - State Departments, Institutions, and Commissions (Continuation) | 78 |
| Chapter 143 - State Departments, Institutions, and Commissions (Continuation) | 79 |
| Chapter 143 - State Departments, Institutions, and Commissions (Continuation) | 80 |
| Chapter 143A - State Government Reorganization | 80 |
| Chapter 143B - Executive Organization Act of 1973 | 80 |
| Chapter 143B - Executive Organization Act of 1973 (Continuation) | 81 |
| Chapter 143B - Executive Organization Act of 1973 (Continuation) | 82 |
| Chapter 143C - State Budget Act | 83 |
| Chapter 143D - The State Governmental Accountability and Internal Control Act | 83 |
| Chapter 144 - State Flag, Official Governmental Flags, Motto, and Colors | 83 |
| Chapter 145 - State Symbols and Other Official Adoptions. | 83 |
| Chapter 146 - State Lands | 83 |
| Chapter 147 - State Officers | 83 |
| Chapter 148 - State Prison System | 84 |
| Chapter 149 - State Song and Toast | 84 |
| Chapter 150 - Uniform Revocation of Licenses [Repealed.] | 84 |
| Chapter 150A - Administrative Procedure Act [Recodified.] | 84 |
| Chapter 150B - Administrative Procedure Act | 84 |
| Chapter 151 - Constables [Repealed.] | 84 |
| Chapter 152 - Coroners | 84 |
| Chapter 152A - County Medical Examiner [Repealed.] | 84 |
| Chapter 152A - County Medical Examiner [Repealed.] (Continuation) | 85 |
| Chapter 153 - Counties and County Commissioners [Repealed.] | 85 |
| Chapter 153A - Counties | 85 |
| Chapter 153B - Mountain Resources Planning Act | 85 |
| Chapter 153C - Uwharrie Regional Resources Act | 85 |
| Chapter 154 - County Surveyor [Repealed.] | 85 |
| Chapter 155 - County Treasurer [Repealed.] | 85 |
| Chapter 156 - Drainage | 85 |

| | |
|---|---|
| Chapter 156 – Drainage (Continuation) | 86 |
| Chapter 157 - Housing Authorities and Projects | 86 |
| Chapter 157A - Historic Properties Commissions [Transferred.] | 86 |
| Chapter 158 - Local Development | 86 |
| Chapter 159 - Local Government Finance | 86 |
| Chapter 159 - Local Government Finance (Continuation) | 87 |
| Chapter 159A - Pollution Abatement and Industrial Facilities Financing Act [Unconstitutional.] | 87 |
| Chapter 159B - Joint Municipal Electric Power and Energy Act | 87 |
| Chapter 159C - Industrial and Pollution Control Facilities Financing Act | 87 |
| Chapter 159D - The North Carolina Capital Facilities Financing Act | 87 |
| Chapter 159E - Registered Public Obligations Act | 87 |
| Chapter 159F - North Carolina Energy Development Authority [Repealed.] | 87 |
| Chapter 159G - Water Infrastructure | 87 |
| Chapter 159H - [Reserved.] | 87 |
| Chapter 159I - Solid Waste Management Loan Program and Local Government Special Obligation Bonds | 87 |
| Chapter 160 - Municipal Corporations [Repealed And Transferred.] | 87 |
| Chapter 160A - Cities and Towns | 88 |
| Chapter 160A - Cities and Towns (Continuation) | 89 |
| Chapter 160B - Consolidated City-County Act | 89 |
| Chapter 160C - Baseball Park Districts [Repealed.] | 90 |
| Chapter 161 - Register of Deeds | 90 |
| Chapter 162 - Sheriff | 90 |
| Chapter 162A - Water and Sewer Systems | 90 |
| Chapter 162B Continuity of Local Government in Emergency. | 90 |
| Chapter 163 Elections and Election Laws. | 90 |
| Chapter 163 Elections and Election Laws. (Continuation) | 91 |
| Chapter 164 Concerning the General Statutes of North Carolina. | 92 |
| Chapter 165 Veterans. | 92 |
| Chapter 166 Civil Preparedness Agencies [Repealed.] | 92 |
| Chapter 166A North Carolina Emergency Management Act. | 92 |
| Chapter 167 State Civil Air Patrol [Repealed.] | 92 |
| Chapter 168 Persons with Disabilities. | 92 |
| Chapter 168A Persons With Disabilities Protection Act. | 92 |

§ 116-44.5. Special provisions applicable to identified constituent institutions of the University of North Carolina.

In addition to the powers granted by G.S. 116-44.4, the board of trustees of each of the constituent institutions enumerated hereinafter shall have the additional powers prescribed:

(1) The Board of Trustees of the University of North Carolina at Chapel Hill may by ordinance prohibit, regulate, and limit the parking of motor vehicles on those portions of the following public streets in the Town of Chapel Hill where parking is not prohibited by an ordinance of the Town of Chapel Hill:

a. Battle Lane;

b. Country Club Road, between Raleigh Street and South Road;

c. Manning Drive;

d. McCauley Street, between Columbia Street and Pittsboro Street;

e. Pittsboro Street, between South Columbia Street and Cameron Avenue;

f. Boundary Street, between Country Club Road and East Franklin Street;

g. Park Place, between Boundary Street and East Franklin Street;

h. South Columbia Street, between Franklin Street and Manning Drive;

i. Cameron Avenue, between South Columbia Street and Raleigh Street;

j. Raleigh Street;

k. Ridge Road;

l. South Road, between Columbia Street and Country Club Road.

In addition, the Board of Trustees of the University of North Carolina at Chapel Hill may regulate traffic on Cameron Avenue, between Raleigh Street and South Columbia Street, and on Raleigh Street, in any manner not inconsistent with ordinances of the Town of Chapel Hill.

(2) The Board of Trustees of Appalachian State University may by ordinance prohibit, regulate, and limit the parking of motor vehicles on those portions of the following public streets in the Town of Boone where parking is not prohibited by an ordinance of the Town of Boone:

a. Rivers Street, between U.S. 221-U.S. 321 (Hardin Street) and Water Street;

b. Stadium Drive, between Rivers Street and Hemlock Drive;

c. College Street, to the extent that it is bounded on both sides by the university campus;

d. Appalachian Street, between Locust Street and Howard Street;

e. Brown Street, between Locust Street and Howard Street;

f. Hill Street, only on the half of Hill Street bounded by the university campus;

g. Stansberry Circle, from Holmes Drive to the end of Stansberry Circle;

h. Locust Street, from U.S. 221-U.S. 321 (Hardin Street) to the end of Locust Street; and

i. Dale Street, from State Farm Road to the end of Dale Street.

(3) The Board of Trustees of the University of North Carolina at Charlotte may by ordinance prohibit, regulate, and limit the parking of motor vehicles on those portions of the following public roads in the County of Mecklenburg where parking is not prohibited by ordinance or other source of legal regulation of the County of Mecklenburg or other governmental entity with jurisdiction to regulate parking on such public road:

a. Mary Alexander Boulevard (State Road No. 2834), between its intersection with N.C. Highway 49 and its intersection with Mallard Creek Church Road.

In addition, the Board of Trustees of the University of North Carolina at Charlotte may regulate traffic on Mary Alexander Boulevard (State Road No. 2834), between its intersection with N.C. Highway 49 and its intersection with Mallard

Creek Church Road, in any manner not inconsistent with any ordinances or other sources of legal regulation of the County of Mecklenburg or other governmental entity with jurisdiction to regulate traffic on such public road.

(3a) The Board of Trustees of the University of North Carolina at Wilmington may by ordinance prohibit, regulate, and limit the parking of motor vehicles on those portions of the following public streets in the City of Wilmington where parking is not prohibited by an ordinance of the City of Wilmington:

a. "H" Street.

(3b) The Board of Trustees of the University of North Carolina at Greensboro may by ordinance prohibit, regulate, and limit the parking of motor vehicles for those portions of any of the following public streets in the City of Greensboro where parking is not prohibited by an ordinance of the City of Greensboro:

a. Forest Street between Oakland Avenue and Spring Garden Street.

b. Highland Avenue between Oakland Avenue and Spring Garden Street.

c. Jefferson Street between Spring Garden Street and the Walker/Aycock parking lot.

d. Kenilworth Street between Oakland Avenue and Walker Avenue.

e. McIver Street between Walker Avenue and West Market Street.

f. Stirling Street between Oakland Avenue and Walker Avenue.

g. Theta Street between Kenilworth Street and Stirling Street.

h. Walker Avenue between Aycock Street and Jackson Library and between Tate Street and McIver Street.

(3c) The Board of Trustees of North Carolina Agricultural and Technical State University may by ordinance prohibit, regulate, and limit the parking of motor vehicles on those portions of the following streets in the City of Greensboro where parking is not prohibited by an ordinance of the City of Greensboro:

a. Dudley Street between Market Street and Bluford Street.

b.  Bluford Street between Regan Street and Luther Street.

c.  Laurel Street between Lindsay Street and East Market Street.

d.  Benbow Road between Sullivan Street and East Market Street.

e.  Sullivan Street between O'Henry Boulevard overpass and Lindsay Street.

f.  Beech Street between Bluford Street and Lindsay Street.

g.  Obermeyer Street between Bluford Street and Market Street.

h.  Daniel Street between Bluford Street and Market Street.

i.  Nocho Street between Bluford Street and Market Street.

In addition, the Board of Trustees of North Carolina A&T State University may regulate traffic on the following streets for the portion of those streets that abut the university: Benbow Road, Dudley Street, Lindsay Street, and Market Street, provided that the regulation is not inconsistent with ordinances of the City of Greensboro.

(4)  This section does not diminish the authority of any affected municipality, county or other governmental entity to prohibit parking on any public street or road listed herein. It is intended only to authorize the respective boards of trustees of the constituent institutions identified hereinabove to further prohibit, regulate, and limit parking on certain public streets and roads running through or adjacent to the campuses of the constituent institutions where parking is not prohibited by ordinance or other law of any affected municipality, county or other governmental entity. When an ordinance or other law of an affected municipality, county or other governmental entity is adopted to prohibit parking on any portion of any public street or road then regulated by an ordinance of a board of trustees, the ordinance of the board of trustees is superseded and the University, upon request of the municipality, county or other governmental entity, shall immediately remove any signs, devices, or markings erected or placed by the University on that portion of the street or road pursuant to the superseded ordinance. (1973, c. 495, s. 1; 1979, c. 238; 2001-170, s. 1; 2003-213, s. 1; 2005-165, s. 1.)

Part 7. Fire Safety.

§ 116-44.6. Definitions.

Unless the context clearly requires another meaning, the following definitions apply in this Part:

(1)     Fraternity or sorority. - A social, professional, or educational incorporated organization that, by official recognition, is affiliated or identified with a public or nonpublic institution of higher education in this State and which maintains a living facility that provides accommodations for five or more students enrolled at the recognition-granting institution of higher education.

(2)     Fund. - The Fire Safety Loan Fund authorized by this Part.

(3)     Living facility. - A sleeping facility capable of overnight accommodation and other capabilities which support continuous occupancy.

(4)     Residence hall. - A living facility maintained by a public or nonpublic institution of higher education in North Carolina or by the North Carolina School of Science and Mathematics for use by enrolled students.

(5)     Supplemental fire safety protection system. - A water system capability which is sized to accommodate the added water supply pressure and volume required for building fire protection.

(6)     Water system. -

a.     A city, county, or sanitary district; or

b.     A water and sewer authority, a metropolitan water district, or county water and sewer district, established pursuant to Chapter 162A of the General Statutes. (1996, 2nd Ex. Sess., c. 18, s. 16.5(a).)


§ 116-44.7. Exemption from certain fees and charges.

No water system serving a residence hall or fraternity or sorority housing shall levy or collect any water-meter fee, water-hydrant fee, tap fee, or similar service fee on a residence hall or fraternity or sorority house with respect to supporting a supplemental fire safety protection system in excess of the marginal cost to the water system to support the fire safety protection system. (1996, 2nd Ex. Sess., c. 18, s. 16.5(a); 1997-443, s. 10.14.)

§ 116-44.8. Fire Safety Loan Fund.

(a) There is established the Fire Safety Loan Fund. The Fund shall be a revolving loan fund for installing fire safety equipment and systems in fraternity and sorority housing.

(b) The Fund shall be administered by the Office of the State Treasurer, and that office may establish the policies and procedures that it deems appropriate for the operation of the Fund. The Office of the State Treasurer may enlist the assistance of other State departments or entities which have expertise that would be useful in administering the Fund, and those State departments or entities shall provide the assistance requested.

(c) The Fund shall be operated on a revolving basis with proceeds from the repayment of prior loans being made available for subsequent loans.

(d) Loans from the Fund shall be secured by a first or second mortgage or other pledge. Loans shall be made for a period not to exceed 10 years. Interest shall not be charged on loans from the Fund. (1996, 2nd Ex. Sess., c. 18, s. 16.5(a).)

§ 116-44.9. Reserved for future codification purposes.

Article 1A.

Regional Universities.

§§ 116-44.10 through 116-44.16: Repealed by Session Laws 1971, c. 1244, s. 1.

Article 2.

Western Carolina University, East Carolina University, Appalachian State University, North Carolina Agricultural and Technical State University.

§ 116-45: Repealed by Session Laws 1971, c. 1244, s. 1.

§ 116-45.1. Repealed by Session Laws 1969, c. 801, s. 7.

§ 116-45.2. Repealed by Session Laws 1969, c. 297, s. 6.

§ 116-46. Repealed by Session Laws 1971, c. 1244, s. 1.

§ 116-46.1. Transferred to § 116-42.1 by Session Laws 1971, c. 1244, s. 11.

§ 116-46.1A. Transferred to § 116-42.2 by Session Laws 1971, c. 1244, s. 11.

§ 116-46.1B. Transferred to § 116-42.3 by Session Laws 1971, c. 1244, s. 11.

§ 116-46.2. Transferred to § 116-17 by Session Laws 1971, c. 1244, s. 3.

§§ 116-46.3 through 116-46.4: Transferred to §§ 116-40.3 and 116-40.4 by Session Laws 1971, c. 1244, s. 10.

Article 3.

Community Colleges.

§§ 116-47 through 116-62.1: Repealed by Session Laws 1991, c. 542, s. 2.

Article 4.

North Carolina School of the Arts.

§ 116-63. Policy.

It is hereby declared to be the policy of the State to foster, encourage and promote, and to provide assistance for, the cultural development of the citizens of North Carolina, and to this end the General Assembly does create and provide for a training center for instruction in the performing arts. (1963, c. 1116.)

§ 116-64. Establishment of school.

There is hereby established, and there shall be maintained, a school for the professional training of students having exceptional talent in the performing arts which shall be defined as an educational institution of the State, to serve the students of North Carolina and other states, particularly other states of the South. The school shall be designated the 'North Carolina School of the Arts, redesignated effective August 1, 2008, as the "University of North Carolina School of the Arts."' (1963, c. 1116; 1971, c. 1244, s. 13; 2008-192, s. 7.)

§ 116-65. To be part of University of North Carolina; membership of Board of Trustees.

The North Carolina School of Arts, redesignated effective August 1, 2008, as the "University of North Carolina School of the Arts," is a part of the University of North Carolina and subject to the provisions of Article 1, Chapter 116, of the General Statutes; provided, however, that notwithstanding the provisions of G.S. 116-31, the Board of Trustees of said school shall consist of 15 persons, 13 of whom are selected in accordance with provisions of G.S. 116-31, and the conductor of the North Carolina Symphony, or the conductor's designee, and the Secretary of the Department of Cultural Resources, both serving ex officio and nonvoting. (1963, c. 1116; 1971, c. 320, s. 4; c. 1244, s. 13; 1979, c. 562; 2003-215, s. 1; 2008-192, s. 8.)

§ 116-66. Powers of various boards.

The Board of Governors of the University of North Carolina and the Board of Trustees of the school shall be advised and assisted by the State Board of Education. Entrance requirements shall be prescribed so that the professional training offered shall be available only to those students who possess exceptional talent in the performing arts. In developing curricula the school shall utilize, pursuant to agreement with institutions of higher education or with any local administrative school unit, existing facilities and such academic nonarts courses and programs of instruction as may be needed by the students of the school, and, in the discretion of the Board of Governors, personnel may be employed jointly with any such institution or unit on a cooperative, cost-sharing basis. Curricula below the collegiate level shall be developed with the advice and approval of the State Board of Education. The school shall confer and cooperate with the Southern Regional Education Board and with other regional and national organizations to obtain wide support and to establish the school as the center in the South for the professional training and performance of artists. The chancellor of the school shall preferably be a noted composer or dramatist. (1963, c. 1116; 1971, c. 1244, s. 13; 1985, c. 101, s. 2.)

§ 116-67: Repealed by Session Laws 1985, c. 101, s. 1.

§ 116-68. Endowment fund.

The Board of Trustees is authorized to establish a permanent endowment fund, and shall perform such duties in relation thereto as are prescribed by the provisions of Article 1, Chapter 116, of the General Statutes. The proceeds in this fund are appropriated as provided by G.S. 116-36. (1963, c. 1116; 1971, c. 1244, s. 13; 2006-203, s. 51.1.)

§ 116-68.1. Fees.

The Board of Governors of The University of North Carolina may set fees, not inconsistent with the actions of the General Assembly, to be paid by in-State high school students enrolled at the University of North Carolina School of the Arts to assist with expenses of the institution. The Board of Trustees may recommend to the Board of Governors of The University of North Carolina that fees be set, not inconsistent with actions of the General Assembly, to be paid by in-State high school students enrolled at the University of North Carolina School of the Arts to assist with expenses of the institution. The University of North

Carolina School of the Arts may charge and collect fees established as provided by this section from in-State high school students enrolled at the University of North Carolina School of the Arts. (2013-360, s. 11.8(a).)

§ 116-69. Purpose of school program.

The primary purpose of the school shall be the professional training, as distinguished from liberal arts instruction, of talented students in the fields of music, drama, the dance, and allied performing arts, at both the high school and college levels of instruction, with emphasis placed upon performance of the arts, and not upon academic studies of the arts. The said school may also offer high school and college instruction in academic subjects, and such other programs as are deemed necessary to meet the needs of its students and of the State, consistent with appropriations made and gifts received therefor, and may cooperate, if it chooses, with other schools which provide such courses of instruction. The school, on occasion, may accept elementary grade students of rare talent, and shall arrange for such students, in cooperation with an elementary school, a suitable educational program. (1963, c. 1116.)

§ 116-69.1. Display of the United States and North Carolina flags and the recitation of the Pledge of Allegiance.

The school shall (i) display the United States and North Carolina flags in each classroom when available, (ii) require the recitation of the Pledge of Allegiance on a daily basis, and (iii) provide instruction on the meaning and historical origins of the flag and the Pledge of Allegiance. The school shall not compel any person to stand, salute the flag, or recite the Pledge of Allegiance. If flags are donated or are otherwise available, flags shall be displayed in each classroom. (2006-137, s. 3.)

§§ 116-70 through 116-70.1. Repealed by Session Laws 1971, c. 1244, s. 13.

Article 5.

Loan Fund for Prospective College Teachers.

§ 116-71. Purpose of Article.

The purpose of this Article is to encourage, assist, and expedite the postgraduate-level education and training of competent teachers for the public and private universities, colleges and community colleges in this State by the granting of loans to finance such study. The funds shall be used to increase the number of teaching faculty as distinguished from research specialists. (1965, c. 1148, s. 1; 1987, c. 564, s. 22.)


§ 116-72. Fund established.

There is established a loan fund for prospective college teachers to assist capable persons to pursue study and training leading to masters or doctorate degrees in preparation to become teachers in the public and private institutions of education beyond the high school in North Carolina. Both private and public sources may be solicited in the creation of the fund. (1965, c. 1148, s. 1.)


§ 116-73. Joint committee for administration of fund; rules and regulations.

"The Scholarship Loan Fund for Prospective College Teachers" shall be the responsibility of the Board of Governors of the University of North Carolina and the State Board of Education and will be administered by them through a joint committee, "The College Scholarship Loan Committee." This Committee will operate under the following rules and regulations and under such further rules and regulations as the Board of Governors of the University of North Carolina and the State Board of Education shall jointly promulgate.

(1) The nomination of applicants and recommendations of renewals shall be the responsibility of the College Scholarship Loan Committee.

(2) Loans should be made for a single academic year (nine months) with renewal possible for two successive years for students successfully pursuing masters or doctoral programs. Loans shall not exceed two thousand dollars

($2,000) for single students and three thousand dollars ($3,000) for married students.

(3)     All scholarship loans shall be evidenced by notes, with sufficient sureties, made payable to the State Board of Education, and shall bear interest at the rate of four percent (4%) per annum from and after September 1 following the awarding of the candidate's degree.

(4)     Recipients of loans may have them repaid by teaching in a college or other educational institution beyond the high school level in North Carolina upon completion of their masters or doctorate degree program, at the rate of one hundred dollars ($100.00) per month for each month of such teaching. If a student supported by a loan in this program should fail to so teach in a North Carolina institution, the loan would become repayable to the State, with interest, for that part of the teaching commitment not met, said note to be repaid according to the terms thereof.

(5)     Loans for 12 weeks of summer study, carrying stipends not to exceed five hundred dollars ($500.00) for single and married students, should be available to students who do not plan to attend postgraduate school as full-time students during the regular academic year. Recipients should be eligible for up to three renewals over a four-year period. The obligation to teach in a North Carolina college or other educational institution, or failing that, to repay the State, shall apply proportionally as indicated above. (1965, c. 1148, s. 1; 1971, c. 1244, s. 14.)

§ 116-74. Duration of fund; use of repaid loans and interest.

The Scholarship Loan Fund for Prospective College Teachers shall continue in effect until terminated by action of the General Assembly of North Carolina. Such amounts of loans as shall be repaid from time to time under the provisions of this Article, together with such amounts of interest as may be received on account of loans made shall become a part of the principal amount of said loan fund. These funds shall be administered for the same purposes and under the same provisions as are set forth herein to the end that they may be utilized in addition to such further amounts as may be privately donated or appropriated from time to time by public or corporate bodies. (1965, c. 1148, s. 1.)

§§ 116-74.1 through 116-74.5. Reserved for future codification purposes.

Article 5A.

Center for Advancement of Teaching.

§ 116-74.6: Recodified as G.S. 115C-296.5 by Session Laws 2009-451, s. 9.13(b), effective July 1, 2009.

§ 116-74.7: Recodified as G.S. 115C-296.6 by Session Laws 2009-451, s. 9.13(d), effective July 1, 2009.

§§ 116-74.8 through 116-74.20. Reserved for future codification purposes.

Article 5B.

School Administrator Training Programs.

§ 116-74.21. Establishment of a competitive proposal process for school administrator programs.

(a) The Board of Governors shall develop and implement a competitive proposal process and criteria for assessing proposals to establish school administrator training programs within the constituent institutions of The University of North Carolina. To facilitate the development of the programs, program criteria, and the proposal process, the Board of Governors may convene a panel of national school administrator program experts and other professional training program experts to assist it in designing the program, the proposal process, and criteria for assessing the proposals.

(b) No more than 12 school administrator programs shall be established under the competitive proposal program. In selecting campus sites, the Board of Governors shall be sensitive to the racial, cultural, and geographic diversity of the State. Special priority shall be given to the following factors: (i) the historical background of the institutions in training educators; (ii) the ability of the sites to serve the geographic regions of the State, such as, the far west, the west, the triad, the piedmont, and the east; and, (iii) whether the type of roads and terrain in a region make commuting difficult. A school administrator program may provide for instruction at one or more campus sites.

(c) The Board of Governors shall study the issue of supply and demand of school administrators to determine the number of school administrators to be trained in the programs in each year of the biennium and report the results of this study to the Joint Legislative Education Oversight Committee no later than April 15 annually.

(d) The Board of Governors shall develop a budget for the programs established under subsection (a) of this section that reflects the resources necessary to establish and operate school administrator programs that meet the vision of the report submitted to the 1993 General Assembly by the Educational Leadership Task Force.

(e) Repealed by Session Laws 2005-276, s. 9.23, effective July 1, 2005. (1993, c. 199, s. 1; 1993 (Reg. Sess., 1994), c. 677, s. 13; 1995, c. 507, s. 27.2(a); 1998-212, s. 11.13(a); 2001-424, s. 31.10(a); 2005-276, s. 9.23; 2010-31, s. 9.3(b).)


§§ 116-74.22 through 116-74.40. Reserved for future codification purposes.


Article 5C.

North Carolina Principal Fellows Program.

§ 116-74.41. North Carolina Principal Fellows Commission established; membership.

(a) There is established the North Carolina Principal Fellows Commission. The Commission shall exercise its powers and duties independently of the Board of Governors of The University of North Carolina. The Director of the Principal Fellows Program shall staff the Commission. The State Education Assistance Authority (SEAA) as created in G.S. 116-203 shall be responsible for implementing scholarship loan agreements, monitoring, cancelling through service, collecting and otherwise enforcing the agreements for the Principal Fellows Program scholarship loans established in accordance with G.S. 116-74.42.

(a1)     All funds appropriated to, or otherwise received by, the Principal Fellows Program for scholarships, all funds received as repayment of scholarship loans, and all interest earned on these funds shall be placed in an institutional trust fund pursuant to G.S. 116-36.1.

(b)     The Commission shall consist of 12 members appointed as follows:

(1)     One member of the Board of Governors of The University of North Carolina appointed by the chair of that board, notwithstanding G.S. 116-7(b).

(2)     One member of the State Board of Education appointed by the State Board chair.

(3)     Two deans of schools of education appointed by the President of The University of North Carolina.

(4)     One public school teacher appointed by the General Assembly upon the recommendation of the President Pro Tempore of the Senate.

(5)     One public school principal appointed by the General Assembly upon the recommendation of the Speaker of the House of Representatives.

(6)     A local superintendent chosen by the State Superintendent of Public Instruction.

(7)     One member to represent business and industry appointed by the Governor.

(8)     One local school board member appointed by the chair of the State Board of Education.

(9)     One parent of a public school child appointed by the State Superintendent of Public Instruction.

(10)     The chairperson of the Board of the State Education Assistance Authority.

(11)     The director of the Principal Fellows Program. The director shall chair the Commission.

(c)     Initial appointments shall be made no later than September 15, 1993. Initial terms of those members appointed to fill the teacher, principal, parent, superintendent, and the local school board member seats shall expire July 1, 1995. Initial terms of those members appointed to fill the Board of Governors of The University of North Carolina, State Board of Education, deans of schools of education, and the member of business and industry seats shall expire July 1, 1997. Thereafter, all appointments for these seats shall be for four-year terms.

(d)     Except as otherwise provided, if a vacancy occurs in the membership, the appointing authority shall appoint another person to serve for the balance of the unexpired term. In the discretion of the appointing authority, a State Board of Education member or a member of the Board of Governors of The University of North Carolina may complete a term on the Commission after the member's appointment from the appointing board has expired.

(e)     Commission members shall receive per diem, subsistence, and travel allowances in accordance with G.S. 138-5 or G.S. 138-6, as appropriate.

(f)     The Commission shall meet regularly, at times and places deemed necessary by the chair. (1993, c. 321, s. 85(a); 2006-203, s. 51.2.)


§ 116-74.42.  Principal Fellows Program established; administration.

(a)     A Principal Fellows Program shall be administered by the North Carolina Principal Fellows Commission in collaboration with the State Education Assistance Authority. The Principal Fellows Program shall provide up to a two-year scholarship loan to selected recipients and shall provide extracurricular enhancement activities for recipients. The North Carolina Principal Fellows Commission shall determine selection criteria, methods of selection, and shall select recipients to receive scholarship loans made under the Principal Fellows Program.

(b)     The Board of Governors of The University of North Carolina shall appoint a director of the Principal Fellows Program. The director shall chair and staff the Principal Fellows Commission, and shall administer the extracurricular enhancement activities of the program. The Board of Governors shall provide office space and clerical support staff for the program.

(c) The Principal Fellows Program shall provide a two-year scholarship loan in the amount specified in subsection (c1) of this section to persons who may be eligible to be selected as school administrators in the public schools of the State by completing a full-time program in school administration in an approved program. Approved programs are those chosen by the Commission from among school administrator programs within the State. No more than 200 principal fellow scholarship loan awards shall be made in each year. The final number of scholarship loan awards per year shall be made in accordance with the Board of Governors' findings concerning the supply and demand of administrators, the State's need for school administrator candidates and within funds appropriated for the scholarship loans. Effective September 1, 1995, and in accordance with school administrator training programs established by the Board of Governors of The University of North Carolina, recipients shall be required to complete an approved full-time academic program during the first year of the scholarship loan program and a full-time internship during the second year of the program. In order to attract fellows as interns, local school administrative units may use all or part of the funds allotted for an assistant principal salary for each intern accepted by the local school administrative unit; however, interns shall not serve as assistant principals.

(c1) The scholarship loan shall be thirty thousand dollars ($30,000) per participant for the first year of participation. For the second year of participation, the amount of the scholarship loan per participant shall be sixty percent (60%) of the beginning salary for an assistant principal plus four thousand one hundred dollars ($4,100) for tuition, fees, and books. The Commission may adjust the amount of the scholarship loan specified in this subsection to take into account increases in tuition, fees, and the cost of books, increases in the State principal assistant salary schedule, and changes in the stipend paid to participants in the program during the second year internship.

(d) The Commission shall adopt stringent standards, which may include standardized test scores, undergraduate performance, job experience and performance, leadership and management abilities, and other standards deemed appropriate by the Commission, to ensure that only the best potential students receive scholarship loans under the Principal Fellows Program. The Commission shall consider the qualifications of all applicants fairly, regardless of gender or race, and shall consider the geographic diversity of the State. Scholarship loans under the Principal Fellows Program shall be awarded only to applicants who meet the standards set by the Commission, are domiciled in North Carolina, and who agree to work as school administrators in a North Carolina public school or at a school operated by the United States government in North Carolina upon completion of the two-year school administrator program supported by the loan.

(e) The Commission shall develop and administer the Principal Fellows Program in cooperation with school administrator programs at institutions approved by the Commission. The Commission shall develop criteria and a process for the approval of campus program sites. Extracurricular enhancement activities shall be coordinated with each fellow's campus program and shall focus on the leadership development of program fellows.

(f) The Commission may form regional review committees to assist it in identifying the best applicants for the program. The Commission and the review committees shall make an effort to identify and encourage women and minorities and others who may not otherwise consider a career in school administration to apply for the Principal Fellows Program.

(g) Upon the naming of recipients of the scholarship loans by the Principal Fellows Commission, the Commission shall transfer to the State Education Assistance Authority (SEAA) its decisions. The SEAA shall perform all of the administrative functions necessary to implement this Article, which functions shall include: rule making, dissemination of information, disbursement, receipt, liaison with participating educational institutions, determination of the acceptability of service repayment agreements, and all other functions necessary for the execution, payment, and enforcement of promissory notes required under this Article. (1993, c. 321, s. 85(a); 2006-66, ss. 9.16(a), (b).)


§ 116-74.43. Terms of loans; receipt and disbursement of funds.

(a) All scholarship loans shall be evidenced by notes made payable to the State Education Assistance Authority that bear interest at a rate not to exceed ten percent (10%) per year as set by the Authority and beginning 90 days after completion of the school administrator program, or 90 days after termination of the scholarship loan, whichever is earlier. The scholarship loan may be terminated upon the recipient's withdrawal from school or by the recipient's failure to meet the standards set by the Commission.

(b) The State Education Assistance Authority shall forgive the loan and any interest accrued on the loan if, within six years after graduation from a school administrator program, exclusive of any authorized deferment for extenuating circumstances, the recipient serves for four years as a school administrator at a North Carolina public school or at a school operated by the United States government in North Carolina. The SEAA shall also forgive the loan if it finds that it is impossible for the recipient to work for four years, within six years after completion of the two-year school administrator program supported by the scholarship loan at a North Carolina public school, or at a school operated by the United States government in North Carolina, because of the death or permanent disability of the recipient. If the recipient repays the scholarship loan by cash payments, all indebtedness shall be repaid within 12 years after completion of the two-year school administrator program supported by the scholarship loan. If the recipient completes the school administrator program, payment of principal and interest shall begin no later than 27 months after the completion of the program. Should a recipient present extenuating circumstances, the State Education Assistance Authority may extend the period to repay the loan in cash to no more than a total of 15 years.

(c) All funds appropriated to, or otherwise received by, the Principal Fellows Program for scholarships, all funds received as repayment of scholarship loans, and all interest earned on these funds, shall be placed in a university trust fund. This university trust fund may be used only for scholarship loans granted under the Principal Fellows Program and administrative costs associated with the recovery of funds advanced under the program. (1993, c. 321, s. 85(a); 1993 (Reg. Sess., 1994), c. 677, s. 12(a); 2008-204, s. 5.3.)

ARTICLES 6-9.

[Repealed.]

§§ 116-75 through 116-104: Repealed by Session Laws 1957, c. 1142.

Article 10.

State School for the Blind and the Deaf in Raleigh.

§§ 116-105 through 116-119: Transferred to §§ 115-321 to 115-335 by Session Laws 1963, c. 448, s. 28.

Article 11.

North Carolina School for the Deaf at Morganton.

§ 116-120: Transferred to § 115-336 by Session Laws 1963, c. 448, s. 28.

§§ 116-121 through 116-124. Repealed by Session Laws 1963, c. 448, s. 28.

§ 116-124.1. Transferred to § 115-342 by Session Laws 1963, c. 448, s. 28.

§ 116-125. Transferred to § 115-343 by Session Laws 1963, c. 448, s. 28.

Article 11A.

Eastern North Carolina School for the Deaf and North Carolina School for the Deaf at Morganton.

§§ 116-125.1 through 116-125.5. Transferred to §§ 115-337 to 115-341 by Session Laws 1963, c. 448, s. 28.

Article 12.

The Caswell School.

§§ 116-126 through 116-137. Repealed by Session Laws 1963, c. 1184, s. 7.

Article 13.

Colored Orphanage of North Carolina.

§§ 116-138 through 116-142. Transferred to §§ 115-344 to 115-348 by Session Laws 1963, c. 448, s. 28.

Article 13A.

Negro Training School for Feebleminded Children.

§§ 116-142.1 through 116-142.10. Repealed by Session Laws 1963, c. 1184, s. 8.

Article 14.

General Provisions as to Tuition and Fees in Certain State Institutions.

§ 116-143. State-supported institutions of higher education required to charge tuition and fees.

(a)     The Board of Governors of The University of North Carolina shall fix the tuition and fees, not inconsistent with actions of the General Assembly, at the institutions of higher education enumerated in G.S. 116-4 in such amount or amounts as it may deem best, taking into consideration the nature of each institution and program of study and the cost of equipment and maintenance; and each institution shall charge and collect from each student, at the beginning of each semester or quarter, tuition, fees, and an amount sufficient to pay other expenses for the term.

(b)     In the event that said students are unable to pay the cost of tuition and required academic fees as the same may become due, in cash, the said several boards of trustees are hereby authorized and empowered, in their discretion, to accept the obligation of the student or students together with such collateral or security as they may deem necessary and proper, it being the purpose of this Article that all students in State institutions of higher learning shall be required to pay tuition, and that free tuition is hereby abolished. Notwithstanding this section, neither the Board of Governors of The University of North Carolina nor its Board of Trustees shall impose any tuition or mandatory fee at the North Carolina School of Science and Mathematics without the approval of the General Assembly, except as provided in subsection (e) of this section.

(c)     Inasmuch as the giving of tuition and fee waivers, or especially reduced rates, represent in effect a variety of scholarship awards, the said practice is hereby prohibited except when expressly authorized by statute.

(d)     Notwithstanding the above provision relating to the abolition of free tuition, the Board of Governors of The University of North Carolina may, in its discretion, provide regulations under which a full-time faculty member of the rank of full-time instructor or above, and any full-time staff member of The University of North Carolina may during the period of normal employment enroll for not more than two courses per year in The University of North Carolina free of charge for tuition, provided such enrollment does not interfere with normal employment obligations and further provided that such enrollments are not counted for the purpose of receiving general fund appropriations.

(e)     The Board of Governors of The University of North Carolina may approve, upon the recommendation of the Board of Trustees of the North Carolina School of Science and Mathematics, the imposition of fees not inconsistent with actions of the General Assembly for distance education services provided by the North Carolina School of Science and Mathematics to nonresidents and for students participating in extracurricular enrichment programs sponsored by the School. (1933, c. 320, s. 1; 1939, cc. 178, 253; 1949, c. 586; 1961, c. 833, s. 16.1; 1963, c. 448, s. 27.1; 1965, c. 903; 1971, c. 845, ss. 6, 10; c. 1086, s. 2; c. 1244, s. 12; 1973, c. 116, s. 1; 1977, c. 605; 1981, c. 859, s. 41.4; 2006-66, s. 9.11(i); 2009-451, ss. 9.21, 9.22(a); 2011-145, s. 9.13(a); 2013-360, s. 11.7(b).)


§ 116-143.1.  Provisions for determining resident status for tuition purposes.

(a)     As defined under this section:

(1)     A "legal resident" or "resident" is a person who qualifies as a domiciliary of North Carolina; a "nonresident" is a person who does not qualify as a domiciliary of North Carolina.

(2)     A "resident for tuition purposes" is a person who qualifies for the in-State tuition rate; a "nonresident for tuition purposes" is a person who does not qualify for the in-State tuition rate.

(3)     "Institution of higher education" means any of the constituent institutions of the University of North Carolina and the community colleges under the jurisdiction of the State Board of Community Colleges.

(b)     To qualify as a resident for tuition purposes, a person must have established legal residence (domicile) in North Carolina and maintained that legal residence for at least 12 months immediately prior to his or her classification as a resident for tuition purposes. Every applicant for admission shall be required to make a statement as to his length of residence in the State.

(c) To be eligible for classification as a resident for tuition purposes, a person must establish that his or her presence in the State currently is, and during the requisite 12-month qualifying period was, for purposes of maintaining a bona fide domicile rather than of maintaining a mere temporary residence or abode incident to enrollment in an institution of higher education.

(d) An individual shall not be classified as a resident for tuition purposes and, thus, not rendered eligible to receive the in-State tuition rate, until he or she has provided such evidence related to legal residence and its duration as may be required by officials of the institution of higher education from which the individual seeks the in-State tuition rate.

(e) When an individual presents evidence that the individual has living parent(s) or court-appointed guardian of the person, the legal residence of such parent(s) or guardian shall be prima facie evidence of the individual's legal residence, which may be reinforced or rebutted relative to the age and general circumstances of the individual by the other evidence of legal residence required of or presented by the individual; provided, that the legal residence of an individual whose parents are domiciled outside this State shall not be prima facie evidence of the individual's legal residence if the individual has lived in this State the five consecutive years prior to enrolling or reregistering at the institution of higher education at which resident status for tuition purposes is sought.

(f) In making domiciliary determinations related to the classification of persons as residents or nonresidents for tuition purposes, the domicile of a married person, irrespective of sex, shall be determined, as in the case of an unmarried person, by reference to all relevant evidence of domiciliary intent. For purposes of this section:

(1) No person shall be precluded solely by reason of marriage to a person domiciled outside North Carolina from establishing or maintaining legal residence in North Carolina and subsequently qualifying or continuing to qualify as a resident for tuition purposes;

(2) No persons shall be deemed solely by reason of marriage to a person domiciled in North Carolina to have established or maintained a legal residence in North Carolina and subsequently to have qualified or continued to qualify as a resident for tuition purposes;

(3) In determining the domicile of a married person, irrespective of sex, the fact of marriage and the place of domicile of his or her spouse shall be deemed relevant evidence to be considered in ascertaining domiciliary intent.

(g) Any nonresident person, irrespective of sex, who marries a legal resident of this State or marries one who later becomes a legal resident, may, upon becoming a legal resident of this State, accede to the benefit of the spouse's immediately precedent duration as a legal resident for purposes of satisfying the 12-month durational requirement of this section.

(h) No person shall lose his or her resident status for tuition purposes solely by reason of serving in the Armed Forces of the United States outside this State.

(h1) Any member of a North Carolina National Guard unit who is a nonresident shall be eligible to be charged the in-State tuition rate and shall pay the full amount of the in-State tuition rate and applicable mandatory fees. This subsection applies to members in a reserve or active duty status.

(i) A person who, having acquired bona fide legal residence in North Carolina, has been classified as a resident for tuition purposes but who, while enrolled in a State institution of higher education, loses North Carolina legal residence, shall continue to enjoy the in-State tuition rate for a statutory grace period. This grace period shall be measured from the date on which the culminating circumstances arose that caused loss of legal residence and shall continue for 12 months; provided, that a resident's marriage to a person domiciled outside of North Carolina shall not be deemed a culminating circumstance even when said resident's spouse continues to be domiciled outside of North Carolina; and provided, further, that if the 12-month period ends during a semester or academic term in which such a former resident is enrolled at a State institution of higher education, such grace period shall extend, in addition, to the end of that semester or academic term.

(j) Notwithstanding the prima facie evidence of legal residence of an individual derived pursuant to subsection (e), notwithstanding the presumptions of the legal residence of a minor established by common law, and notwithstanding the authority of a judicially determined custody award of a minor, for purposes of this section, the legal residence of a minor whose parents are divorced, separated, or otherwise living apart shall be deemed to be North Carolina for the time period relative to which either parent is entitled to claim and does in fact claim the minor as a dependent for North Carolina individual income tax purposes. The provisions of this subsection shall pertain only to a minor who is claimed as a dependent by a North Carolina legal resident.

Any person who immediately prior to his or her eighteenth birthday would have been deemed under this subsection a North Carolina legal resident but who achieves majority before enrolling at an institution of higher education shall not lose the benefit of this subsection if that person:

(1) Upon achieving majority, acts, to the extent that the person's degree of actual emancipation permits, in a manner consistent with bona fide legal residence in North Carolina; and

(2) Begins enrollment at an institution of higher education not later than the fall academic term next following completion of education prerequisite to admission at such institution.

(k) Notwithstanding other provisions of this section, a minor who satisfies the following conditions immediately prior to commencement of an enrolled term at an institution of higher education, shall be accorded resident tuition status for that term:

(1) The minor has lived for five or more consecutive years continuing to such term in North Carolina in the home of an adult relative other than a parent, domiciled in this State; and

(2) The adult relative has functioned during those years as a de facto guardian of the minor and exercised day-to-day care, supervision, and control of the minor.

A person who immediately prior to his or her eighteenth birthday qualified for or was accorded resident status for tuition purposes pursuant to this subsection shall be deemed upon achieving majority to be a legal resident of North Carolina of at least 12 months' duration; provided, that the legal residence of such an adult person shall be deemed to continue in North Carolina only so long as the person does not abandon legal residence in this State.

(l) Any person who ceases to be enrolled at or graduates from an institution of higher education while classified as a resident for tuition purposes and subsequently abandons North Carolina domicile shall be permitted to reenroll at an institution of higher education as a resident for tuition purposes without necessity of meeting the 12-month durational requirement of this section if the person reestablishes North Carolina domicile within 12 months of abandonment of North Carolina domicile and continuously maintains the reestablished North Carolina domicile at least through the beginning of the academic term(s) for which in-State tuition status is sought. The benefit of this subsection shall be accorded not more than once to any one person.

(m)     Notwithstanding subsection (b) of this section, a person who is a full-time employee of The University of North Carolina, or is the spouse or dependent child of a full-time employee of The University of North Carolina, and who is a legal resident of North Carolina, qualifies as a resident for tuition purposes without having maintained that legal residence for at least 12 months immediately prior to his or her classification as a resident for tuition purposes. (1971, c. 845, ss. 7-9; 1973, cc. 710, 1364, 1377; 1975, c. 436; 1979, cc. 435, 836; 1981, cc. 471, 905; 1987, c. 564, s. 19; 1989, c. 728, s. 1.3; 1991 (Reg. Sess., 1992), c. 1030, s. 32; 2004-130, s. 2; 2005-276, s. 9.25(a); 2011-183, s. 83.)

§ 116-143.2. Expired.

§ 116-143.3. Tuition of Armed Forces personnel and their dependents.

(a)     Definitions. - The following definitions apply in this section:

(1)     The term "abode" shall mean the place where a person actually lives, whether temporarily or permanently; the term "abide" shall mean to live in a given place.

(2)     The term "Armed Forces" shall mean the United States Air Force, Army, Coast Guard, Marine Corps, and Navy; the North Carolina National Guard; and any reserve component of the foregoing.

(3)     Repealed by Session Laws 2007-484, s. 15, effective August 30, 2007.

(b)     Any active duty member of the Armed Forces qualifying for admission to an institution of higher education as defined in G.S. 116-143.1(a)(3) but not qualifying as a resident for tuition purposes under G.S. 116-143.1 shall be charged the in-State tuition rate and applicable mandatory fees for enrollments while the member of the Armed Forces is abiding in this State incident to active military duty in this State. In the event the active duty member of the Armed

Forces is reassigned outside of North Carolina or retires, the member shall continue to be eligible for the in-State tuition rate and applicable mandatory fees so long as the member is continuously enrolled in the degree or other program in which the member was enrolled at the time the member is reassigned. In the event the active duty member of the Armed Forces receives an Honorable Discharge from military service, the member shall continue to be eligible for the in-State tuition rate and applicable mandatory fees so long as the member establishes residency in North Carolina within 30 days after the discharge and is continuously enrolled in the degree or other program in which the member was enrolled at the time the member is discharged.

(b1), (b2) Repealed by Session Laws 2004-130, s. 1, effective August 1, 2004.

(c) Any dependent relative of a member of the Armed Forces who is abiding in this State incident to active military duty, as defined by the Board of Governors of The University of North Carolina and by the State Board of Community Colleges while sharing the abode of that member shall be eligible to be charged the in-State tuition rate, if the dependent relative qualifies for admission to an institution of higher education as defined in G.S. 116-143.1(a)(3). The dependent relatives shall comply with the requirements of the Selective Service System, if applicable, in order to be accorded this benefit. In the event the member of the Armed Forces is reassigned outside of North Carolina or retires, the dependent relative shall continue to be eligible for the in-State tuition rate and applicable mandatory fees so long as the dependent relative is continuously enrolled in the degree or other program in which the dependent relative was enrolled at the time the member is reassigned or retires. In the event the member of the Armed Forces receives an Honorable Discharge from military service, the dependent relative shall continue to be eligible for the in-State tuition rate and applicable mandatory fees so long as the dependent relative establishes residency within North Carolina within 30 days after the discharge and is continuously enrolled in the degree or other program in which the dependent relative was enrolled at the time the member is discharged.

(d) The person applying for the benefit of this section has the burden of proving entitlement to the benefit.

(e) A person charged less than the out-of-state tuition rate solely by reason of this section shall not, during the period of receiving that benefit, qualify for or be the basis of conferring the benefit of G.S. 116-143.1(g), (h), (i), (j), (k), or (l). (1983 (Reg. Sess., 1984), c. 1034, s. 57; 1985, c. 39, s. 1; c. 479, s. 69; c. 757,

s. 154; 1987, c. 564, § 7; 1997-443, s. 10.2; 2003-284, s. 8.16(a); 2004-130, s. 1; 2005-276, s. 9.38; 2005-345, s. 14; 2005-445, s. 7; 2007-484, s. 15; 2011-183, s. 84.)

§ 116-143.4. Admissions status of persons charged in-State tuition.

A person eligible for the in-State tuition rate pursuant to this Article shall be considered an in-State applicant for the purpose of admission; provided that, a person eligible for in-State tuition pursuant to G.S. 116-143.3(c) shall be considered an in-State applicant for the purpose of admission only if at the time of seeking admission he is enrolled in a high school located in North Carolina or enrolled in a general education development (GED) program in an institution located in this State. (1989 (Reg. Sess., 1990), c. 907.)

§ 116-143.5: Repealed by Session Laws 2011-145, s. 9.13(b), effective July 1, 2011.

§ 116-143.6. Full scholarship students attending constituent institutions.

(a) Notwithstanding any other provision of law, if the Board of Trustees of a constituent institution of The University of North Carolina elects to do so, it may by resolution adopted consider as residents of North Carolina all persons who receive full scholarships, unless the scholarship is for athletics, to the institution from entities recognized by the institution and attend the institution as undergraduate students. The aforesaid persons shall be considered residents of North Carolina for all purposes by The University of North Carolina.

(b) The following definitions apply in this section:

(1) "Full cost" means an amount calculated by the constituent institution that is no less than the sum of tuition, required fees, and on-campus room and board.

(2) "Full scholarship" means a grant that meets the full cost for a student to attend the constituent institution for an academic year.

(c) This section shall not be applied in any manner that violates federal law.

(d) This section shall be administered by the electing constituent institution so as to have no fiscal impact.

(e) In administering this section, the electing constituent institution shall maintain at least the current number of North Carolina residents admitted to that constituent institution. (2005-276, s. 9.27(a); 2010-31, s. 9.25.)

§ 116-143.7. Tuition surcharge.

(a) The Board of Governors of The University of North Carolina shall impose a fifty percent (50%) tuition surcharge on students who take more than 140 degree credit hours to complete a baccalaureate degree in a four-year program or more than one hundred ten percent (110%) of the credit hours necessary to complete a baccalaureate degree in any program officially designated by the Board of Governors as a five-year program. Courses and credit hours taken include those taken at that constituent institution or accepted for transfer. In calculating the number of degree credit hours taken:

(1) Included are courses that a student:

a. Fails.

b. Does not complete unless the course was officially dropped by the student pursuant to the academic policy of the appropriate constituent institution.

(2) Excluded are credit hours earned through:

a. The College Board's Advanced Placement Program, CLEP examinations, or similar programs.

b. Institutional advanced placement, course validation, or any similar procedure for awarding course credit.

c. Summer term or extension programs.

(b) No surcharge shall be imposed on any student who exceeds the degree credit hour limits within the equivalent of four academic years of regular term enrollment or within five academic years of regular term enrollment in a degree program officially designated by the Board of Governors as a five-year program.

(c) Upon application by a student, the tuition surcharge shall be waived if the student demonstrates that any of the following have substantially disrupted or interrupted the student's pursuit of a degree: (i) a military service obligation, (ii) serious medical debilitation, (iii) a short-term or long-term disability, or (iv) other extraordinary hardship. The Board of Governors shall establish the appropriate procedures to implement the waiver provided by this subsection.

(d) Each constituent institution shall implement procedures to notify students and parents regarding the tuition surcharge and to provide appropriate advance notice to a student when the student is approaching the credit hour limit regarding the tuition surcharge. The procedures shall comply with the tuition surcharge notification principles established by the Board of Governors. (2009-451, s. 9.10(a), (b); 2013-325, s. 1.)


§ 116-144. Higher tuition to be charged nonresidents.

The Board of Governors shall fix the tuition and required fees charged nonresidents of North Carolina who attend the institutions enumerated in G.S. 116-4 at rates higher than the rates charged residents of North Carolina and comparable to the rates charged nonresident students by comparable public institutions nationwide, except that a person who serves as a graduate teaching assistant or graduate research assistant or in a similar instructional or research assignment and is at the same time enrolled as a graduate student in the same institution may, in the discretion of the Board of Governors, be charged a lower rate fixed by the Board, provided the rate is not lower than the North Carolina resident rate. (1933, c. 320, s. 3; 1983, c. 761, s. 112.)


Article 15.

Educational Advantages for Children of World War Veterans.

§§ 116-145 through 116-148.1. Repealed by Session Laws 1951, c. 1160, s. 1.

§§ 116-149 through 116-153. Repealed by Session Laws 1967, c. 1060, s. 10.

Article 16.

State Board of Higher Education.

§§ 116-154 through 116-157. Repealed by Session Laws 1971, c. 1244, s. 14.

§ 116-158. Powers and duties generally.

The Board shall have the following specific powers and duties, in the exercise and performance of which it shall be subject to the provisions of Article 1, Chapter 143 of the General Statutes except as herein otherwise provided:

(1) to (8) Repealed by Session Laws 1971, c. 1244, s. 14.

(9) Transferred to G.S. 116-18 by Session Laws 1971, c. 1244, s. 4 (1955, c. 1186, s. 5; 1959, c. 326, ss. 2-7; 1965, c. 1096, s. 3; 1971, c. 1244, ss. 4, 14.)

§§ 116-158.1 through 116-158.4. Transferred to §§ 116-19 to 116-22 by Session Laws 1971, c. 1244, s. 5.

§§ 116-159 through 116-167. Repealed by Session Laws 1971, c. 1244, s. 14.

Article 17.

College Revolving Fund.

§§ 116-168 through 116-170: Repealed by Session Laws 1983, c. 717, s. 34.

Article 18.

Scholarship Loan Fund for Prospective Teachers.

§§ 116-171 through 116-174: Transferred to §§ 115C-468 to 115C-471 by Session Laws 1983 (Regular Session 1984), c. 1034, s. 10.1.


Article 18A.

Contracts of Minors Borrowing for Higher Education; Scholarship Revocation.

§ 116-174.1. Minors authorized to borrow for higher education; interest; requirements of loans.

All minors in North Carolina of the age of 17 years and upwards shall have full power and authority to enter into written contracts of indebtedness, at a rate of interest not exceeding the contract rate authorized in Chapter 24 of the General Statutes, with persons and educational institutions or with firms and corporations licensed to do business in North Carolina and to execute notes evidencing such indebtedness. Such loans shall be:

(1)     Unsecured by the conveyance of any property as security, whether real, personal or mixed;

(2)     For the sole purpose of borrowing money to obtain post-secondary education at an accredited college, university, junior college, community college, business or trade school provided, however, that none of the proceeds of such loans shall be used to pay for any correspondence courses;

(3)     The proceeds of any loan shall be disbursed either directly to the educational institution for the benefit of the borrower or jointly to the borrower and the educational institution. (1963, c. 780; 1969, c. 1073; 1987, c. 564, s. 36.)


§ 116-174.2. Grounds for revocation of scholarships.

Any student regularly registered and enrolled as an undergraduate, graduate, or professional student in a state-supported college, university or community college who shall be convicted, enter a plea of guilty or nolo contendere upon an indictment or charge for engaging in a riot, inciting a riot, unlawful demonstration or assembly, seizing or occupying a building or facility, sitting down in buildings they have seized, or lying down in entrances to buildings or any facilities, or on the campus of any college, university, or community college, or any student, whether an undergraduate, graduate or professional student who shall forfeit an appearance bond on an indictment or charge of any of the above-named offenses, shall have revoked and withdrawn from his benefit all state-supported scholarships or any State funds granted to him for educational assistance. It shall be the duty of all persons or officials having charge of and authority over the granting of state-supported scholarships or any other form of financial assistance to immediately revoke and withdraw same in the event and upon the happening of any of the conditions or matters above enumerated; provided, however, that in subsequent academic terms any such student shall be eligible to be considered for and to be granted financial assistance from State funds. (1969, c. 1019.)

Article 19.

Revenue Bonds for Student Housing.

§ 116-175. Definitions.

As used in this Article, the following words and terms shall have the following meanings, unless the context shall indicate another or different meaning or intent.

(1)     The word "Board" shall mean the Board of Governors of the University of North Carolina.

(2)     The word "cost" as applied to a project shall include the cost of acquisition or construction, the cost of all labor, materials and equipment, the cost of all lands, property, rights and easements acquired, financing charges, interest prior to and during construction and, if deemed advisable by the Board, for one year after completion of construction, cost of plans and specifications, surveys and estimates of cost and/or revenues, cost of engineering and legal services, and all other expenses necessary or incident to such acquisition or

construction, administrative expense and such other expenses, including reasonable provision for initial operating expenses, as may be necessary or incident to the financing herein authorized. Any obligation or expense incurred by the Board prior to the issuance of bonds under the provisions of this Article in connection with any of the foregoing items of cost may be regarded as a part of such cost.

(3)   The word "institution" shall mean each of the institutions enumerated in G.S. 116-2.

(4)   The word "project" shall mean and shall include any one or more buildings for student housing of any size or type approved by the Board of Governors of the University of North Carolina, and the Director of the Budget, and any enlargements or improvements thereof or additions thereto, so approved for the housing of students at either institution, together with the necessary land and equipment. The approval of a project by the Board of Governors of the University of North Carolina and the Director of the Budget shall specify a time within which construction contracts shall be awarded. (1957, c. 1131, s. 1; 1963, cc. 421, 422; c. 448, s. 20.1; c. 1158, ss. 1, 11/2; 1965, c. 31, s. 3; 1967, c. 1038; 1969, c. 297, s. 7; c. 388; c. 608, s. 1; c. 801, ss. 2-4; 1971, c. 1244, s. 16; 1983, c. 577, s. 6.)


§ 116-175.1:  Repealed, effective July 1, 2007, and applicable to the budget for the 2007-2009 biennium and each subsequent biennium thereafter, by Session Laws 2006-203, s. 52.


§ 116-176.  Issuance of bonds.

The Board is hereby authorized to issue, subject to the approval of the Director of the Budget, at one time or from time to time, revenue bonds of the Board for the purpose of acquiring or constructing any project or projects. The bonds of each issue shall be dated, shall mature at such time or times not exceeding 50 years from their date or dates, shall bear interest at such rate or rates as may be determined by the Board, and may be redeemable before maturity, at the option of the Board, at such price or prices and under terms and conditions as may be fixed by the Board prior to the issuance of the bonds. The Board shall determine the form and manner of execution of the bonds, including any interest coupons to be attached thereto, and shall fix the denomination or denominations of the bonds and the place or places of payment of principal and interest, which may be at any bank or trust company within or without the State. In case any officer whose signature or a facsimile of whose signature shall appear on any bonds or coupons shall cease to be such officer before the delivery of such bonds, such signature or such facsimile shall nevertheless be valid and sufficient for all purposes the same as if he had remained in office until such delivery. Notwithstanding any of the other provisions of this Article or any recitals in any bonds issued under the provisions of this Article, all such bonds shall be deemed to be negotiable instruments under the laws of this State. The bonds may be issued in coupon or registered form or both, as the Board may determine, and provision may be made for the registration of any coupon bonds as to principal alone and also as to both principal and interest, and for the reconversion into coupon bonds of any bonds registered as to both principal and interest. The Board may sell such bonds in such manner, at public or private sale, and for such price, as it may determine to be in the best interest of the Board.

The proceeds of the bonds of each issue shall be used solely for the purpose for which such bonds shall have been authorized and shall be disbursed in such manner and under such restrictions, if any, as the Board may provide in the resolution authorizing the issuance of such bonds or in the trust agreement hereinafter mentioned securing the same. Unless otherwise provided in the authorizing resolution or in the trust agreement securing such bonds, if the proceeds of such bonds, by error of estimates or otherwise, shall be less than such cost, additional bonds may in like manner be issued to provide the amount of such deficit and shall be deemed to be of the same issue and shall be entitled to payment from the same fund without preference or priority of the bonds first issued for the same purpose.

The resolution providing for the issuance of revenue bonds, and any trust agreement securing such bonds, may also contain such limitations upon the issuance of additional revenue bonds as the Board may deem proper, and such additional bonds shall be issued under such restrictions and limitations as may be prescribed by such resolution or trust agreement.

Prior to the preparation of definitive bonds, the Board may, under like restrictions, issue interim receipts or temporary bonds, with or without coupons, exchangeable for definitive bonds when such bonds shall have been executed and are available for delivery. The Board may also provide for the replacement of any bonds which shall become mutilated or be destroyed or lost.

Bonds may be issued by the Board under the provisions of this Article, subject to the approval of the Director of the Budget, but without obtaining the consent of any other commission, board, bureau or agency of the State, and without any other proceedings or the happening of any other conditions or things than those consents, proceedings, conditions or things which are specifically required by this Article.

Revenue bonds issued under the provisions of this Article shall not be deemed to constitute a debt of the State of North Carolina or a pledge of the faith and credit of the State, but such bonds shall be payable solely from the funds herein provided therefor and a statement to that effect shall be recited on the face of the bonds.

The Board may enter into or negotiate a note with an acceptable bank or trust company in lieu of issuing bonds for the financing of projects covered under this Article. The terms and conditions of any note of this nature shall be in accordance with the terms and conditions surrounding issuance of bonds. (1957, c. 1131, s. 2; 1969, c. 1158, s. 1; 1971, c. 511, s. 1; 1975, c. 233, s. 1; 1983, c. 577, s. 6.)

§ 116-177. Revenues for payment of bonds; rules for use of facilities.

So long as any bonds issued under this Article shall be outstanding the Board shall fix, and may revise from time to time, rentals for the facilities to be furnished by any project financed under this Article or for the right to use any such facilities or to receive any such services. Such rentals shall be fixed and revised so that the revenues received by the Board from any project or projects, together with any other available funds, will be sufficient at all times

(1) To pay the cost of maintaining, repairing and operating such project or projects, including reserves for such purposes, and

(2) To pay when added to increased rentals from existing facilities the principal of and the interest on the bonds for the payment of which such revenues are pledged and to provide reserves therefor.

The Board shall increase the rentals for the facilities furnished by any existing dormitories at any institution to provide, to the extent necessary, additional funds to liquidate in full any revenue bonds issued under this Article.

The Board is further authorized to make and enforce and to contract to make and enforce parietal rules that shall insure the maximum use of any project or existing facilities. (1957, c. 1131, s. 3.)

§ 116-178. Trust agreement.

In the discretion of the Board and subject to the approval of the Director of the Budget, each or any issue of revenue bonds may be secured by a trust agreement by and between the Board and a corporate trustee, which may be any trust company or bank having the powers of a trust company within or without the State. The resolution authorizing the issuance of the bonds or such trust agreement may pledge to the extent necessary the revenues to be received from any project or projects at any institution and from any similar existing facilities described in G.S. 116-175(4) at the same institution, in excess of amounts now charged to each occupant of such project, but shall not convey or mortgage any such project or existing facilities, and may contain such provisions for protecting and enforcing the rights and remedies of the bondholders as may be reasonable and proper and not in violation of law, including covenants setting forth the duties of the Board in relation to the acquisition or construction of such project or projects and in relation to the maintenance, repair, operation and insurance of such project or projects and such existing facilities, the fixing and revising of rentals and other charges; and, the custody, safeguarding and application of all moneys, and for the employment of consulting engineers or architects in connection with such acquisition, construction or operation. Notwithstanding the provisions of any other law the Board may carry insurance on any such project or projects in such amounts and covering such risks as it may deem advisable. It shall be lawful for any bank or trust company incorporated under the laws of the State of North Carolina which may act as depository of the proceeds of bonds or of revenues to furnish such indemnifying bonds or to pledge such securities as may be required by the Board. Such resolution or trust agreement may set forth the rights and remedies of the bondholders and of the trustees, if any, and may restrict the individual right of action by bondholders. Such resolution or trust agreement may contain such other provisions in addition to the foregoing as the Board may deem reasonable and proper for the security of the bondholders.

The Board may provide for the payment of the proceeds of the sale of the bonds and the revenues of any project or existing facilities or part thereof to such officer, board or depository as it may designate for the custody thereof, and for the method of disbursement thereof, with such safeguards and restrictions as it may determine. All expenses incurred in carrying out the provisions of such resolution or trust agreement may be treated as a part of the cost of operation.

All pledges of revenues under the provisions of this Article shall be valid and binding from the time when such pledges are made. All such revenues so pledged and thereafter received by the Board shall immediately be subject to the lien of such pledges without any physical delivery thereof or further action, and the lien of such pledges shall be valid and binding as against all parties having claims of any kind in tort, contract or otherwise against the Board, irrespective of whether such parties have notice thereof. (1957, c. 1131, s. 4; 1983, c. 577, s. 6.)


§ 116-179. Sale of bonds; functions performed by executive committee.

The Board may authorize its executive committee to sell any bonds which the Board has, with the approval of the Director of the Budget, authorized to be issued under this Article in such manner and under such limitations or conditions as the Board shall prescribe and to perform such other functions under this Article as the Board shall determine. (1957, c. 1131, s. 5; 1983, c. 577, s. 6.)


§ 116-180. Moneys received deemed trust funds.

All moneys received pursuant to the authority of this Article shall be deemed to be trust funds, to be held and applied solely as provided in this Article. The resolution authorizing the issuance of bonds or the trust agreement securing such bonds shall provide that any officer to whom, or bank, trust company or fiscal agent to which, such moneys shall be paid shall act as trustee of such moneys and shall hold and apply the same for the purposes hereof, subject to such regulations as such resolution or trust agreement may provide. (1957, c. 1131, s. 6.)


§ 116-181. Remedies.

Any holder of revenue bonds issued under the provisions of this Article or of any of the coupons appertaining thereto, and the trustee under any trust agreement, except to the extent that the rights herein given may be restricted by the resolution authorizing the issuance of such bonds or by such trust agreement, may, either at law or in equity, by suit, action, mandamus or other proceeding, protect and enforce any and all rights under the laws of the State of North Carolina or granted hereunder or under such resolution or trust agreement, and may enforce and compel the performance of all duties required by this Article or by such resolution or trust agreement to be performed by the Board or by any officer thereof, including the fixing, charging and collecting of fees, rentals and other charges. (1957, c. 1131, s. 7.)

§ 116-182. Refunding bonds.

The Board is hereby authorized, subject to the approval of the Director of the Budget, to issue from time to time revenue refunding bonds for the purpose of refunding any revenue bonds issued by the Board in connection with any project or projects at any one institution, including the payment of any redemption premium thereon and any interest accrued or to accrue to the date of redemption of such bonds. The Board is further authorized, subject to the approval of the Director of the Budget, to issue from time to time revenue refunding bonds for the combined purpose of

(1) Refunding any revenue bonds or revenue refunding bonds issued by the Board in connection with any project or projects at any one institution, including the payment of any redemption premium thereon and any interest accrued or to accrue to the date of redemption of such bonds, and

(2) Paying all or any part of the cost of acquiring or constructing any additional project or projects at the same institution.

The issuance of such bonds, the maturities and other details thereof, the rights and remedies of the holders thereof, and the rights, powers, privileges, duties and obligations of the Board with respect to the same, shall be governed by the foregoing provisions of this Article insofar as the same may be applicable. (1957, c. 1131, s. 8; 1983, c. 577, s. 6.)

§ 116-183. Acceptance of grants; exemption from taxation.

The Board is hereby authorized, subject to the approval of the Director of the Budget, to accept grants of money or materials or property of any kind for any project from a federal agency, private agency, corporation or individual, upon such terms and conditions as such federal agency, private agency, corporation or individual may impose. The bonds issued under this Article are exempt from all State, county, and municipal taxation or assessment, direct or indirect, general or special, whether imposed for the purpose of general revenue or otherwise, excluding inheritance and gift taxes, income taxes on the gain from the transfer of the bonds and notes, and franchise taxes. The interest on the bonds and notes is not subject to taxation as income. (1957, c. 1131, s. 9; 1983, c. 577, s. 6; 1995, c. 46, s. 6.)

§ 116-184. Article cumulative.

This Article shall be deemed to provide an additional and alternative method for the doing of the things authorized hereby and shall be regarded as supplemental and additional to powers conferred by other laws, and shall not be regarded as in derogation of or as repealing any powers now existing under any other law, either general, special or local; provided, however, that the issuance of revenue bonds or revenue refunding bonds under the provisions of this Article need not comply with the requirements of any other law applicable to the issuance of bonds. (1957, c. 1131, s. 10.)

§ 116-185. Inconsistent laws declared inapplicable.

All general, special or local laws, or parts thereof, inconsistent herewith are hereby declared to be inapplicable to the provisions of this Article. (1957, c. 1131, s. 11.)

Article 20.

Motor Vehicles of Students.

§ 116-186. Transferred to § 116-42.4 by Session Laws 1971, c. 1244, s. 11.

Article 21.

Revenue Bonds for Student Housing, Student Activities, Physical Education and Recreation.

§ 116-187. Purpose of Article.

The purpose of this Article is to authorize the Board of Governors of the University of North Carolina to issue revenue bonds, payable from rentals, charges, fees (including student fees) and other revenues but with no pledge of taxes or the faith and credit of the State or any agency or political subdivision thereof, to pay the cost, in whole or in part, of buildings and other facilities for the housing, health, welfare, recreation and convenience of students enrolled at the institutions hereinafter designated, housing of faculty, adult or continuing education programs and for revenue-producing parking decks or structures, and for University of North Carolina Hospitals at Chapel Hill. (1963, c. 847, s. 1; 1967, c. 1148, s. 1; 1971, c. 1061, s. 1; c. 1244, s. 16; 1979, c. 731, s. 6; 1989, c. 141, s. 4.)

§ 116-187.1: Repealed by Session Laws 2006-203, s. 53, effective July 1, 2007, and applicable to the budget for the 2007-2009 biennium and each subsequent biennium thereafter.

§ 116-188. Credit and taxing power of State not pledged; statement on face of bonds.

Revenue bonds issued as in this Article provided shall not be deemed to constitute a debt or liability of the State or any political subdivision thereof or a pledge of the faith and credit of the State or of any such political subdivision, but shall be payable solely from the funds herein provided therefor from revenues. All such revenue bonds shall contain on the face thereof a statement to the effect that neither the State nor the Board (herein mentioned) shall be obligated to pay the same or the interest thereon except from revenues as herein defined and that neither the faith and credit nor the taxing power of the State or of any political subdivision or instrumentality thereof is pledged to the payment of the principal of or the interest on such bonds. The issuance of revenue bonds hereunder shall not directly or indirectly or contingently obligate the State or any political subdivision thereof to levy or to pledge any taxes whatsoever therefor. (1963, c. 847, s. 2.)


§ 116-189. Definitions.

As used in this Article, the following words and terms shall have the following meanings, unless the context shall indicate another or different meaning or intent:

(1) The word "Board" shall mean the Board of Governors of the University of North Carolina.

(2) The word "cost," as applied to any project, shall include the cost of acquisition or construction, the cost of acquisition of all property, both real and personal, or interests therein, the cost of demolishing, removing or relocating any buildings or structures on land so acquired, including the cost of acquiring any lands to which such buildings or structures may be moved or relocated, the cost of all labor, materials, equipment and furnishings, financing charges, interest prior to and during construction and, if deemed advisable by the Board, for a period not exceeding one year after completion of such construction, provisions for working capital, reserves for debt service and for extensions, enlargements, additions and improvements, cost of engineering, financial and legal services, plans, specifications, studies, surveys, estimates of cost and of revenues, administrative expenses, expenses necessary or incident to determining the feasibility or practicability of constructing the project, and such other expenses as may be necessary or incident to the acquisition or construction of the project, the financing of such acquisition or construction, and the placing of the project in operation. Any obligation or expense incurred by the Board prior to the issuance of bonds under the provisions of this Article in connection with any of the foregoing items of cost may be regarded as a part of such cost.

(3) The term "existing facilities" shall mean buildings and facilities then existing any part of the revenues of which are pledged under the provisions of

any resolution authorizing the issuance of revenue bonds hereunder to the payment of such bonds.

(4)     The word "institution" shall mean each of the institutions enumerated in G.S. 116-2, the University of North Carolina Health Care System, and the University of North Carolina General Administration.

(5)     The word "project" shall mean and shall include any one or more buildings, structures, or facilities of any size or type now or hereafter existing for (i) the housing, health, welfare, recreation, and convenience of students, (ii) the housing of faculty, (iii) academic, research, patient care, and community services, and (iv) parking at an institution or institutions, that has been approved by the Board and the Director of the Budget and any improvements or additions so approved to any such buildings, structures, or facilities, including, but without limiting the generality thereof, dormitories and other student, faculty, and adult or continuing education housing, dining facilities, student centers, gymnasiums, field houses and other physical education and recreation buildings, infirmaries and other health care buildings, academic facilities, furnishings, equipment, parking facilities, and necessary land and interest in land. Any project may include, without limiting the generality thereof, facilities for services such as lounges, restrooms, lockers, offices, stores for books and supplies, snack bars, cafeterias, restaurants, laundries, cleaning, postal, banking and similar services, rooms and other facilities for guests and visitors, and facilities for meetings and for recreational, cultural, and entertainment activities.

(6)     The word "revenues" shall mean all or any part of the rents, charges, fees (including student fees) and other income revenues derived from or in connection with any project or projects and existing facilities, and may include receipts and other income derived from athletic games and public events. (1963, c. 847, s. 3; 1965, c. 31, s. 3; 1967, c. 1038; c. 1148, s. 2; 1969, c. 297, s. 8; c. 388; c. 608, s. 1; c. 801, ss. 2-4; 1971, c. 1061, s. 2; c. 1244, s. 16; 1979, c. 731, s. 6; 1983, c. 577, s. 8; 1989, c. 141, s. 5; 2000-168, ss. 4, 5.)

§ 116-190. General powers of Board of Governors.

The Board is authorized, subject to the requirements of this Article:

(1)     To determine the location and character of any project or projects and to acquire, construct and provide the same and to maintain, repair and operate

and enter into contracts for the management, lease, use or operation of all or any portion of any project or projects and any existing facilities;

(2) To issue revenue bonds as hereinafter provided to pay all or any part of the cost of any project or projects, and to fund or refund the same;

(3) To fix and revise from time to time and charge and collect (i) student fees from students enrolled at the institution operated by the Board, (ii) rates, fees, rents and charges for the use of and for the services furnished by all or any portion of any project or projects and (iii) admission fees for athletic games and other public events;

(4) To establish and enforce, and to agree through any resolution or trust agreement authorizing or securing bonds under this Article to make and enforce, rules and regulations for the use of and services rendered by any project or projects and any existing facilities, including parietal rules, when deemed desirable by the Board, to provide for the maximum use of any project or projects and any existing facilities;

(5) To acquire, hold, lease and dispose of real and personal property in the exercise of its powers and the performance of its duties hereunder and to lease all or any part of any project or projects and any existing facilities for such period or periods of years, not exceeding 40 years, upon such terms and conditions as the Board determines subject to the provisions of G.S. 143-341;

(6) To employ consulting engineers, attorneys, accountants, construction and financial experts, superintendents, managers and such other employees and agents as may be necessary in its judgment in connection with any project or projects and existing facilities, and to fix their compensation;

(7) To make and enter into all contracts and agreements necessary or incidental to the performance of its duties and the execution of its powers under this Article;

(8) To receive and accept from any federal, State or other public agency and any private agency, person or other entity donations, loans, grants, aid or contributions of any money, property, labor or other things of value for any project or projects, and to agree to apply and use the same in accordance with the terms and conditions under which the same are provided; and

(9) To do all acts and things necessary or convenient to carry out the powers granted by this Article. (1963, c. 847, s. 4; 1971, c. 1244, s. 14.)

§ 116-191. Issuance of bonds and bond anticipation notes.

The Board is hereby authorized to issue, subject to the approval of the Director of the Budget, at one time or from time to time, revenue bonds of the Board for the purpose of paying all or any part of the cost of acquiring, constructing or providing any project or projects. The bonds of each issue shall be dated, shall mature at such time or times not exceeding 50 years from their date or dates, shall bear interest at such rate or rates as may be determined by the Board, and may be redeemable before maturity, at the option of the Board, at such price or prices and under such terms and conditions as may be fixed by the Board prior to the issuance of the bonds. The Board shall determine the form and manner of execution of the bonds, including any interest coupons to be attached thereto, and shall fix the denomination or denominations of the bonds and the place or places of payment of principal and interest, which may be at any bank or trust company within or without the State. In case any officer whose signature or a facsimile of whose signature shall appear on any bonds or coupons shall cease to be such officer before the delivery of such bonds, such signature or such facsimile shall nevertheless be valid and sufficient for all purposes the same as if he had remained in office until such delivery. Notwithstanding any of the other provisions of this Article or any recitals in any bonds issued under the provisions of this Article, all such bonds shall be deemed to be negotiable instruments under the laws of this State, subject only to the provisions for registration in any resolution authorizing the issuance of such bonds or any trust agreement securing the same. The bonds may be issued in coupon or registered form or both, as the Board may determine, and provision may be made for the registration of any coupon bonds as to principal alone and also as to both principal and interest, and for the reconversion into coupon bonds of any bonds registered as to both principal and interest. The Board may sell such bonds in such manner, at public or private sale, and for such price, as it may determine to be for the best interests of the Board.

The proceeds of the bonds of each issue shall be used solely for the purpose for which such bonds shall have been authorized and shall be disbursed in such manner and under such restrictions, if any, as the Board may provide in the resolution authorizing the issuance of such bonds or in the trust agreement hereinafter mentioned securing the same. Unless otherwise provided in the authorizing resolution or in the trust agreement securing such bonds, if the proceeds of such bonds, by error of estimates or otherwise, shall be less than such cost, additional bonds may in like manner be issued to provide the amount of such deficit and shall be deemed to be of the same issue and shall be entitled to payment from the same fund without preference or priority of the bonds first issued for the same purpose.

The resolution providing for the issuance of revenue bonds, and any trust agreement securing such bonds, may also contain such limitations upon the issuance of additional revenue bonds as the Board may deem proper, and such additional bonds shall be issued under such restrictions and limitations as may be prescribed by such resolution or trust agreement.

Prior to the preparation of definitive bonds, the Board may, under like restrictions, issue interim receipts or temporary bonds, with or without coupons, exchangeable for definitive bonds when such bonds shall have been executed and are available for delivery. The Board may also provide for the replacement of any bonds which shall become mutilated or be destroyed or lost.

Except as herein otherwise provided, bonds may be issued under this Article and other powers vested in the Board under this Article may be exercised by the Board without obtaining the consent of any department, division, commission, board, bureau or agency of the State and without any other proceedings or the happening of any other conditions or things than those proceedings, conditions or things which are specifically required by this Article.

The Board may enter into or negotiate a note with an acceptable bank or trust company in lieu of issuing bonds for the financing of projects covered under this section. The terms and conditions of any note of this nature shall be in accordance with the terms and conditions surrounding issuance of bonds.

The Board is hereby authorized to issue, subject to the approval of the Director of the Budget, at one time or from time to time, revenue bond anticipation notes of the Board in anticipation of the issuance of bonds authorized pursuant to the provisions of this Article. The principal of and the interest on such notes shall be payable solely from the proceeds of bonds or renewal notes or, in the event bond or renewal note proceeds are not available, any available revenues of the project or projects for which such bonds shall have been authorized. The notes of each issue shall be dated, shall mature at such time or times not exceeding two years from their date or dates, shall bear interest at such rate or rates as may be determined by the Board, and may be redeemable before maturity, at the option of the Board, at such price or prices and under such terms and conditions as may be fixed by the Board prior to the issuance of the notes. The Board shall determine the form and the manner of execution of the notes, including any interest coupons to be attached thereto, and shall fix the denomination or denominations of the notes and the place or places of payment of principal and interest, which may be at any bank or trust company within or without the State. In case any officer, whose signature or a facsimile of whose signature shall appear on any notes or coupons, shall cease to be such officer before the delivery of such notes, such signature or such facsimile shall nevertheless be valid and sufficient for all purposes the same as if he had remained in office until such delivery. Notwithstanding any of the other provisions of this Article or any recitals in any notes issued under the provisions of this Article, all such notes shall be deemed to be negotiable instruments under the laws of this State, subject only to the provisions for registration in any resolution authorizing the issuance of such notes or any trust agreement securing the bonds in anticipation of which such notes are being issued. The notes may be issued in coupon or registered form or both, as the Board may determine, and provision may be made for the registration of any coupon notes as to principal alone and also as to both principal and interest, and for the reconversion into coupon notes of any notes registered as to both principal and interest. The Board may sell such notes in such manner, at public or private sale, and for such price, as it may determine to be for the best interests of the Board.

The proceeds of the notes of each issue shall be used solely for the purpose for which the bonds in anticipation of which such notes are being issued shall have been authorized, and such note proceeds shall be disbursed in such manner and under such restrictions, if any, as the Board may provide in the resolution authorizing the issuance of such notes or bonds or in the trust agreement securing such bonds.

The resolution providing for the issuance of notes, and any trust agreement securing the bonds in anticipation of which such notes are being authorized, may also contain such limitations upon the issuance of additional notes as the Board may deem proper, and such additional notes shall be issued under such restrictions and limitations as may be prescribed by such resolution or trust agreement. The Board may also provide for the replacement of any notes which shall become mutilated or be destroyed or lost.

Except as herein otherwise provided, notes may be issued under this Article and other powers vested in the Board under this Article may be exercised by the

Board without obtaining the consent of any department, division, commission, board, bureau or agency of the State and without any other proceedings or the happening of any other conditions or things than those proceedings, conditions or things which are specifically required by this Article.

Unless the context shall otherwise indicate, the word "bonds," wherever used in this Article, shall be deemed and construed to include the words "bond anticipation notes." (1963, c. 847, s. 5; 1969, c. 1158, s. 2; 1971, c. 511, s. 2; 1973, c. 662; 1975, c. 233, s. 2; 1983, c. 577, s. 8.)

§ 116-192. Trust agreement; money received deemed trust funds; insurance; remedies.

In the discretion of the Board and subject to the approval of the Director of the Budget, any revenue bonds issued under this Article may be secured by a trust agreement by and between the Board and a corporate trustee (or trustees) which may be any trust company or bank having the powers of a trust company within or without the State. Such trust agreement or the resolution providing for the issuance of such bonds may pledge or assign the revenues to be received, but shall not convey or mortgage any project or projects or any existing facilities or any part thereof. Such trust agreement or resolution providing for the issuance of such bonds may contain such provisions for protecting and enforcing the rights and remedies of the holders of such bonds as may be reasonable and proper and not in violation of law, including covenants setting forth the duties of the Board in relation to the acquisition, construction or provision of any project or projects, the maintenance, repair, operation and insurance of any project or projects and any existing facilities, student fees and admission fees and charges and other fees, rents and charges to be fixed and collected, and the custody, safeguarding and application of all moneys. It shall be lawful for any bank or trust company incorporated under the laws of the State which may act as depositary of the proceeds of bonds or revenues to furnish such indemnifying bonds or to pledge such securities as may be required by the Board. Any such trust agreement or resolution may set forth the rights and remedies of the holders of the bonds and the rights, remedies and immunities of the trustee or trustees, if any, and may restrict the individual right of action by such holders. In addition to the foregoing, any such trust agreement or resolution may contain such other provisions as the Board may deem reasonable and proper for the security of such holders. All expenses incurred in carrying out the provisions of such trust agreement or resolution may be treated as a part of the cost of the project or projects for which such bonds are issued or as an expense of operation of such project or projects, as the case may be.

All moneys received pursuant to the authority of this Article, whether as proceeds from the sale of bonds or as revenues, shall be deemed to be trust funds to be held and applied solely as provided in this Article. The Board may provide for the payment of the proceeds of the sale of the bonds and the revenues, or part thereof, to such officer, board or depositary as it may designate for the custody thereof, and for the method of disbursement thereof, with such safeguards and restrictions as it may determine. Any officer with whom, or any bank or trust company with which, such moneys shall be deposited shall act as trustee of such moneys and shall hold and apply the same for the purposes hereof, subject to such requirements as are provided in this Article and in the resolution or trust agreement authorizing or securing such bonds.

Notwithstanding the provisions of any other law the Board may carry insurance on any project or projects and any existing facilities in such amounts and covering such risks as it may deem advisable.

Any holder of bonds issued under this Article or of any of the coupons appertaining thereto, and the trustee or trustees under any trust agreement, except to the extent the rights herein given may be restricted by such trust agreement or the resolution authorizing the issuance of such bonds, may, either at law or in equity, by suit, action, mandamus or other proceedings, protect and enforce any and all rights under the laws of the State or granted hereunder or under such trust agreement or resolution, and may enforce and compel the performance of all duties required by this Article or by such trust agreement or resolution to be performed by the Board or by any officer thereof, including the fixing, charging and collecting of fees, rents and charges. (1963, c. 847, s. 6; 1983, c. 577, s. 8.)

§ 116-193. Fixing fees, rents and charges; sinking fund.

For the purpose of aiding in the acquisition, construction or provision of any project and the maintenance, repair and operation of any project or any existing facilities, the Board is authorized to fix, revise from time to time, charge and collect from students enrolled at the institution under its jurisdiction such student fee or fees for such privileges and services and in such amount or amounts as the Board shall determine, and to fix, revise from time to time, charge and collect other fees, rents and charges for the use of and for the services furnished or to be furnished by any project or projects and any existing facilities, or any portion thereof, and admission fees for athletic games and other public events, and to contract with any person, partnership, association or corporation for the lease, use, occupancy or operation of, or for concessions in, any project or projects and any existing facilities, or any part thereof, and to fix the terms, conditions, fees, rents and charges for any such lease, use, occupancy, operation or concession. So long as bonds issued hereunder and payable therefrom are outstanding, such fees, rents and charges shall be so fixed and adjusted, with relation to other revenues available therefor, as to provide funds pursuant to the requirements of the resolution or trust agreement authorizing or securing such bonds at least sufficient with such other revenues, if any, (i) to pay the cost of maintaining, repairing and operating any project or projects and any existing facilities any part of the revenues of which are pledged to the payment of the bonds issued for such project or projects, (ii) to pay the principal of and the interest on such bonds as the same shall become due and payable, and (iii) to create and maintain reserves for such purposes. Such fees, rents and charges shall not be subject to supervision or regulation by any other commission, board, bureau or agency of the State. A sufficient amount of the revenues, except such part thereof as may be necessary to pay such cost of maintenance, repair and operation and to provide such reserves therefor and for renewals, replacements, extensions, enlargements and improvements as may be provided for in the resolution authorizing the issuance of such bonds or in the trust agreement securing the same, shall be set aside at such regular intervals as may be provided in such resolution or such trust agreement in a sinking fund which is hereby pledged to, and charged with, the payment of the principal of and the interest on such bonds as the same shall become due and the redemption price or the purchase price of bonds retired by call or purchase as therein provided. Such pledge shall be valid and binding from the time when the pledge is made, the fees, rents and charges and other revenues or other moneys so pledged and thereafter received by the Board shall immediately be subject to the lien of such pledge without any physical delivery thereof or further act, and the lien of any such pledge shall be valid and binding as against all parties having claims of any kind in tort, contract or otherwise against the Board, irrespective of whether such parties have notice thereof. Neither the resolution nor any trust agreement by which a pledge is created need be filed or recorded except in the records of the Board. The use and disposition of moneys to the credit of such sinking fund shall be subject to the provisions of the resolution authorizing the issuance of such bonds or of the trust agreement securing the same. (1963, c. 847, s. 7.)

§ 116-194. Vesting powers in executive committee.

The Board may authorize its executive committee to sell any bonds which the Board has, with the approval of the Director of the Budget, authorized to be issued under this Article in such manner and under such limitations or conditions as the Board shall prescribe and to perform such other functions under this Article as the Board shall determine. (1963, c. 847, s. 8; 1983, c. 577, s. 8.)

§ 116-195. Refunding bonds.

The Board is hereby authorized, subject to the approval of the Director of the Budget, to issue from time to time revenue refunding bonds for the purpose of refunding any revenue bonds or revenue refunding bonds issued by the Board under Chapter 1289 of the 1955 Session Laws of North Carolina or under G.S. 116-175 to 116-185, inclusive, or under this Article, including the payment of any redemption premium thereon and any interest accrued or to accrue to the date of redemption of such bonds. The Board is further authorized, subject to the approval of the Director of the Budget, to issue from time to time revenue refunding bonds for the combined purpose of (i) refunding any such revenue bonds or revenue refunding bonds issued by the Board under said Chapter 1289 or under said G.S. 116-175 to 116-185, inclusive, or under this Article, including the payment of any redemption premium thereon and any interest accrued or to accrue to the date of redemption of such bonds, and (ii) paying all or any part of the cost of acquiring or constructing any additional project or projects.

The issuance of such refunding bonds, the maturities and other details thereof, the rights and remedies of the holders thereof, and the rights, powers, privileges, duties and obligations of the Board with respect to the same, shall be governed by the foregoing provisions of this Article insofar as the same may be applicable. (1963, c. 847, s. 9; 1983, c. 577, s. 8.)

§ 116-196. Exemption from taxation; bonds eligible for investment or deposit.

Any bonds issued under this Article shall at all times be exempt from all taxes or assessment, direct or indirect, general or special, whether imposed for the purpose of general revenue or otherwise, which are levied or assessed by the State or by any county, political subdivision, agency or other instrumentality of the State, excluding inheritance and gift taxes, income taxes on the gain from the transfer of the bonds, and franchise taxes. The interest on the bonds is not subject to taxation as income. Bonds issued by the Board under the provisions of this Article are hereby made securities in which all public officers and public bodies of the State and its political subdivisions, all insurance companies, trust companies, banking associations, investment companies, executors, administrators, trustees and other fiduciaries may properly and legally invest funds, including capital in their control or belonging to them. Such bonds are hereby made securities which may properly and legally be deposited with and received by any State or municipal officer or any agency or political subdivision of the State for any purpose for which the deposit of bonds or obligations of the State is now or may hereafter be authorized by law. (1963, c. 847, s. 10; 1995, c. 46, s. 7.)


§ 116-197. Article provides additional and alternative method.

This Article shall be deemed to provide an additional and alternative method for the doing of the things authorized hereby and shall be regarded as supplemental and additional to powers conferred by other laws, including G.S. 116-175 to 116-185, inclusive, and shall not be regarded as in derogation of or as repealing any powers now existing under any other law, either general, special or local; provided, however, that the issuance of revenue bonds or revenue refunding bonds under the provisions of this Article need not comply with the requirements of any other law applicable to the issuance of bonds. (1963, c. 847, s. 11.)


§ 116-198. Inconsistent laws declared inapplicable.

All general, special or local laws, or parts thereof, inconsistent herewith are hereby declared to be inapplicable to the provisions of this Article. (1963, c. 847, s. 12.)


§§ 116-198.1 through 116-198.5. Reserved for future codification purposes.

Article 21A.

Higher Educational Facilities Finance Act.

§§ 116-198.6 through 116-198.30: Not in effect.


Article 21B.

The Centennial Campus, the Horace Williams Campus,

and the Millenial Campuses Financing Act.

§ 116-198.31. Purpose of Article.

The purpose of this Article is to authorize the Board of Governors of The University of North Carolina to issue revenue bonds, payable from any leases, rentals, charges, fees, and other revenues but with no pledge of taxes or the faith and credit of the State or any agency or political subdivision thereof, to pay the cost, in whole or part, of buildings, structures, or other facilities for the Centennial Campus, located at North Carolina State University at Raleigh, for the Horace Williams Campus located at the University of North Carolina at Chapel Hill, and for any Millennial Campus as defined by G.S. 116-198.33(4b). (1987, c. 336, s. 1; 1999-234, s. 3; 2000-177, ss. 3, 4.)


§ 116-198.32. Credit and taxing power of State not pledged; statement on face of bonds.

Revenue bonds issued as in this Article provided shall not be deemed to constitute a debt or liability of the State or any political subdivision thereof or a pledge of the faith and credit of the State or of any such political subdivision, but shall be payable solely from the funds herein provided therefor from revenues. All such revenue bonds shall contain on the face thereof a statement to the effect that neither the State nor the Board (herein mentioned) shall be obligated to pay the same or the interest thereon except from revenues as herein defined and that neither the faith and credit nor the taxing power of the State or of any political subdivision or instrumentality thereof is pledged to the payment of the principal of or the interest on such bonds. The issuance of revenue bonds hereunder shall not directly or indirectly or contingently obligate the State or any political subdivision thereof to levy or to pledge any taxes whatsoever therefor. (1987, c. 336.)

§ 116-198.33. Definitions.

As used in this Article, the following words and terms shall have the following meanings, unless the context shall indicate another or different meaning or intent:

(1) The word "Board" shall mean the Board of Governors of The University of North Carolina.

(2) The word "cost" as applied to any project, shall include the cost of acquisition or construction; the cost of acquisition of all property, both real and personal, or interests therein; the cost of demolishing, removing, or relocating any buildings or structures on land so acquired, including the cost of acquiring any lands to which such buildings or structures may be removed or relocated; the cost of all labor, materials, equipment and furnishings, financing charges, interest prior to and during construction and, if deemed advisable by the Board, for a period not exceeding one year after completion of such construction; provisions for working capital, reserves for debt service and for extensions, enlargements, additions, and improvements; cost of engineering, financial, and legal services, plans, specifications, studies, surveys, and estimates of cost and of revenues; administrative expenses; expenses necessary or incident to determining the feasibility or practicability of constructing the project; and such other expenses as may be necessary or incident to acquisition or construction with respect to the project or to the placing of the project in operation. Any obligation or expense incurred by the Board prior to the issuance of bonds under the provisions of this Article in connection with any of the foregoing items of cost may be regarded as a part of such cost.

(3) The word "Institution" shall mean North Carolina State University at Raleigh and the University of North Carolina at Chapel Hill, or a constituent institution of The University of North Carolina with a Millennial Campus as defined by G.S. 116-198.33(4b).

(4) The term "Centennial Campus" means all of the following properties:

a. The real property and appurtenant facilities bounded by Blue Ridge Road, Hillsborough Street, Wade Avenue, and Interstate 440 that are the sites of the College of Veterinary Medicine, the University Club, and the Agricultural Turf Grass Management Program.

b. The real property and appurtenant facilities that are the former Dix Hospital properties and other contiguous parcels of property that are adjacent to Centennial Boulevard.

c. All other real property and appurtenant facilities designated by the Board of Governors as part of the Centennial Campus. The properties designated by the Board of Governors do not have to be contiguous with the Centennial Campus to be designated as part of that Campus.

(4a) The term "Horace Williams Campus" means all of the following properties:

a. The real property and appurtenant facilities left to the University of North Carolina at Chapel Hill by the Will of Henry Horace Williams.

b. All other real property and appurtenant facilities designated by the Board of Governors as part of the Horace Williams Campus. The properties designated by the Board of Governors do not have to be contiguous with the Horace Williams Campus to be designated as part of that Campus.

(4b) The term "Millennial Campus" means all real property and appurtenant facilities designated by the Board of Governors as part of a Millennial Campus of a constituent institution of The University of North Carolina other than North Carolina State University or the University of North Carolina at Chapel Hill. The properties designated by the Board of Governors do not have to be contiguous with the constituent institution to be designated as part of the institution's Millennial Campus.

(5) The term "existing facilities" shall mean buildings and facilities, then existing, any part of the revenues of which are pledged under the provisions of any resolution authorizing the issuance of revenue bonds hereunder to the payment of such bonds.

(6) The word "project" shall mean and shall include any one or more buildings, structures, administration buildings, libraries, research or instructional facilities, housing maintenance, storage, or utility facilities, and any facilities

related thereto or required or useful for conducting of research or the operation of the Centennial Campus, the Horace Williams Campus, or of a Millennial Campus as defined by G.S. 116-198.33(4b), including roads, water, sewer, power, gas, greenways, parking, or any other support facilities essential or convenient for the orderly conduct of the Centennial Campus, the Horace Williams Campus, or a Millennial Campus, respectively.

(7)  The word "revenues" shall mean all or any part of the rents, leases, charges, fees, and other income revenues derived from or in connection with any project or projects and existing facilities. (1987, c. 336, s. 1; 1998-159, s. 2; 1999-234, s. 4; 2000-177, s. 5.)


§ 116-198.34. General powers of Board of Governors.

The Board may exercise any one or more of the following powers:

(1)  To determine the location and character of any project or projects, and to acquire, construct, and provide the same, and to maintain, repair, and operate, and to enter into contracts for the management, lease, use, or operation of all or any portion of any project or projects and any existing facilities.

(2)  To issue revenue bonds as hereinafter provided to pay all or any part of the cost of any project or projects, and to fund or refund the same.

(3)  To fix and revise from time to time and charge and collect rates, fees, rents, and charges for the use of, and for the services furnished by, all or any portion of any project or projects.

(4)  To establish and enforce, and to agree through any resolution or trust agreement authorizing or securing bonds under this Article to make and enforce, rules and regulations for the use of and services rendered by any project or projects and any existing facilities, to provide for the maximum use of any project or projects and any existing facilities.

(5)  (Effective until June 30, 2015) To acquire, hold, lease, and dispose of real and personal property in the exercise of its powers and the performance of its duties hereunder and to lease all or any part of any project or projects and any existing facilities upon such terms and conditions as the Board determines,

subject to the provisions of G.S. 143-341 and Chapter 146 of the General Statutes.

Notwithstanding G.S. 143-341 and Chapter 146 of the General Statutes, an acquisition for a period of 10 years or less or a disposition of 65 years or less by easement, lease, or rental agreement of real property or space in any building on the Centennial Campus, on the Horace Williams Campus, on a Millennial Campus, or on a Kannapolis Research Campus shall not require the approval of the Governor and the Council of State. The Board shall report the acquisitions or dispositions described in this paragraph of this subdivision to the Department of Administration for inclusion in the inventory maintained by Department pursuant to G.S. 143-341(4)a. and b. and the information regarding those transactions that is required by G.S. 143-341(4)a. and b. All other acquisitions and dispositions made under this subdivision for a period in excess of the terms described in this paragraph of this subdivision are subject to the provisions of G.S. 143-341 and Chapter 146 of the General Statutes.

(5)     (Effective June 30, 2015) To acquire, hold, lease, and dispose of real and personal property in the exercise of its powers and the performance of its duties hereunder and to lease all or any part of any project or projects and any existing facilities upon such terms and conditions as the Board determines, subject to the provisions of G.S. 143-341 and Chapter 146 of the General Statutes.

Notwithstanding G.S. 143-341 and Chapter 146 of the General Statutes, a disposition by easement, lease, or rental agreement of space in any building on the Centennial Campus, on the Horace Williams Campus, or on a Millennial Campus made for a period of 10 years or less shall not require the approval of the Governor and the Council of State. All other acquisitions and dispositions made under this subdivision are subject to the provisions of G.S. 143-341 and Chapter 146 of the General Statutes.

(6)     To employ consulting engineers, architects, attorneys, accountants, construction and financial experts, superintendents, managers, and such other employees and agents as may be necessary in its judgment in connection with any project or projects and existing facilities, and to fix their compensation.

(7)     To make and enter into all contracts and agreements necessary or incidental to the performance of its duties and the execution of its powers under this Article.

(8) To receive and accept from any federal, State, or other public agency and any private agency, person or other entity donations, loans, grants, aid, or contributions of any money, property, labor, or other things of value for any project or projects, and to agree to apply and use the same in accordance with the terms and conditions under which the same are provided.

(8a) To designate the real property and appurtenant facilities to be included as part of the Centennial Campus, the Horace Williams Campus, or a Millennial Campus.

(8b) Acting on recommendation made by the President of The University of North Carolina after consultation by the President with the Chancellor and the Board of Trustees of a constituent institution, to designate real property held by, or to be acquired by, a constituent institution as a "Millennial Campus" of the institution. That designation shall be based on an express finding by the Board of Governors that the institution desiring to create a "Millennial Campus" has the administrative and fiscal capability to create and maintain such a campus and provided further, that the Board of Governors has found that the creation of the constituent institution's "Millennial Campus" will enhance the institution's research, teaching, and service missions as well as enhance the economic development of the region served by the institution. Upon formal request by the constituent institutions, the Board of Governors may authorize two or more constituent institutions which meet the requirements of this section to create a joint Millennial Campus.

(9) To do all acts and things necessary or convenient to carry out the powers granted by this Article. (1987, c. 336, s. 1; 1998-159, s. 3; 1999-234, s. 5; 2000-177, s. 6; 2012-142, s. 9.10(b); 2013-360, s. 11.10(a), (b); 2013-363, s. 3.12.)


§ 116-198.35. Issuance of bonds and bond anticipation notes.

The Board is hereby authorized to issue, subject to the approval of the Director of the Budget, at one time or from time to time, revenue bonds of the Board for the purpose of paying all or any part of the cost of acquiring, constructing, or providing any project or projects on the Centennial Campus, on the Horace Williams Campus, or on a Millennial Campus. The bonds of each issue shall be dated, shall mature at such time or times not exceeding 40 years from their date or dates, shall bear interest at such rate or rates as may be determined by the

Board, and may be redeemable before maturity, at the option of the Board, at such price or prices and under such terms and conditions as may be fixed by the Board prior to the issuance of the bonds. The Board shall determine the form and manner of execution of the bonds, including any interest coupons to be attached thereto, and shall fix the denomination or denominations of the bonds and the place or places of payment of principal and interest, which may be at any bank or trust company within or without the State. In case any officer whose signature or a facsimile of whose signature shall appear on any bonds or coupons shall cease to be such officer before the delivery of such bonds, such signature or such facsimile shall nevertheless be valid and sufficient for all purposes the same as if he had remained in office until such delivery. Notwithstanding any of the other provisions of this Article or any recitals in any bonds issued under the provisions of this Article, all such bonds shall be deemed to be negotiable instruments under the laws of this State, subject only to the provisions for registration in any resolution authorizing the issuance of such bonds or any trust agreement securing the same. The bonds may be issued in coupon or registered form or both or as book-entry bonds, as the Board may determine, and provision may be made for the registration of any coupon bonds as to principal alone and also as to both principal and interest, and for the reconversion into coupon bonds of any bonds registered as to both principal and interest. The Board may sell such bonds in such manner, at public or private sale, and for such price, as it may determine to be for the best interests of the Board.

The proceeds of the bonds of each issue shall be used solely for the purpose for which such bonds shall have been authorized and shall be disbursed in such manner and under such restrictions, if any, as the Board may provide in the resolution authorizing the issuance of such bonds or in the trust agreement hereinafter mentioned securing the same. Unless otherwise provided in the authorizing resolution or in the trust agreement securing such bonds, if the proceeds of such bonds, by error of estimates or otherwise, shall be less than such cost, additional bonds may in like manner be issued to provide the amount of such deficit and shall be deemed to be of the same issue and shall be entitled to payment from the same fund without preference or priority of the bonds first issued for the same purpose.

The resolution providing for the issuance of revenue bonds, and any trust agreement securing such bonds, may also contain such limitations upon the issuance of additional revenue bonds as the Board may deem proper, and such additional bonds shall be issued under such restrictions and limitations as may be prescribed by such resolution or trust agreement.

Prior to the preparation of definitive bonds, the Board may, under like restrictions, issue interim receipts or temporary bonds, with or without coupons, exchangeable for definitive bonds when such bonds shall have been executed and are available for delivery. The Board may also provide for the replacement of any bonds which shall become mutilated or be destroyed or lost.

Except as herein otherwise provided, bonds may be issued under this Article and other powers vested in the Board under this Article may be exercised by the Board without obtaining the consent of any department, division, commission, board, bureau, or agency of the State and without any other proceedings or the happening of any other conditions or things than those proceedings, conditions, or things which are specifically required by this Article.

The Board may enter into or negotiate a note with an acceptable bank or trust company in lieu of issuing bonds for the financing of projects covered under this section. The terms and conditions of any note of this nature shall be in accordance with the terms and conditions surrounding issuance of bonds.

The Board is hereby authorized to issue, subject to the approval of the Director of the Budget, at one time or from time to time, revenue bond anticipation notes of the Board in anticipation of the issuance of bonds authorized pursuant to the provisions of this Article. The principal of and the interest on such notes shall be payable solely from the proceeds of bonds or renewal notes, or, in the event bond or renewal note proceeds are not available, any available revenues of the project or projects for which such bonds shall have been authorized. The notes of each issue shall be dated, shall mature at such time or times not exceeding two years from their date or dates, shall bear interest at such rate or rates as may be determined by the Board, and may be redeemable before maturity, at the option of the Board, at such price or prices and under such terms and conditions as may be fixed by the Board prior to the issuance of the notes. The Board shall determine the form and the manner of execution of the notes, including any interest coupons to be attached thereto, and shall fix the denomination or denominations of the notes and the place or places of payment of principal and interest, which may be at any bank or trust company within or without the State. In case any officer whose signature or a facsimile of whose signature shall appear on any notes or coupons shall cease to be such officer before the delivery of such notes, such signature or such facsimile shall nevertheless be valid and sufficient for all purposes the same as if he had remained in office until such delivery. Notwithstanding any of the other provisions of this Article or any recitals in any notes issued under the provisions of this Article, all such notes shall be deemed to be negotiable instruments under the laws of this State, subject only to the provisions for registration in any resolution authorizing the issuance of such notes or any trust agreement securing the bonds in anticipation of which such notes are being issued. The notes may be issued in coupon or registered form or both or as book entry notes, as the Board may determine, and provision may be made for the registration of any coupon notes as to principal alone and also as to both principal and interest, and for the reconversion into coupon notes of any notes registered as to both principal and interest. The Board may sell such notes in such manner, at public or private sale, and for such price, as it may determine to be for the best interests of the Board.

The proceeds of the notes of each issue shall be used solely for the purpose for which the bonds in anticipation of which such notes are being issued shall have been authorized, and such note proceeds shall be disbursed in such manner and under such restrictions, if any, as the Board may provide in the resolution authorizing the issuance of such notes or bonds or in the trust agreement securing such bonds.

The resolution providing for the issuance of notes, and any trust agreement securing the bonds in anticipation of which such notes are being authorized, may also contain such limitations upon the issuance of additional notes as the Board may deem proper, and such additional notes shall be issued under such restrictions and limitations as may be prescribed by such resolution or trust agreement. The Board may also provide for the replacement of any notes which shall become mutilated or be destroyed or lost.

Except as herein otherwise provided, notes may be issued under this Article and other powers vested in the Board under this Article may be exercised by the Board without obtaining the consent of any department, division, commission, board, bureau, or agency of the State and without any other proceedings or the happening of any other conditions or things than those proceedings, conditions, or things which are specifically required by this Article.

Unless the context shall otherwise indicate, the word "bonds" wherever used in this Article, shall be deemed and construed to include the words "bond anticipation notes." (1987, c. 336, s. 1; 1999-234, s. 6; 2000-177, s. 7.)

§ 116-198.36. Proceeds of bonds are deemed trust funds.

In the discretion of the Board and subject to the approval of the Director of the Budget, any revenue bonds issued under this Article may be secured by a trust agreement by and between the Board and a corporate trustee (or trustees) which may be any trust company or bank having the powers of a trust company within or without the State. Such trust agreement or the resolution providing for the issuance of such bonds may pledge or assign the revenues to be received but shall not convey or mortgage any project or projects or any existing facilities or any part thereof. Such trust agreement or resolution providing for the issuance of such bonds may contain such provisions for protecting and enforcing the rights and remedies of the holders of such bonds as may be reasonable and proper and not in violation of law, including covenants setting forth the duties of the Board in relation to the acquisition, construction, or provision of any project or projects, the maintenance, repair, operation, and insurance of any project or projects and any existing facilities, student fees and admission fees and charges, and other fees, rents, and charges to be fixed and collected, and the custody, safeguarding, and application of all moneys. It shall be lawful for any bank or trust company incorporated under the laws of the State which may act as depositary of the proceeds of bonds or revenues to furnish such indemnifying bonds or to pledge such securities as may be required by the Board. Any such trust agreement or resolution may set forth the rights and remedies of the holders of the bonds and the rights, remedies, and immunities of the trustee or trustees, if any, and may restrict the individual right of action by such holders. In addition to the foregoing, any such trust agreement or resolution may contain such other provisions as the Board may deem reasonable and proper for the security of such holders. All expenses incurred in carrying out the provisions of such trust agreement or resolution may be treated as a part of the cost of the project or projects for which such bonds are issued or as an expense of operation of such project or projects, as the case may be.

The proceeds of all bonds issued and all revenues and other moneys received pursuant to the authority of this Article shall be deemed to be trust funds, to be held and applied solely as provided in this Article. The Board may provide for the payment of the proceeds of the sale of the bonds and the revenues, or part thereof, to such officer, board, or depositary as it may designate for the custody thereof, and for the method of disbursement thereof, with such safeguards and restrictions as it may determine. Any officer with whom, or any bank, trust company, or fiscal agent with which, such moneys shall be deposited shall act as trustee of such moneys and shall hold and apply the same for the purposes hereof, subject to such requirements as are provided in this Article and in the resolution or trust agreement authorizing or securing such bonds.

Notwithstanding the provisions of any other law, the Board may carry insurance on any project or projects and any existing facilities in such amounts and covering such risks as it may deem advisable.

Any holder of bonds issued under this Article or of any of the coupons appertaining thereto, and the trustee or trustees under any trust agreement, except to the extent the rights herein given may be restricted by such trust agreement or the resolution authorizing the issuance of such bonds, may, either at law or in equity, by suit, action, mandamus, or other proceedings, protect and enforce any and all rights under the laws of the State or granted hereunder or under such trust agreement or resolution, and may enforce and compel the performance of all duties required by this Article or by such trust agreement or resolution to be performed by the Board or by any officer thereof, including the fixing, charging, and collecting of fees, rents, and charges. (1987, c. 336.)

§ 116-198.37. Fixing fees, rents, and charges; sinking fund.

For the purpose of aiding in the acquisition, construction, or provision of any project and the maintenance, repair, and operation of any project or any existing facilities, the Board is authorized to fix, revise from time to time, charge, and collect such fee or fees for such privileges and services and in such amount or amounts as the Board shall determine, and to fix, revise from time to time, charge, and collect other fees, rents, and charges for the use of and for the services furnished or to be furnished by any project or projects and any existing facilities, or any portion thereof, and to contract with any person, partnership, association, or corporation for the lease, use, occupancy, or operation of any project or projects and any existing facilities, or any part thereof, and to fix the terms, conditions, fees, rents, and charges for any such lease, use, occupancy, or operation. So long as bonds issued hereunder and payable therefrom are outstanding, such fees, rents, and charges shall be so fixed and adjusted, with relation to other revenues available therefor, as to provide funds pursuant to the requirements of the resolution or trust agreement authorizing or securing such bonds at least sufficient with such other revenues, if any, (i) to pay the cost of maintaining, repairing, and operating any project or projects and any existing facilities any part of the revenues of which are pledged to the payment of the bonds issued for such project or projects, (ii) to pay the principal of and the interest on such bonds as the same shall become due and payable, and (iii) to create and maintain reserves for such purposes. Any surplus funds remaining after application to the purposes mentioned in (i), (ii), and (iii), above, shall be held in trust and applied by the Board to the development of the Centennial Campus, the Horace Williams Campus, or a Millennial Campus, as applicable. Such fees, rents, and charges shall not be subject to supervision or regulation by any other commission, board, bureau, or agency of the State. A sufficient amount of the revenues, except such part thereof as may be necessary to pay such cost of maintenance, repair, and operation and to provide such reserves therefor and for renewals, replacements, extensions, enlargements, and improvements as may be provided for in the resolution authorizing the issuance of such bonds or in the trust agreement securing the same, shall be set aside at such regular intervals as may be provided in such resolution or such trust agreement in a sinking fund which is hereby pledged to and charged with the payment of the principal of and the interest on such bonds as the same shall become due and the redemption price or the purchase price of bonds retired by call or purchase as therein provided. Such pledge shall be valid and binding from the time when the pledge is made; the fees, rents, and charges and other revenues or other moneys so pledged and thereafter received by the Board shall immediately be subject to the lien of such pledge without any physical delivery thereof or further act; and the lien of any such pledge shall be valid and binding as against all parties having claims of any kind in tort, contract, or otherwise against the Board, irrespective of whether such parties have notice thereof. Neither the resolution nor any trust agreement by which a pledge is created need be filed or recorded except in the records of the Board. The use and disposition of moneys to the credit of such sinking fund shall be subject to the provisions of the resolution authorizing the issuance of such bonds or of the trust agreement securing the same. (1987, c. 336, s. 1; 1999-234, s. 7; 2000-177, s. 8.)

§ 116-198.38. Refunding bonds.

The Board is hereby authorized, subject to the approval of the Director of the Budget, to issue from time to time revenue refunding bonds for the purpose of refunding any revenue bonds or revenue refunding bonds issued by the Board under this Article, including the payment of any redemption premium thereon and any interest accrued or to accrue to the date of redemption of such bonds. The Board is further authorized, subject to the approval of the Director of the Budget, to issue from time to time revenue refunding bonds for the combined purpose of (i) refunding any such revenue bonds or revenue refunding bonds issued by the Board under this Article, including the payment of any redemption premium thereon and any interest accrued or to accrue to the date of redemption of such bonds, and (ii) paying all or any part of the cost of acquiring or constructing any additional project or projects.

The issuance of such refunding bonds, the maturities and other details thereof, the rights and remedies of the holders thereof, and the rights, powers, privileges, duties, and obligations of the Board with respect to the same, shall be governed by the foregoing provisions of this Article insofar as the same may be applicable. (1987, c. 336.)

§ 116-198.39. Bonds are exempt from taxation.

Any bonds issued under this Article shall at all times be exempt from all taxes or assessment, direct or indirect, general or special, whether imposed for the purpose of general revenue or otherwise, which are levied or assessed by the State or by any county, political subdivision, agency, or other instrumentality of the State, excluding inheritance and gift taxes, income taxes on the gain from the transfer of the bonds, and franchise taxes. The interest on the bonds is not subject to taxation as income. Bonds issued by the Board under the provisions of this Article are hereby made securities in which all public officers and public bodies of the State and its political subdivisions, all insurance companies, trust companies, banking associations, investment companies, executors, administrators, trustees, and other fiduciaries may properly and legally invest funds, including capital in their control or belonging to them. Such bonds are hereby made securities which may properly and legally be deposited with and received by any State or municipal officer or any agency or political subdivision of the State for any purpose for which the deposit of bonds or obligations of the State is now or may hereafter be authorized by law. (1987, c. 336, s. 1; 1995, c. 46, s. 8.)

§ 116-198.40. Article provides additional and alternative method of financing; not exclusive.

This Article shall be deemed to provide an additional and alternative method for the doing of the things authorized hereby and shall be regarded as supplemental and additional to powers conferred by other laws, and shall not be regarded as in derogation of or as repealing any powers now existing under any other law, either general, special, or local; provided, however, that the issuance of revenue bonds or revenue refunding bonds under the provisions of this Article need not comply with the requirements of any other law applicable to the issuance of bonds. (1987, c. 336, s. 1.)

Article 22.

Visiting Speakers at State-Supported Institutions.

§§ 116-199 through 116-200: Repealed by Session Laws 1995, c. 379, s. 17.

Article 23.

State Education Assistance.

Part 1. State Education Assistance Authority.

§ 116-201. Purpose and definitions.

(a) The purpose of this Article is to authorize a system of financial assistance, consisting of grants, loans, work-study or other employment, and other aids, to assist qualified students to enable them to obtain an education beyond the high school level by attending public or private educational institutions. The General Assembly has found and hereby declares that it is in the public interest and essential to the welfare and well-being of the State and to the proper growth and development of the State to foster and provide financial assistance to properly qualified students in order to help them to obtain an education beyond the high school level. The General Assembly has further found that many students who are fully qualified to enroll in appropriate educational institutions for furthering their education beyond the high school level lack the financial means and are unable, without financial assistance as authorized under this Article, to pay the cost of such education, with a consequent irreparable loss to the State of valuable talents vital to its welfare. The General Assembly has determined that the establishment of a proper system of financial assistance for such objective purpose serves a public purpose and is fully consistent with the long established policy of the State to encourage, promote and assist education to enhance economic development.

(b)     As used in this Article, the following terms shall have the following meanings unless the context indicates a contrary intent:

(1)     "Article" or "this Article" means Article 23 of Chapter 116 of the General Statutes of North Carolina;

(2)     "Authority" means the State Education Assistance Authority created by this Article or, if the Authority is abolished, the board, body, commission or agency succeeding to its principal functions, or on whom the powers given by this Article to the Authority shall be conferred by law;

(3)     "Bond resolution" or "resolution" when used in relation to the issuance of bonds is deemed to mean either any resolution authorizing the issuance of bonds or any trust agreement or other instrument securing any bonds;

(4)     "Bonds" or "revenue bonds" means the obligations authorized to be issued by the Authority under this Article, which may consist of revenue bonds, revenue refunding bonds, bond anticipation notes and other notes and obligations, evidencing the Authority's obligation to repay borrowed money from revenues, funds and other money pledged or made available therefor by the Authority under this Article;

(5)     "Eligible institution," with respect to student loans, has the same meaning as the term has in section 1085 of Title 20 of the United States Code;

(6)     "Eligible institution," with respect to grants and work-study programs, includes the constituent institutions of The University of North Carolina, all state-supported institutions organized and administered pursuant to Chapter 115A of the General Statutes and all private institutions as defined in subdivision (8) of this subsection;

(7)     "Student obligations" means student loan notes and other debt obligations evidencing loans to students which the Authority may make, take, acquire, buy, sell, endorse or guarantee under the provisions of this Article, and may include any direct or indirect interest in the whole or any part of any such notes or obligations;

(8) "Private institution" means an institution other than a seminary, Bible school, Bible college or similar religious institution in this State that is not owned or operated by the State or any agency or political subdivision thereof, or by any combination thereof, that offers post-high school education and is accredited by the Southern Association of Colleges and Schools or, in the case of institutions that are not eligible to be considered for accreditation, accredited in those categories and by those nationally recognized accrediting agencies that the Authority may designate;

(9) "Reserve Trust Fund" means the trust fund authorized under G.S. 116-209 of this Article;

(10) "State Education Assistance Authority Loan Fund" means the trust fund so designated and authorized by G.S. 116-209.3 of this Article;

(11) "Student," with respect to scholarships, grants, and work-study programs, means a resident of the State, in accordance with definitions of residency that may from time to time be prescribed by the Board of Governors of The University of North Carolina and published in the residency manual of the Board, who, under regulations adopted by the Authority, has enrolled or will enroll in an eligible institution for the purpose of pursuing his education beyond the high school level, who is making suitable progress in his education in accordance with standards acceptable to the Authority and, for the purposes of G.S. 116-209.19, who has not received a bachelor's degree, or qualified for it and who is otherwise classified as an undergraduate under those regulations that the Authority may promulgate;

(12) "Student," with respect to loans, means a resident of the State as defined in (11) of this subsection and an eligible student as defined in 20 U.S.C. 1071 who is enrolled in an eligible institution located in North Carolina; and

(13) "Student loans" means loans to students defined in subdivisions (11) and (12) of this subsection to aid them in pursuing their education beyond the high school level. (1965, c. 1180, s. 1; 1971, c. 392, s. 1; c. 1244, s. 14; 1979, c. 165, s. 1; 1987, c. 227, ss. 1, 2; 2010-31, s. 17.3(b); 2013-410, s. 9.1.)

§ 116-202. Authority may buy and sell students' obligations; undertakings of Authority limited to revenues.

In order to facilitate vocational and college education and to promote the industrial and economic development of the State, the State Education Assistance Authority (hereinafter created) is hereby authorized and empowered to buy and sell obligations of students attending institutions of higher education or post-secondary business, trade, technical, and other vocational schools, which obligations represent loans made to such students for the purpose of obtaining training or education.

No bonds, as this term is defined in this Article, are deemed to constitute a debt of the State, or of any political subdivision thereof or a pledge of the faith and credit of the State or of any political subdivision, but are payable solely from the funds of the Authority. All bonds shall contain on their faces a statement to the effect that neither the State nor the Authority is obligated to pay the same or the interest thereon except from revenues of the Authority and that neither the faith and credit nor the taxing power of the State or of any political subdivision is pledged to the payment of the principal of or the interest on the bonds.

All expenses incurred in carrying out the provisions of this Article shall be payable solely from funds provided under the provisions of this Article and no liability or obligation shall be incurred by the Authority hereunder beyond the extent to which moneys shall have been provided under the provisions of this Article. (1965, c. 1180, s. 1; 1967, c. 955, s. 1; 1979, c. 165, s. 2; 1987, c. 227, s. 3.)


§ 116-203. Authority created as subdivision of State; appointment, terms and removal of board of directors; officers; quorum; expenses and compensation of directors.

(a)     Authority Created. - There is created and constituted a political subdivision of the State to be known as the "State Education Assistance Authority." The exercise by the Authority of the powers conferred by this Article shall be deemed and held to be the performance of an essential governmental function.

(b)     Membership. - The Authority shall be governed by a board of directors consisting of nine members, seven of whom shall be appointed by the Governor and two of whom shall be ex officio. The members shall be as follows:

(1) Seven members appointed by the Governor, three of whom shall have expertise in secondary or higher education, two of whom shall have expertise in finance, one of whom shall be a member of the public at large with an interest in higher education, and one of whom shall be a chief financial officer from a college or university that is a member of North Carolina Independent Colleges and Universities, Inc., appointed upon the recommendation of North Carolina Independent Colleges and Universities, Inc.

(2) The chief financial officer of The University of North Carolina shall serve as an ex officio member.

(3) The chief financial officer of the North Carolina Community College System shall serve as an ex officio member.

(c) Terms. - Members appointed by the Governor shall serve for a term of four years and until their successors are appointed and duly qualified. Immediately after appointment, the directors shall enter upon the performance of their duties.

(d) Vacancies. - A vacancy in an appointment made by the Governor shall be filled by the Governor in the same manner as the original appointment for the remainder of the unexpired term.

(e) Removal. - The Governor may remove any member of the board of directors appointed by the Governor for misfeasance, malfeasance, or nonfeasance.

(f) Officers. - The board shall annually elect one of its members as chair and another as vice-chair and shall also elect annually a secretary, or a secretary-treasurer, who may or may not be a member of the board. The chair, or in the chair's absence, the vice-chair, shall preside at all meetings of the board. In the absence of both the chair and vice-chair, the board shall appoint a chair pro tempore, who shall preside at such meetings.

(g) Quorum. - Five directors shall constitute a quorum for the transaction of the business of the Authority, and no vacancy in the membership of the board shall impair the right of a quorum to exercise all the rights and perform all the duties of the Authority. The favorable vote of at least a majority of the members of the board present at any meeting is required for the adoption of any resolution or motion or for other official action.

(h)     Expenses. - The members of the board shall receive per diem and allowances as provided in G.S. 138-5 and G.S. 138-6. These expenses and compensation shall be paid from funds provided under this Article, or as otherwise provided.  (1965, c. 1180, s. 1; 1979, c. 165, s. 3; 2010-109, s. 1.)


§ 116-204.  Powers of Authority.

The Authority is hereby authorized and empowered:

(1)     To fix and revise from time to time and charge and collect fees for its acts and undertakings;

(2)     To establish rules and regulations concerning its acts and undertakings;

(3)     To acquire, hold and dispose of personal property in the exercise of its powers and the performance of its duties;

(4)     To make and enter into all contracts and agreements necessary or incidental to the performance of its duties and the execution of its powers under this Article;

(5)     To employ, in its discretion, consultants, attorneys, accountants, and financial experts, superintendents, managers and such other employees and agents as may be necessary in its judgment, and to fix their compensation to be payable from funds made available to the Authority by law;

(6)     To receive and accept from any federal or private agency, corporation, association or person grants to be expended in accomplishing the objectives of the Authority, and to receive and accept from the State, from any municipality, county or other political subdivision thereof and from any other source aid or contributions of either money, property, or other things of value, to be held, used and applied only for the purposes for which such grants and contributions may be made;

(7)     To sue and to be sued; to have a seal and to alter the same at its pleasure; and to make and from time to time amend and repeal bylaws, rules and regulations not inconsistent with law to carry into effect the powers and purposes of the Authority;

(8) To do all other acts and things necessary or convenient to carry out the powers expressly granted in this Article; provided, however, that nothing in this Article shall be construed to empower the Authority to engage in the business of banking or insurance.

(9) To collect loan repayments for loans awarded under the Teaching Fellows Program pursuant to G.S. 115C-363.23A if the loan repayment is outstanding for more than 30 days.

(10) To collect loan repayments for loans awarded from the Scholarship Loan Fund for Prospective Teachers pursuant to Article 32A of Chapter 115C of the General Statutes if the loan repayment is outstanding for more than 30 days.

(11) To administer the awarding of scholarship grants to students attending nonpublic schools as provided in Part 2A of Article 39 of Chapter 115C of the General Statutes. (1965, c. 1180, s. 1; 2002-126, s. 9.2(f); 2011-266, s. 1.38(b); 2013-360, ss. 8.29(d), 11.9.)


§ 116-205. Title to property; use of State lands; offices.

(a) Title to any property acquired by the Authority shall be taken in the name of the Authority.

(b) The State hereby consents, subject to the approval of the Governor and Council of State, to the use of any other lands or property owned by the State, which are deemed by the Authority to be necessary for its purposes.

(c) The Authority may establish such offices in state-owned or rented structures as it deems appropriate for its purposes. (1965, c. 1180, s. 1.)


§ 116-206. Acquisition of obligations.

With the proceeds of bonds or any other funds of the Authority available therefor, the Authority may acquire from any bank, insurance company, or educational lending institution, eligible student obligations, or any interest or participation therein in such amount, at such price or prices and upon such terms and conditions as the Authority shall determine to be in the public interest and desirable to carry out the purposes of this Article. The Authority shall take such actions and require the execution of such instruments deemed appropriate by it to permit the recovery, in connection with any such obligations or any interest or participation therein acquired by the Authority, of the amount to which the Authority may be rightfully entitled, and otherwise to enforce and protect its rights and interest thereto. (1965, c. 1180, s. 1; 1967, c. 955, s. 2; 1971, c. 392, s. 2, 1987, c. 227, s. 4.)

§ 116-207. Terms of acquisitions.

The Authority shall prescribe the terms, conditions and limitations upon which it will acquire a contingent or direct interest in any obligation and such terms, conditions and limitations shall include, but without limiting the generality hereof, the interest rate payable upon such obligations, the maturities thereof, the terms for payment of principal and interest, applicable life or other insurance which may be required in connection with any such obligation and who shall pay the premiums thereon, the safekeeping of assets pledged to secure any such undertaking, and any and all matters in connection with the foregoing as will protect the assets of the Authority. (1965, c. 1180, s. 1.)

§ 116-208. Construction of Article.

The provisions of this Article shall be liberally construed to the end that its beneficial purposes may be effectuated. (1965, c. 1180, s. 1.)

§ 116-209. Reserve Trust Fund created; transfer of Escheat Fund; pledge of security interest for payment of bonds; administration.

The appropriation made to the Authority under this Article shall be used exclusively for the purpose of acquiring contingent or vested rights in obligations which it may acquire under this Article; such appropriations, payments, revenue and interest as well as other income received in connection with such obligations is hereby established as a trust fund. Such fund shall be used for the purposes of the Authority other than maintenance and operation.

The maintenance and operating expenses of the Authority shall be paid from funds specifically appropriated for such purposes. No part of the trust fund established under this section shall be expended for such purposes.

The State Treasurer shall be the custodian of the assets of the Authority and shall invest them in accordance with the provisions of G.S. 147-69.2 and 147-69.3. All payments from the accounts thereof shall be made by him issued upon vouchers signed by such persons as are designated by the Authority. A duly attested copy of a resolution of the Authority designating such persons and bearing on its face the specimen signatures of such persons shall be filed with the State Treasurer as his authority for issuing warrants upon such vouchers.

The trust fund is designated "Reserve Trust Fund" and shall be maintained by the Authority, except as otherwise provided, pursuant to the provisions of this Article, as security for or insurance respecting any bonds or other obligations issued by the Authority under this Article. The corpus of the Escheat Fund, including all future additions other than the income, are transferred to, and become, a part of the Reserve Trust Fund and shall be accounted for, administered, invested, reinvested, used and applied as provided in Chapter 116B of the General Statutes. The Authority may pledge and vest a security interest in all or any part of the Reserve Trust Fund by resolution adopted or trust agreement approved by it as security for or insurance respecting the payment of bonds or other obligations issued under this Article. The Reserve Trust Fund shall be held, administered, invested, reinvested, used and applied as provided in any resolution adopted or trust agreement approved by the Authority, subject to the provisions of this Article and Chapter 116B of the General Statutes. (1965, c. 1180, s. 1; 1979, c. 165, s. 4; c. 467, s. 8; 1987, c. 227, s. 5.)

§ 116-209.1. Provisions in conflict.

Any of the foregoing provisions of this Article which shall be in conflict with the provisions hereinbelow set forth shall be repealed to the extent of such conflict. (1967, c. 1177.)

§ 116-209.2. Reserves.

The Authority may provide in any resolution authorizing the issuance of bonds or any trust agreement securing any bonds that proceeds of such bonds may be used to establish reserve accounts in any trustee or banking institution or otherwise as determined by the Authority, for securing such bonds and facilitating the making of student loans and acquiring student obligations, to provide for the payment of interest on such bonds for such period of time as the Authority shall determine, and for such other purposes as will facilitate the issuance of bonds at rates of interest and upon terms deemed reasonable by the Authority and will, in the Authority's judgment, facilitate carrying out the purposes of this Article. (1967, c. 1177; 1971, c. 392, s. 3.)


§ 116-209.3. Additional powers.

The Authority is authorized to develop and administer programs and perform all functions necessary or convenient to promote and facilitate the making and insuring of student loans and providing such other student loan assistance and services as the Authority shall deem necessary or desirable for carrying out the purposes of this Article and for qualifying for loans, grants, insurance and other benefits and assistance under any program of the United States now or hereafter authorized fostering student loans. There shall be established and maintained a trust fund which shall be designated "State Education Assistance Authority Loan Fund" (the "Loan Fund") which may be used by the Authority in making student loans directly or through agents or independent contractors, insuring student loans, acquiring, purchasing, endorsing or guaranteeing promissory notes, contracts, obligations or other legal instruments evidencing student loans made by banks, educational institutions, nonprofit corporations or other eligible lenders, and for defraying the expenses of operation and administration of the Authority for which other funds are not available to the Authority. There shall be deposited to the credit of such Loan Fund the proceeds (exclusive of accrued interest) derived from the sale of its revenue bonds by the Authority and any other moneys made available to the Authority for the making or insuring of student loans or the purchase of obligations. There shall also be deposited to the credit of the Loan Fund surplus funds from time to time transferred by the Authority from the sinking fund. Such Loan Fund shall be maintained as a revolving fund. There is also deposited to the credit of the Loan Fund the income derived from the investment or deposit of the Escheat Fund distributed to the Authority pursuant to G.S. 116B-7. The income shall be held, administered and applied by the Authority as provided in any resolution adopted or trust agreement approved by the Authority, subject to the provisions of Chapter 116B of the General Statutes and this Article.

In lieu of or in addition to the Loan Fund, the Authority may provide in any resolution authorizing the issuance of bonds or any trust agreement securing such bonds that any other trust funds or accounts may be established as may be deemed necessary or convenient for securing the bonds or for making student loans, acquiring obligations or otherwise carrying out its other powers under this Article, and there may be deposited to the credit of any such fund or account proceeds of bonds or other money available to the Authority for the purposes to be served by such fund or account. (1967, c. 1177; 1971, c. 392, s. 4; 1979, c. 165, s. 5; 1987, c. 227, s. 6; 1999-460, s. 12.)


§ 116-209.4. Authority to issue bonds.

The Authority is hereby authorized to provide for the issuance, at one time or from time to time, of revenue bonds of the Authority in such principal amounts as the Board of Directors shall determine to be necessary. The bonds shall be designated, subject to such additions or changes as the Authority deems advisable, "State Education Assistance Authority Revenue Bonds, Series____," inserting in the blank space a letter identifying the particular series of bonds.

The principal of and the interest on such bonds shall be payable solely from the funds herein provided for such payment. The bonds of each issue shall be dated, shall bear interest at such rate or rates, shall mature at such time or times not exceeding 30 years from their date or dates, as may be determined by the Authority, and may be made redeemable before maturity, at the option of the Authority, at such price or prices and under such terms and conditions as may be fixed by the Authority prior to the issuance of the bonds. Prior to the preparation of definitive bonds, the Authority may, under like restrictions, issue interim receipts or temporary bonds, with or without coupons, exchangeable for definitive bonds when such bonds shall have been executed and are available for delivery. The Authority may also provide for the replacement of any bonds which shall become mutilated or shall be destroyed or lost. The Authority shall determine the form and the manner of execution of the bonds, including any interest coupons to be attached thereto, and shall fix the denomination or denominations of the bonds and the place or places of payment of principal and interest, which may be at any bank or trust company within or without the State. In case any officer whose signature or a facsimile of whose signature shall appear on any bonds or coupons shall cease to be such officer before the delivery of such bonds, such signature or such facsimile shall nevertheless be valid and sufficient for all purposes the same as if he had remained in office until such delivery. The Authority may also provide for the authentication of the bonds by a fiscal agent. The bonds may be issued in coupon or in registered form, or both, as the Authority may determine, and provision may be made for the registration of any coupon bonds as to principal alone and also as to both principal and interest, and for the reconversion into coupon bonds of any bonds registered as to both principal and interest, and for the interchange of registered and coupon bonds. The Authority may sell such bonds in such manner, either at public or private sale, and for such price as it may determine will best effectuate the purposes of this Article.

The Authority is authorized to provide in any resolution authorizing the issuance of bonds for pledging or assigning as security for its revenue bonds, subject to any prior pledge or assignment, and for deposit to the credit of the sinking fund, any or all of its income, receipts, funds or other assets, exclusive of bond proceeds and other funds required to be deposited to the credit of the Loan Fund, of whatsoever kind from time to time acquired or owned by the Authority, including all donations, grants and other money or property made available to it, payments received on student loans, such as principal, interest and penalties, if any, premiums on student loan insurance, fees, charges and other income derived from services rendered or otherwise, proceeds of property or insurance, earnings and profits on investments of funds and from sales, purchases, endorsements or guarantees of obligations, as defined in G.S. 116-201 hereof, and other securities and instruments, contract rights, any funds, rights, insurance or other benefits acquired pursuant to any federal law or contract to the extent not in conflict therewith, money recovered through the enforcement of any remedies or rights, and any other funds or things of value which in the determination of the Authority may enhance the marketability of its revenue bonds. Money in the sinking fund shall be disbursed in such manner and under such restrictions as the Authority may provide in the resolution authorizing the issuance of such bonds. Unless otherwise provided in the bond resolution, the revenue bonds at any time issued hereunder shall be entitled to payment from the sinking fund without preference or priority of the bonds first issued. Bonds may be issued under the provisions of this Article without obtaining, except as otherwise expressly provided in this Article, the consent of any department, division, commission, board, body, bureau or agency of the State, and without any other proceedings or the happening of any conditions or things other than those proceedings, conditions or things which are specifically required by this

Article and the provisions of the resolution authorizing the issuance of such bonds.

The Authority is authorized to provide by resolution or in any trust agreement for the issuance of revenue refunding bonds of the Authority for the purpose of refunding, or advance refunding and paying, any bonds then outstanding, which have been issued under the provisions of this Article, including the payment of any redemption premium and of any interest accrued or to accrue up to the date of redemption of the bonds, and, if deemed advisable by the Authority, for making student loans or acquiring obligations under this Article. The issuance of the revenue refunding bonds, the maturities and other details, the rights of the holders and the rights, duties and obligations of the Authority, shall be governed by the appropriate provisions of this Article relating to the issuance of revenue bonds. Revenue refunding bonds issued under this section may be sold or exchanged for outstanding bonds issued under this Article. If sold, in addition to any other authorized purpose, the proceeds may be deposited in an escrow or other trust fund and invested, in whole or in part, and with the earnings from the investments, may be applied to the purchase or to the redemption prior to, or to payment at maturity, of outstanding bonds, all as provided by resolution or in trust agreement securing the bonds. (1967, c. 1177; 1971, c. 392, ss. 5-7; 1979, c. 165, s. 6.)

§ 116-209.5. Bond resolution.

The resolution providing for the issuance of such bonds may contain such provisions for protecting and enforcing the rights and remedies of the bondholders as may be reasonable and proper and not in violation of law, including covenants setting forth the duties of the Authority in relation to the purchase or sale of obligations, the making of student loans, the insurance of student loans, the fees, charges and premiums to be fixed and collected, the terms and conditions for the issuance of additional bonds and the custody, safeguarding and application of all moneys. It shall be lawful for any bank or trust company incorporated under the laws of the State which may act as depositary of the proceeds of bonds, revenues or other money hereunder to furnish such indemnifying bonds or to pledge such securities as may be required by the Authority. Any such resolution may set forth the rights and remedies of the bondholders and may restrict the individual right of action by bondholders. All expenses incurred in carrying out the provisions of such resolution may be treated as a part of the cost of administering this Article and may be payable, together with other expenses of operation and administration under this Article incurred by the Authority, from the Loan Fund.

In the discretion of the Authority, any bonds issued under the provisions of this Article may be secured by a trust agreement by and between the Authority and a corporate trustee, which may be any trust company or bank having powers of a trust company within or without the State. Such trust agreement or the resolution providing for the issuance of such bonds may pledge or assign the fees, penalties, charges, proceeds from collections, grants, subsidies, donations and other funds and revenues to be received therefor. Such trust agreement or resolution providing for the issuance of such bonds may contain such provisions for protecting and enforcing the rights and remedies of the holders of such bonds as may be reasonable and proper and not in violation of law, including covenants setting forth the duties of the Authority in relation to student loans, the acquisition of obligations, insurance, the fees, penalties and other charges to be fixed and collected, the sale or purchase of obligations or any part thereof, or other property, the terms and conditions for the issuance of additional bonds, and the custody, safeguarding and application of all moneys. It shall be lawful for any bank or trust company incorporated under the laws of the State which may act as depositary of the proceeds of bonds, revenues or other money hereunder to furnish such indemnifying bonds or to pledge such securities as may be required by the Authority. Any such trust agreement or resolution may set forth the rights and remedies of the bondholders and of the trustee, and may restrict the individual right of action by bondholders. In addition to the foregoing, any such trust agreement or resolution may contain such other provisions as the Authority may deem reasonable and proper for the security of the bondholders. All expenses incurred in carrying out the provisions of such trust agreement or resolution may be treated as a part of the cost of carrying out the purposes for which such bonds shall be issued.

In addition to all other powers granted to the Authority by this Article, the Authority is hereby authorized to pledge to the payment of the principal of and the interest on any bonds under the provisions of this Article any moneys received or to be received by it under any appropriation made to it by the General Assembly, unless the appropriation is restricted by the General Assembly to specific purposes of the Authority or such pledge is prohibited by the law making such appropriation; provided, however, that nothing herein shall be construed to obligate the General Assembly to make any such appropriation. (1967, c. 1177; 1971, c. 392, s. 8.)

§ 116-209.6.  Revenues.

The Authority is authorized to fix and collect fees, charges, interest and premiums for making or insuring student loans, purchasing, endorsing or guaranteeing obligations and any other services performed under this Article. The Authority is further authorized to contract with the United States of America or any agency or officer thereof and with any person, partnership, association, banking institution or other corporation respecting the carrying out of the Authority's functions under this Article. The Authority shall at all times endeavor to fix and collect such fees, charges, receipts, premiums and other income so as to have available in the sinking fund at all times an amount which, together with any other funds made available therefor, shall be sufficient to pay the principal of and the interest on such bonds as the same shall become due and payable and to create reserves for such purposes. Money in the sinking fund, except such part thereof as may be necessary to provide such reserves for the bonds as may be provided for in the resolution authorizing the issuance of such bonds, shall be set aside in the sinking fund at such regular intervals as may be provided in such resolution and is hereby pledged to, and charged with, the payment of the principal of and the interest on such bonds as the same shall become due and the redemption price or the purchase price of bonds retired by call or purchase as therein provided. Such pledge shall be valid and binding from the time when the pledge is made. The fees, charges, receipts, proceeds and other revenues and moneys so pledged and thereafter received by the Authority shall immediately be subject to the lien of such pledge without any physical delivery thereof or further act, and the lien of any such pledge shall be valid and binding as against all parties having claims of any kind in tort, contract or otherwise against the Authority, irrespective of whether such parties have notice thereof. The resolution by which a pledge is created need not be filed or recorded except in the records of the Authority. The use and disposition of money to the credit of the sinking fund shall be subject to the provisions of the resolution authorizing the issuance of such bonds. Any such resolution may, in the discretion of the Authority, provide for the transfer of surplus money in the sinking fund to the credit of the Loan Fund. Except as may otherwise be provided in such resolution, such sinking fund shall be a fund for all such bonds without distinction or priority of one over another. (1967, c. 1177.)

§ 116-209.7.  Trust funds.

Notwithstanding any other provisions of law to the contrary, all money received pursuant to the authority of the Article, whether as proceeds from the sale of bonds, sale of property or insurance, or as payments of student loans, whether principal, interest or penalties, if any, thereon, or as insurance premiums, or from the purchase or sale of obligations, or as any other receipts or revenues derived hereunder, shall be deemed to be trust funds to be held and applied solely as provided in this Article. The resolution authorizing the bonds of any issue may provide that any of such money may be temporarily invested pending the disbursement thereof and shall provide that any officer with whom, or any bank or trust company with which, such money shall be deposited shall act as trustee of such money and shall hold and apply the same for the purposes hereof, subject to such regulations as this Article and such resolution may provide. (1967, c. 1177.)

§ 116-209.8. Remedies.

Any holder of bonds issued under the provisions of this Article or any of the coupons appertaining thereto, except to the extent the rights herein given may be restricted by such resolution authorizing the issuance of such bonds, may either at law or in equity, by suit, action, mandamus or other proceeding, protect and enforce any and all rights under the laws of the State or granted hereunder or under such resolution authorizing the issuance of such bonds, or under any contract executed by the Authority pursuant to this Article, and may enforce and compel the performance of all duties required by this Article or by such resolution to be performed by the Authority or by any officer thereof, including the fixing, charging and collecting of fees, charges and premiums and the collection of principal, interest and penalties, if any, on student loans or obligations evidencing such loans. The Authority may provide in any trust agreement securing the bonds that any such rights may be enforced for and on behalf of the holders of bonds by the trustee under such trust agreement. (1967, c. 1177; 1971, c. 392, s. 9.)

§ 116-209.9. Negotiability of bonds.

All bonds issued under the provisions of this Article shall have and are hereby declared to have all the qualities and incidents, including negotiability, of investment securities under the Uniform Commercial Code of the State but no provision of such Code respecting the filing of a financial statement to perfect a security interest shall be deemed applicable to or necessary for any security interest created in connection with the issuance of any such bonds. (1967, c. 1177; 1971, c. 392, s. 10.)

§ 116-209.10. Bonds eligible for investment.

Bonds issued by the Authority under the provisions of this Article are hereby made securities in which all public officers and public bodies of the State and its political subdivisions, all insurance companies, trust companies, banking associations, investment companies, executors, administrators, trustees and other fiduciaries may properly and legally invest funds, including capital in their control or belonging to them. Such bonds are hereby made securities which may properly and legally be deposited with and received by any State or municipal officer or any agency or political subdivision of the State for any purpose for which the deposit of bonds or obligations of the State is now or may hereafter be authorized by law. (1967, c. 1177.)

§ 116-209.11. Additional pledge.

Notwithstanding any other provision to the contrary herein, the Authority is hereby authorized to pledge as security for any bonds issued hereunder any contract between the Authority and the United States of America under which the United States agrees to make funds available to the Authority for any of the purposes of this Article, to insure or guarantee the payment of interest or principal on student loans, or otherwise to aid in promoting or facilitating student loans. (1967, c. 1177.)

§ 116-209.12. Credit of State not pledged.

Bonds issued under the provisions of this Article shall not be deemed to constitute a debt, liability or obligation of the State or of any political subdivision thereof or a pledge of the faith and credit of the State or of any such political subdivision, but shall be payable solely from the revenues and other funds provided therefor. Each bond issued under this Article shall contain on the face thereof a statement to the effect that the Authority shall not be obligated to pay the same nor the interest thereon except from the revenues, proceeds and other funds pledged therefor and that neither the faith and credit nor the taxing power of the State or of any political subdivision thereof is pledged to the payment of the principal of or the interest on such bonds. Expenses incurred by the Authority in carrying out the provisions of this Article may be made payable from funds provided pursuant to this Article and no liability or obligation shall be incurred by the Authority hereunder beyond the extent to which moneys shall have been so provided. (1967, c. 1177.)

§ 116-209.13. Tax exemption.

The exercise of the powers granted by this Article in all respects will be for the benefit of the people of the State, for their well-being and prosperity and for the improvement of their social and economic conditions, and the Authority shall not be required to pay any taxes on any property owned by the Authority under the provisions of this Article or upon the income therefrom, and the bonds issued under the provisions of this Article shall at all times be free from taxation by the State or any local unit or political subdivision or other instrumentality of the State, excepting inheritance or gift taxes, income taxes on the gain from the transfer of the bonds, and franchise taxes. The interest on the bonds is not subject to taxation as income. (1967, c. 1177; 1995, c. 46, s. 9.)

§ 116-209.14. Annual reports.

The Authority shall, following the close of each fiscal year, publish an annual report of its activities for the preceding year to the Governor and the General Assembly. Each report shall set forth a complete operating and financial statement covering the operations of the Authority during the year. The operations of the Authority shall be subject to the oversight of the State Auditor pursuant to Article 5A of Chapter 147 of the General Statutes. (1967, c. 1177; 1979, c. 165, s. 7; 1983, c. 913, s. 20.)

§ 116-209.15. Merger of trust fund.

The Authority may merge into the Loan Fund the trust fund established pursuant to G.S. 116-209 hereof and may transfer from such trust fund to the credit of the Loan Fund all money, investments and other assets and resources credited to such trust fund, for application and use in accordance with the provisions of this Article pertaining to the Loan Fund, including the power to pay expenses of the Authority from the Loan Fund to the extent that other funds are not available therefor. (1967, c. 1177.)

§ 116-209.16. Other powers; criteria.

The Authority, in addition to all the powers more specifically vested hereunder, shall have all other powers necessary or convenient to carry out and effectuate the purposes and provisions of this Article, including the power to receive, administer and comply with the conditions and requirements respecting any gift, grant or donation of any property or money, any insurance or guarantee of any student loan or student obligations, any loans, advances, contributions, interest subsidies or any other assistance from any federal or State agency or other entity; to pledge or assign any money, charges, fees or other revenues and any proceeds derived by the Authority from any student loans, obligations, sales of property, insurance or other sources; to borrow money and to issue in evidence thereof revenue bonds of the Authority for the purposes of this Article and to issue revenue refunding bonds; to conduct studies and surveys respecting the needs for financial assistance of residents of the State respecting education beyond the high school level.

In carrying out the powers vested and the responsibilities imposed under this Article, the Authority shall be guided by and shall observe the following criteria and requirements, the determination of the Authority as to compliance with such criteria and requirements being final and conclusive:

(1) Any student loan, grant or other assistance provided by the Authority to any student shall be necessary to enable the student to pursue his education above the high school level; and

(2) No student loan, grant or other financial assistance shall be provided to any student by the Authority except in conformity with the provisions of this Article and to carry out the purposes hereof.

The Authority shall by rules and regulations prescribe other conditions, criteria and requirements that it shall deem necessary or desirable for providing financial assistance to students under this Article upon a fair and equitable basis, giving due regard to the needs and qualifications of the students and to the purposes of this Article. (1971, c. 392, s. 11.)

§ 116-209.17. Establishment of student assistance program.

The Authority is authorized, in addition to all other powers and duties vested or imposed under this Article, to establish and administer a statewide student assistance program for the purpose of removing, insofar as may be possible, the financial barriers to education beyond the high school level for eligible needy students at public or private institutions in this State and, with respect to loans, public, and private institutions located elsewhere. This objective shall be accomplished, consistent with Federal law or regulation, through a comprehensive program under which the financial ability of each student and of his family, under standards prescribed by the Authority, is measured against the reasonable costs, as determined by the Authority, of the educational program which the student proposes to pursue. Needs of students for financial assistance shall, to the extent of the availability of funds from federal, State, institutional or other sources, be met through work-study programs, loans, grants and out-of-term employment, or a combination of these forms of assistance. With respect to grants made pursuant to this Article, no student is eligible to receive benefits under this student assistance program for a total of more than 45 months of full-time, post-high school level education. (1971, c. 392, s. 11; 1979, c. 165, s. 8; 1987, c. 227, s. 7.)

§ 116-209.18. Powers of Authority to administer student assistance program.

In order to accomplish the purposes of this Article the Authority is authorized:

(1) To receive from the general fund or other sources such sums as the General Assembly may authorize from time to time for such purposes, and to receive from any other donor, public or private, such sums as may be made available, and to cause such sums to be disbursed for the purposes for which they have been provided;

(2) To establish such criteria as the Authority shall deem necessary or desirable for determining the need of students for grants under this Article, as

opposed to other forms of financial assistance, and for deciding who shall receive grants;

(3)   To prescribe the form and to regulate the submission of applications for assistance and to prescribe the procedures for considering and approving such applications;

(4)   To provide for the making of, and to make, grants under this Article under such terms and conditions as the Authority shall deem advisable;

(5)   To encourage educational institutions to increase the resources available for financial assistance; to prescribe such formulas for institutional maintenance of effort as the Authority may determine to be consistent with the purposes of this Article;

(6)   To provide by contract for the administration of all or any portion of the student assistance program by nonprofit organizations or corporations, pursuant to regulations and criteria established by the Authority;

(7)   To serve, on designation by the Governor, or as may otherwise be provided by federal law, as the State agency to administer such statewide programs of student assistance as shall be established from time to time under federal law; and

(8)   To have all other powers and authority necessary to carry out the purposes of the student assistance program, including, without limitation, all the powers given to the Authority by G.S. 116-204 and by other provisions of the General Statutes. (1971, c. 392, s. 11.)


§ 116-209.19.  Grants to students.

The Authority is authorized to make grants to eligible students enrolled or to be enrolled in eligible institutions in North Carolina out of such money as from time to time may be appropriated by the State or as may otherwise be available to the Authority for such grants. The Authority, subject to the provisions of this Article and any applicable appropriation act, shall adopt rules, regulations and procedures for determining the needs of the respective students for grants and for the purpose of making such grants. The amount of any grant made by the Authority to any student, whether enrolled or to be enrolled in any private institution or any tax-supported public institution, shall be determined by the Authority upon the basis of substantially similar standards and guides that shall be set forth in the Authority's rules, regulations and procedures; provided, however, that grants made in any fiscal year to students enrolled or to be enrolled in private institutions may be increased to compensate, in whole or in part, for the average annual State appropriated tuition subsidy for such fiscal year, determined as provided herein. The average annual State appropriated subsidy for each fiscal year shall be determined by the Secretary of Administration, after consultation with the Board of Governors of the University of North Carolina and the Authority, for each of the two categories of tax-supported institutions, being (i) institutions, presently 16, that provide education of the collegiate grade and grant baccalaureate degrees and (ii) institutions, such as community colleges and technical institutes created and existing under Chapter 115A of the General Statutes and community colleges created and existing under Chapter 115D of the General Statutes. The average annual State appropriated subsidy for each of such two categories of institutions shall mean the amount of the total appropriations of the State for the respective fiscal years under the current operations budgets, pursuant to the State Budget Act reasonably allocable to undergraduate students enrolled in such institutions exclusive of the Division of Health Affairs of the University of North Carolina and the North Carolina School of the Arts, redesignated effective August 1, 2008, as the "University of North Carolina School of the Arts" for all institutions in such category, all as shall be determined by the Secretary of Administration after consultation as above provided, divided by the budgeted number of North Carolina undergraduate students to be enrolled in such fiscal year.

The Authority, in determining the needs of students for grants, may among other factors, give consideration to the amount of other financial assistance that may be available to the students, such as nonrepayable awards under the Pell Grant Program, the Health Professions Education Assistance Act or other student assistance programs created by federal law. (1971, c. 392, s. 11; c. 1244, s. 14; 1975, c. 879, s. 46; 1979,c. 165, s. 9; 1983, c. 717, s. 35; 1985 (Reg. Sess., 1986), c.955, ss. 38, 39; 1987, c. 227, s. 8; c. 564, s. 23; 2006-203, s. 54; 2008-192, s. 9.)


§ 116-209.19A. Limit semesters eligible for need-based grants and scholarships.

The Authority administers the following need-based grant and scholarship programs: the Education Lottery Scholarships, North Carolina Community College Grant Program, The University of North Carolina Need-Based Financial Aid Program, and Need-Based Scholarships for Students Attending Private Institutions of Higher Education. G.S. 115C-499.2A, 115D-40.2, 116-25.1, and 116-281.1 limit the number of semesters that a student may receive a grant or scholarship from any of those programs and also provide the circumstances in which a waiver to those limits may be granted by the appropriate postsecondary institution. The Authority shall enforce these limitations in administering these programs so that unless a waiver is granted by the appropriate postsecondary institution, no student shall receive a grant or scholarship from any of those programs or any combination of those financial aid programs while pursuing a degree, diploma, or certificate for more than any of the following time periods: (i) 10 full-time academic semesters or its equivalent if enrolled part-time or (ii) 12 full-time academic semesters or its equivalent if the student is enrolled in a program officially designated as a five-year degree program.

A postsecondary institution that grants a waiver under G.S. 115C-499.2A, 115D-40.2, 116-25.1, or 116-281.1 shall certify the granting of the waiver in a manner acceptable to the Authority and shall also maintain documentation substantiating the reason for the waiver. (2013-360, s. 11.15(g).)

§ 116-209.20. Public purpose.

No expenditure of funds under this Article shall be made for any purpose other than a public purpose. (1971, c. 392, s. 11.)

§ 116-209.21. Cooperation of the Board of Governors of the University of North Carolina.

The Board of Governors of the University of North Carolina shall provide the secretariat for the Authority. The Executive Director of the Authority, who shall be its principal executive officer, shall be elected by the Board of Directors of the Authority on nomination of the President of the University of North Carolina. (1971, c. 392, s. 11; c. 1244, s. 14.)

§ 116-209.22. Constitutional construction.

The provisions of this Article are severable, and if any of its provisions shall be held unconstitutional by any court of competent jurisdiction, the decision of such court shall not affect or impair any of the remaining provisions. (1971, c. 392, s. 11.)

§ 116-209.23. Inconsistent laws inapplicable.

Insofar as the provisions of this Article are inconsistent with the provisions of any general or special laws, or parts thereof, the provisions of this Article shall be controlling, except that no provision of the 1971 amendments to this Article shall apply to scholarships for children of war veterans as set forth in Article 4 of Chapter 165, as amended. (1971, c. 392, s. 11.)

§ 116-209.24. Parental loans.

(a) Policy. - The General Assembly of North Carolina hereby finds and declares that the making and insuring of loans to the eligible parents of students is fully consistent with and furthers the long established policy of the State to encourage, promote and assist education as more fully set forth in G.S. 116-201(a).

(b) Definitions. - As used in this section, the following terms shall have the following meanings:

(1) "Obligations", "student obligations", or "student loan obligations" as defined under G.S. 116-201(b)(7) includes, unless the context indicates a contrary intent, parental obligations.

(2) "Parent" means a student's mother, father, adoptive parent, or legal guardian of the student if such guardian is required by court order to use his or her own financial resources to support that student.

(3) "Parental loans" means loans made or guaranteed by the Authority to a parent of an eligible student.

(4) "Parental obligations" means obligations evidencing loans made pursuant to subsection (c) of this section.

(5) "Student loans" includes, unless the context indicates a contrary intent, parental loans.

(c) Parental Assistance. - The Authority is authorized to develop and administer programs and perform all functions necessary or convenient to promote and facilitate the making and insuring of loans to parents of students in order to facilitate the vocational and college education of such students who are enrolled or to be enrolled in eligible institutions. The Authority is also authorized to provide such other services and loan assistance to parents of students as the Authority shall deem necessary or desirable for carrying out the purpose of this section and for qualifying for loans, grants, insurance, and other benefits and assistance under any program of the United States now or hereafter authorized fostering loans to eligible parents of students.

(d) Authorization to Buy and Sell Parental Obligations. - The Authority is hereby authorized and empowered to buy and sell parental obligations.

(e) Authorization to Issue Bonds. - The Authority is hereby authorized to provide for the issuance, at one time or from time to time, of bonds or revenue bonds, as such terms are defined in G.S. 116-201(4), in conformity with provisions of this section. (1981, c. 794, s. 1; 1987, c. 227, s. 9.)


§ 116-209.25. Parental Savings Trust Fund.

(a) Policy. - The General Assembly of North Carolina hereby finds and declares that encouraging parents and other interested parties to save for the postsecondary education expenses of eligible students is fully consistent with and furthers the long-established policy of the State to encourage, promote, and assist education as more fully set forth in G.S. 116-201(a).

(b) Parental Savings Trust Fund. - There is established a parental savings trust fund to be administered by the State Education Assistance Authority to enable qualified parents to save funds to meet the costs of the postsecondary education expenses of eligible students.

(c) Contributions to the Trust Funds. - The Authority is authorized to accept, hold, invest, and disburse contributions, and interest earned on such contributions, from qualified parents and other interested parties as trustee of the Parental Savings Trust Fund. The Authority shall hold all contributions to the Parental Savings Trust Fund, and any earnings thereon, in a separate trust fund and shall invest the contributions in accordance with this section. The assets of the Parental Savings Trust Fund shall at all times be preserved, invested, and expended solely for the purposes of the trust fund and shall be held in trust for the parents and other interested parties and their designated beneficiaries. Nothing in this Article shall be construed to prohibit the Authority from accepting, holding, and investing contributions from persons who reside outside of North Carolina. Neither the contributions to the Parental Savings Trust Fund, nor the earnings thereon, shall be considered State moneys, assets of the State, or State revenue for any purpose.

(c1) Investments. - The Authority shall determine an appropriate investment strategy for the Parental Savings Trust Fund. The strategy may include a combination of fixed income assets and preferred or common stocks issued by any company incorporated, or otherwise located within or without the United States, or other appropriate investment instruments to achieve long-term return through a combination of capital appreciation and current income. The Authority may deposit all or any portion of the Parental Savings Trust Fund for investment either with the State Treasurer, or in the individual, common, or collective trust funds of an investment manager or managers that meet the requirements of this subsection. Contributions to the Parental Savings Trust Fund on deposit with the State Treasurer shall be invested by the State Treasurer as authorized in G.S. 147-69.2(b)(1) through (6) and the applicable provisions of G.S. 147-69.3. Contributions to the Parental Savings Trust Fund may be invested in the individual, common, or collective trust funds of an investment manager provided that the investment manager meets both of the following conditions:

(1) The investment manager has assets under management of at least one hundred million dollars ($100,000,000) at all times.

(2) The investment manager is subject to the jurisdiction and regulation of the United States Securities and Exchange Commission.

(d) Administration of the Trust Fund. - The Authority is authorized to develop and perform all functions necessary and desirable to administer the Parental Savings Trust Fund and to provide such other services as the Authority shall deem necessary to facilitate participation in the Parental Savings Trust

Fund. The Authority is further authorized to obtain the services of such investment advisors or program managers as may be necessary for the proper administration and marketing and investment strategy for the Parental Savings Trust Fund.

(e)     Loan Program. - The Authority is authorized to develop and administer a loan program in conjunction with the Parental Savings Trust Fund to provide loan assistance to qualified parents and interested parties in order to facilitate the postsecondary education of eligible students. All funds appropriated to, or otherwise received by the Authority for loans under this section, all funds received as repayment of such loans, and all interest earned on these funds shall be placed in an institutional trust fund. This institutional trust fund may be used only for loans made to qualified parents and interested parties who contributed to the Parental Savings Trust Fund and administrative costs associated with the recovery of funds advanced under this loan program.

(f)     Limitations. - Nothing in this section shall be construed to create any obligation of the Authority, the State Treasurer, the State, or any agency or instrumentality of the State to guarantee for the benefit of any parent, other interested party, or designated beneficiary the rate of return or other return for any contribution to the Parental Savings Trust Fund and the payment of interest or other return on any contribution to the Parental Savings Trust Fund. (1996, 2nd Ex. Sess., c. 18, s. 16.7; 2000-177, s. 11; 2001-243, s. 1; 2002-159, s. 19.)

§ 116-209.26: Repealed by Session Laws 2009-451, s. 9.2(e), effective July 1, 2010.

§ 116-209.27.  Reserved for future codification purposes.

§ 116-209.28.  Reserved for future codification purposes.

§ 116-209.29.  Reserved for future codification purposes.

§ 116-209.30:  Repealed by Session Laws 2011-74, s. 9(a), effective July 1, 2012.

§ 116-209.31: Reserved for future codification purposes.

§ 116-209.32: Reserved for future codification purposes.

§ 116-209.33: Repealed by Session Laws 2011-74, s. 7(a), effective July 1, 2012.

§ 116-209.34: Repealed by Session Laws 2011-74, s. 7(a), effective July 1, 2012.

§ 116-209.35: Repealed by Session Laws 2011-74, s. 8, effective July 1, 2012.

§ 116-209.36: Repealed by Session Laws 2008-107, s. 9.1(a), effective July 1, 2008.

§ 116-209.37: Reserved for future codification purposes.

§ 116-209.38: Repealed by Session Laws 2009-451, s. 9.18(c), effective July 1, 2011.

§ 116-209.39: Reserved for future codification purposes.

§ 116-209.40: Repealed by Session Laws 2013-360, s. 11.2(d), effective July 1, 2013.

§ 116-209.45. Forgivable Education Loans for Service Program and Fund.

(a)     Policy. - The General Assembly finds that it is in the public interest to provide financial assistance in the form of forgivable loans for service to qualified students who are committed to working in the State in order to respond to critical employment shortages.

(b)     Definitions. - The following definitions apply in this section:

(1)     Eligible Institution. - Notwithstanding G.S. 116-201(b)(5) and G.S. 116-201(b)(6) and for purposes of this section only, an institution of higher education that is any of the following:

a.      A postsecondary constituent institution of The University of North Carolina as defined in G.S. 116-2(4).

b.      A community college as defined in G.S. 115D-2(2).

c. through e. Repealed by Session Laws 2012-142, s. 9.2(a), effective July 1, 2012.

f. Another public or nonprofit postsecondary institution offering a program of study not otherwise available in North Carolina that is deemed to be eligible under rules promulgated by the Authority.

g. An eligible private postsecondary institution as defined in G.S. 116-280(3).

(2) Fund. - The Forgivable Education Loans for Service Fund.

(3) Loan. - A forgivable loan made under the Program.

(4) Program. - The Forgivable Education Loans for Service Program.

(c) Establish Forgivable Education Loans for Service Program. - There is established the Forgivable Education Loans for Service Program to be administered by the Authority. The purpose of the Program is to facilitate and promote the making, insuring, and collection of loans from the Forgivable Education Loans for Service Fund. The Program shall initially target future teachers, nurses, and allied health professionals.

(d) Establish Forgivable Loans for Service Fund. - There is established the Forgivable Education Loans for Service Fund to be administered by the Authority. The purpose of the Fund is to provide financial assistance to qualified students to enable them to obtain the requisite education beyond the high school level to work in North Carolina in certain high-need professions as identified by the General Assembly and to respond to current as well as future employment shortages in North Carolina.

(e) Eligibility for Loans. - The Authority shall establish the criteria for initial and continuing eligibility to participate in the Program. All loan recipients shall be residents of North Carolina and shall attend an eligible institution.

The Authority shall adopt standards deemed appropriate by the Authority to ensure that only qualified, potential recipients receive a loan under the Program. The standards may include minimum grade point average and satisfactory academic progress.

(f) Loan Terms and Conditions. - The following terms and conditions shall apply to each loan made pursuant to this section:

(1) Promissory note. - All loans shall be evidenced by promissory notes made payable to the Authority.

(2) Interest. - All promissory notes shall bear an interest rate established by the Authority that does not exceed ten percent (10%) and is in relation to the current interest rate for nonneed-based federal loans made pursuant to Title IV of the Higher Education Act of 1965, as amended. Interest shall accrue from the date of disbursement of the loan funds.

(3) Loan amount. - The Authority shall establish the amount of the loan based on funds available and factors such as the recipient's educational program, enrollment status, and field of study.

(4) Repayment. - The Authority shall establish the criteria for loan forgiveness for employment in a designated field in North Carolina. These criteria may provide for accelerated repayment and less than full-time employment options. The Authority shall collect cash repayments when service repayment is not completed. The Authority shall establish the terms for cash repayment, including a minimum monthly repayment amount and maximum period of time to complete repayment.

(5) Death and disability. - The Authority may forgive all or part of a loan if it determines that it is impossible for the recipient to repay the loan in cash or service because of the death or disability of the recipient.

(6) Hardship. - The Authority may grant a forbearance, a deferment, or both in hardship circumstances when a good faith effort has been made to repay the loan in a timely manner.

(7) Other. - The Authority may establish other terms and conditions that are necessary or convenient to effectuate the Program.

(g) Advisory Group. - The Authority shall appoint an advisory group composed of, at minimum, appropriate representatives from higher education institutions and health and labor departments, agencies, or commissions to make recommendations to the Authority regarding the Authority's future apportionment and distribution of Program loans based on projected labor market shortages, higher education enrollment projections, and other relevant information.

(h)     Use of Fund Monies. - All funds appropriated to or otherwise received by the Authority to provide loans through the Program, all funds received as repayment of loans, and all interest earned on these funds shall be placed in the Fund. The Fund shall be used only for loans made pursuant to this section and for administrative costs of the Authority.

(i)     Rule-making Authority. - The Authority may adopt rules necessary to implement, administer, and enforce the provisions of this section.

(j)     Report to the General Assembly. - The Authority shall report no later than December 1, 2013, and annually thereafter to the Joint Legislative Education Oversight Committee regarding the Fund and loans awarded from the Fund. (2011-74, s. 1; 2012-142, s. 9.2(a).)


Part 2. North Carolina National Guard Tuition Assistance Act of 1975.

§ 116-209.50.  Short title.

This Part shall be known and may be cited as the North Carolina National Guard Tuition Assistance Act of 1975.  (1975, c. 917, s. 2; 2010-31, s. 17.3(b).)


§ 116-209.51.  Purpose.

The General Assembly of North Carolina, recognizing that the North Carolina National Guard is the only organized, trained and equipped military force subject to the control of the State, hereby establishes a program of tuition assistance for qualifying guard members for the purpose of encouraging voluntary membership in the North Carolina National Guard, improving the educational level of its members, and thereby benefiting the State as a whole. (1975, c. 917, s. 3; 2009-281, s. 1; 2010-31, s. 17.3(b); 2011-183, s. 85.)


§ 116-209.52.  Definitions.

(a) Academic Year. - Any period of 365 days beginning with the first day of enrollment for a course of instruction.

(a1) Business or Trade School. - Any school within the State of North Carolina which is licensed by the State Board of Education and listed by that Board as an approved private business school or an approved private trade school.

(b) Private Educational Institutions. - Any junior college, senior college or university which is operated and governed by private interests not under the control of the federal, State or any local government, which is located within and licensed by the State of North Carolina, which does not operate for profit, whose curriculum is primarily directed toward the awarding of associate, baccalaureate or graduate degrees, which agrees to the applicable administration and funding provisions of this Part.

(c) Repealed by Session Laws 2010-31, s. 17.3(c), effective July 1, 2010.

(d) State Educational Institutions. - Any of the constituent institutions of the University of North Carolina, or any community college operated under the provisions of Chapter 115D of the General Statutes of North Carolina.

(e) Repealed by Session Laws 2008-94, s. 2, effective July 1, 2008.

(f) Student Loan. - A loan or loans made to eligible students or parents of students to aid in attaining an education beyond the high school level. (1975, c. 917, s. 4; 1977, c. 70, s. 2; c. 228, s. 1; 1987, c. 564, s. 24; 2008-94, s. 2; 2010-31, s. 17.3(b), (c).)


§ 116-209.53. Benefit.

The benefit provided under this Part shall consist of a monetary educational assistance grant not to exceed the highest amount charged by a State educational institution per academic year or a lesser amount, as prescribed by the Authority, to remain within the funds appropriated, to qualifying members of the North Carolina National Guard. Benefits provided under G.S. 116-209.55(g) shall be payable for a period of one year at a time, renewable at the option of the Authority. All other benefits provided under this Part shall be payable for a period of one academic year at a time, renewable at the option of the Authority.

(1975, c. 917, s. 5; 1977, c. 228, s. 2; 1983 (Reg. Sess., 1984), c. 1034, ss. 99, 100; 1993 (Reg. Sess., 1994), c. 769, s. 22.3; 2000-67, s. 18; 2005-444, s. 1; 2008-94, s. 3; 2010-31, s. 17.3(b), (c).)

§ 116-209.54. Eligibility.

(a)     Active members of the North Carolina National Guard who are enrolled or who shall enroll in any business or trade school, private educational institution, or State educational institution shall be eligible to apply for this tuition assistance benefit: Provided, that the applicant has a minimum obligation of two years remaining as a member of the North Carolina National Guard from the end of the academic period for which tuition assistance is provided or that the applicant commit himself or herself to extended membership for at least two additional years from the end of that academic period.

(b)     This tuition assistance benefit shall be applicable to students in the following categories:

(1)     Students seeking to achieve completion of their secondary school education at a community college or technical institute.

(2)     Students seeking trade or vocational training or education.

(3)     Students seeking to achieve a two-year associate degree.

(4)     Students seeking to achieve a four-year baccalaureate degree.

(5)     Students seeking to achieve a graduate degree.

(c)     The following persons shall be eligible to apply for disbursements to pay outstanding student loans pursuant to G.S. 116-209.55(g):

(1)     Persons described in subsections (a) and (b) of this section.

(2)     Active members of the North Carolina National Guard who were previously enrolled in any business or trade school, private educational institution, or State educational institution, but only if:

a. The applicant has a minimum obligation of two years remaining as a member of the North Carolina National Guard from the time of the application; or

b. The applicant commits himself or herself to extended membership for at least two additional years from the time of the application. (1975, c. 917, s. 6; 1977, c. 228, ss. 3, 4; 2008-94, s. 4; 2010-31, s. 17.3(b), (c); 2011-183, s. 86(a), (b).)

§ 116-209.55. Administration and funding.

(a) The Authority is charged with the administration of the tuition assistance program under this Part.

(b) The Authority shall determine the eligibility of applicants, select the benefit recipients, establish the effective date of the benefit, and may suspend or revoke the benefit if the Authority finds that the recipient does not maintain an adequate academic status, or if the recipient engages in riots, unlawful demonstrations, the seizure of educational buildings, or otherwise engages in disorderly conduct, breaches of the peace, or unlawful assemblies. The Authority shall maintain such records and shall promulgate such rules and regulations as the Authority deems necessary for the orderly administration of this program. The Authority may require of business or trade schools or State or private educational institutions such reports and other information as the Authority may need to carry out the provisions of this Part and the Authority shall disburse benefit payments for recipients upon certification of enrollment by the enrolling institutions.

(c) All tuition benefit disbursements shall be made to the business or trade school or State or private educational institution concerned, for credit to the tuition account of each recipient. Funds disbursed pursuant to subsection (g) of this section shall be made to the student loan creditor concerned to be applied against the outstanding student loans of each North Carolina National Guard member beneficiary.

(d) The participation by any business or trade school or private educational institution in this program shall be subject to the applicable provisions of this Part and to examination by the State Auditor of the accounts of the benefit recipients attending or having attended such private schools or institutions. The

Authority may defer making an award or may suspend an award in any business or trade school or private educational institution which does not comply with the provisions of this Part relating to said institutions. The manner of payment to any business or trade school or private educational institution shall be as prescribed by the Authority.

(e) Irrespective of other provisions of this Part, the Authority may prescribe special procedures for adjusting the accounts of benefit recipients who, for reasons of illness, physical inability to attend classes or for other valid reason satisfactory to the Authority, may withdraw from any business or trade school or State or private educational institution prior to the completion of the term, semester, quarter or other academic period being attended at the time of withdrawal.

(f) Any balance of the monetary educational assistance grant up to the maximum for the academic year remaining after tuition is paid pursuant to subsection (c) of this section may be disbursed to the recipient as reimbursement for required course books and materials. The manner of obtaining the reimbursement payment for these required books and materials shall be as prescribed by the Authority.

(g) Any funds not needed to accomplish the other purposes of this Part may be used to help members of the North Carolina National Guard repay outstanding student loans in accordance with rules to be adopted by the Authority. These rules shall provide that the length of a member's deployment may be considered in determining whether or not, and in what amount, a member receives assistance pursuant to this subsection. There shall be no reimbursement under this subsection for payments already made on student loans, and funds shall not be provided under this subsection for the purpose of paying student loans obtained for courses from which the member withdrew or for which the member did not receive a passing grade. Payments for outstanding loans shall not exceed the maximum benefit available under G.S. 116-209.53. (1975, c. 917, s. 7; 1977, c. 70, s. 2; 2005-444, ss. 2, 3; 2008-94, s. 1; 2010-31, s. 17.3(b), (c); 2011-183, s. 87.)

Article 24.

Learning Institute of North Carolina.

§§ 116-210 through 116-211: Repealed by Session Laws 1979, c. 744, s. 8.

Article 25.

Disruption on Campuses of State-Owned Institutions of Higher Education.

§ 116-212.  Campus of state-supported institution of higher education subject to curfew.

The chancellor or president of any state-supported institution of higher learning may designate periods of time during which the campuses of such institutions and designated buildings and facilities connected therewith are off-limits and subject to a curfew as to all persons who are not faculty members, staff personnel, currently enrolled students of that institution, local law-enforcement officers, members of the National Guard on active duty, members of the General Assembly, the Governor of North Carolina and/or his designated agents, persons authorized by the chief administrative officer of the institution or his designated agent, and any person who satisfactorily identifies himself as a reporter for any newspaper, magazine, radio or television station. Any person not herein authorized who comes onto or remains on said campus in violation of this section shall be punished as set out in G.S. 116-213.  (1969, c. 860, s. 1; 2009-281, s. 1.)


§ 116-213.  Violation of curfew a misdemeanor; punishment.

(a)     Any person who during such period of curfew utilizes sound-amplifying equipment of any kind or nature upon the premises subject to such curfew in an educational, administrative building, or in any facility owned or controlled by the State or a State institution of higher learning, or upon the campus or grounds of any such institution, without the permission of the administrative head of the institution or his designated agent, shall be guilty of a Class 2 misdemeanor. For the purposes of this section the term "sound-amplifying equipment" shall mean any device, machine, or mechanical contrivance which is capable of amplifying sound and capable of delivering an electrical input of one or more watts to the loudspeaker, but this section shall not include radios and televisions.

(b)     Any person convicted of violating any provision of G.S. 116-212 or 116-213, or who shall enter a plea of guilty to such violation or a plea of nolo contendere, shall be guilty of a Class 2 misdemeanor.  (1969, c. 860, ss. 2, 3; 1993, c. 539, s. 895; 1994, Ex. Sess., c. 24, s. 14(c).)

§§ 116-214 through 116-218. Reserved for future codification purposes.

Article 26.

Liability Insurance or Self-Insurance.

§ 116-219. Authorization to secure insurance or provide self-insurance.

The Board of Governors of the University of North Carolina (hereinafter referred to as "the Board") is authorized through the purchase of contracts of insurance or the creation of self-insurance trusts, or through combination of such insurance and self-insurance, to provide individual health-care practitioners with coverage against claims of personal tort liability based on conduct within the course and scope of health-care functions undertaken by such individuals as employees, agents, or officers of (i) the University of North Carolina, (ii) any constituent institution of the University of North Carolina, (iii) the University of North Carolina Hospitals at Chapel Hill, or (iv) any health-care institution, agency or entity which has an affiliation agreement with the University of North Carolina, with a constituent institution of the University of North Carolina, or with the University of North Carolina Hospitals at Chapel Hill. The types of health-care practitioners to which the provisions of this Article may apply include, but are not limited to, medical doctors, dentists, nurses, residents, interns, medical technologists, nurses' aides, and orderlies. Subject to all requirements and limitations of this Article, the coverage to be provided, through insurance or self-insurance or combination thereof, may include provision for the payment of expenses of litigation, the payment of civil judgments in courts of competent jurisdiction, and the payment of settlement amounts, in actions, suits or claims to which this Article applies. (1975, 2nd Sess., c. 976; 1989, c. 141, s. 6.)

§ 116-220. Establishment and administration of self-insurance trust funds; rules and regulations; defense of actions against covered persons; application of § 143-300.6.

(a)     In the event the Board elects to act as self-insurer of a program of liability insurance, it may establish one or more insurance trust accounts to be used only for the purposes authorized by this Article: Provided, however, said program of liability insurance shall not be subject to regulation by the

Commissioner of Insurance. The Board is authorized to receive and accept any gift, donation, appropriation or transfer of funds made for the purposes of this section and to deposit such funds in the insurance trust accounts. All expenses incurred in collecting, receiving, and maintaining such funds and in otherwise administering the self-insured program of liability insurance shall be paid from such insurance trust accounts.

(b) Subject to all requirements and limitations of this Article, the Board is authorized to adopt rules and regulations for the establishment and administration of the self-insured program of liability insurance, including, but not limited to, rules and regulations concerning the eligibility for and terms and conditions of participation in the program, the assessment of charges against participants, the management of the insurance trust accounts, and the negotiation, settlement, litigation, and payment of claims.

(c) The Board is authorized to create a Liability Insurance Trust Fund Council composed of not more than 13 members; one member each shall be appointed by the State Attorney General, the State Insurance Commissioner, the Director of the Office of State Budget and Management, and the State Treasurer; the remaining members shall be appointed by the Board. Subject to all requirements and limitations of this Article and to any rules and regulations adopted by the Board under the terms of subsection (b) of this section, the Board may delegate to the Liability Insurance Trust Fund Council responsibility and authority for the administration of the self-insured liability insurance program and of the insurance trust accounts established pursuant to such program.

(d) Defense of all suits or actions against an individual health-care practitioner who is covered by a self-insured program of liability insurance established by the Board under the provisions of this Article may be provided by the Attorney General in accordance with the provisions of G.S. 143-300.3 of Article 31A of Chapter 143; provided, that in the event it should be determined pursuant to G.S. 143-300.4 that defense of such a claim should not be provided by the State, or if it should be determined pursuant to G.S. 143-300.5 and G.S. 147-17 that counsel other than the Attorney General should be employed, or if the individual health-care practitioner is not an employee of the State as defined in G.S. 143-300.2, then private legal counsel may be employed by the Liability Insurance Trust Fund Council and paid for from funds in the insurance trust accounts.

(e) For purposes of the requirements of G.S. 143-300.6, the coverage provided State employees by any self-insured program of liability insurance established by the Board pursuant to the provisions of this Article shall be deemed to be commercial liability insurance coverage within the meaning of G.S. 143-300.6(c).

(f) By rules or regulations adopted by the Board in accordance with G.S. 116-220(b) of this Article, the Board may provide that funds maintained in insurance trust accounts under such a self-insured program of liability insurance may be used to pay any expenses, including damages ordered to be paid, which may be incurred by the University of North Carolina, a constituent institution of the University of North Carolina, or the University of North Carolina Hospitals at Chapel Hill with respect to any tort claim, based on alleged negligent acts in the provision of health-care services, which may be prosecuted under the provisions of Article 31 of Chapter 143 of the General Statutes. (1975, 2nd Sess., c. 976; 1987, c. 263, s. 1; 1989, c. 141, s. 7; 2000-140, s. 93.1(a); 2001-424, s. 12.2(b); 2009-136, s. 4.)


§ 116-220.1. Funding of self-insurance program.

(a) If the Board elects to establish a self-insurance trust fund, the initial contribution to the fund shall be determined by an independent actuary but shall be no less than three hundred thousand dollars ($300,000). Annual contributions to said fund shall be made in an amount to be determined each year by the Trust Fund Council upon the advice of an independent actuary and shall include amounts necessary to pay all costs of administration of the self-insurance program and claims adjustment including litigation in addition to amounts necessary to pay claims. Contributions shall be no less than one hundred fifty percent (150%) of the amounts actually paid each year on medical malpractice claims until such time as the Trust Fund Council, with the advice of an independent actuary and the approval of the Board of Governors, determines that an annual contribution in a lesser amount will not impair the adequacy of the fund to satisfy existing and potential health care malpractice claims for a period of one year.

(b) Claims certified to be paid from the fund shall be paid in the order of award or settlement. In the event that the fund created hereunder shall at any time have insufficient funds to assure that both existing and future claims will be paid, the Board is hereby authorized to borrow necessary amounts up to thirty million dollars ($30,000,000) per established self-insurance trust fund account to replenish the fund. The Board shall maintain funds in each self-insurance trust at no less than one hundred thousand dollars ($100,000) at all times.

(c)     Funds borrowed by the Board to replenish the trust fund account may be secured by pledging noncapital assets of the members. Members shall mean those entities, agencies, departments or divisions of the University which directly contribute funds to the self-insurance trust. In no event shall individual health care providers be deemed members for the purposes of this section.

(d)     Obligations issued under the provisions of this Article shall not be deemed to constitute a debt, liability or obligation of the State or of any political subdivision thereof or a pledge of the faith and credit of the State or of any such political subdivision but shall be payable solely from the revenues or assets of the members. Each obligation issued under this Article shall contain on the face thereof a statement to the effect that the University shall not be obligated to pay the same nor the interest thereon except from the revenues or assets pledged therefor and that neither the faith and credit nor the taxing power of the State or of any political subdivision thereof is pledged to the payment of the principal of or the interest on such obligation. (1977, c. 523, s. 2; 1987, c. 263, s. 2.)


§ 116-220.2.  Termination of fund.

Any fund created hereunder may be terminated by the Board of Governors upon their determination that other satisfactory and adequate arrangements have been made to assure that both existing and future health care malpractice claims or judgments against the participants in the self-insurance program will be paid and satisfied. Upon the termination of any fund pursuant to this section, the full amount remaining in such fund upon termination less any outstanding indebtedness shall promptly be repaid to the University and allocated among the participating entities according to their respective contributions as determined by the Board of Governors. (1977, c. 523, s. 2.)


§ 116-221.  Sovereign immunity.

Nothing in this Article shall be deemed to waive the sovereign immunity of the State. (1975, 2nd Sess., c. 976.)

§ 116-222. Confidentiality of records.

Records pertaining to the liability insurance program, including all information, correspondence, investigations, or interviews, concerning or pertaining to claims or potential claims against participants in the self-insurance program or to the program or applications for participation in the program shall not be considered public records under General Statutes Chapter 132 and shall not be subject to discovery under the Rules of Civil Procedure, General Statutes Chapter 1A. (1975, 2nd Sess., c. 976; 1977, c. 523, s. 1.)


§ 116-223. Further action.

The Board of Governors of the University of North Carolina is hereby authorized to take all action necessary to effectuate the purposes and provisions of this Article. (1977, c. 523, s. 2.)


§ 116-224. Appropriation.

The funds described by this Article are appropriated and shall be used only as provided by this Article. (2006-203, s. 54.1.)

§ 116-225. Reserved for future codification purposes.

§ 116-226. Reserved for future codification purposes.

§ 116-227. Reserved for future codification purposes.

§ 116-228. Reserved for future codification purposes.

Article 27.

Private Institution Towing Procedures.

§ 116-229. Post-towing procedures.

If a private college or university employs law-enforcement officers so that Article 7A, Chapter 20, would otherwise apply to the removal and disposal of motor vehicles, the governing body of that college or university may by rule or ordinance provide an alternative hearing procedure for the owner. For purposes of this section, the definitions in G.S. 20-219.9 apply.

(1) If the college or university operates in such a way that the person who tows the vehicle is responsible for collecting towing fees, all provisions of Article 7A, Chapter 20, apply.

(2) If the college or university operates in such a way that it is responsible for collecting towing fees, it shall:

a. Provide by contract or ordinance for a schedule of reasonable towing fees,

b. Provide a procedure for a prompt fair hearing to contest the towing,

c. Provide for an appeal to district court from that hearing,

d. Authorize release of the vehicle at any time after towing by the posting of a bond or paying of the fees due, and

e. If the college or university chooses to enforce its authority by sale of the vehicle, provide a sale procedure similar to that provided in G.S. 44A-4, 44A-5, and 44A-6, except that no hearing in addition to the probable cause hearing is required. If no one purchases the vehicle at the sale and if the value of the vehicle is less than the amount of the lien, the college or university may destroy it. (1983, c. 420, s. 6.)


Article 27A.

Disclosure of Student Data and Records by Private Institutions.

§ 116-229.1. Disclosure of student data and records by private colleges and universities.

(a) A private college or university that discloses personally identifiable information in student data or records according to the terms of a written agreement with a State agency, local school administrative unit, community college, constituent institution of The University of North Carolina, or the North Carolina Independent Colleges and Universities, Inc., in compliance with the Family Educational Rights and Privacy Act, 20 U.S.C. § 1232g, shall not be liable for a breach of confidentiality, disclosure, use, retention, or destruction of the student data or records if the breach, disclosure, use, retention, or destruction results from actions or omissions of either (i) the State agency, local school administrative unit, community college, or constituent institution of The University of North Carolina to which the data was provided or (ii) persons provided access to the data or records by those entities.

(b)     The North Carolina Independent Colleges and Universities, Inc., shall not be liable for a breach of confidentiality, disclosure, use, retention, or destruction of student data or records transferred on behalf of a private college or university to a State agency, local school administrative unit, community college, or constituent institution of The University of North Carolina if the breach, disclosure, use, retention, or destruction results from actions or omissions of either (i) the State agency, local school administrative unit, community college, or constituent institution of The University of North Carolina to which the data was provided or (ii) persons provided access to the data or records by those entities. (2012-133, s. 3.)


Article 28.

North Carolina-Israel Visiting Scholar Program.

§ 116-230.  North Carolina-Israel Visiting Scholar Program.

(a)     There is created the North Carolina-Israel Visiting Scholar Program for the purpose of granting funds to members of the faculties of the constituent institutions of The University of North Carolina and institutions of higher education in Israel to assist in their travel and living expenses while participating in the program.

(b)     The President of The University of North Carolina shall appoint a North Carolina Committee to work with a committee from Israel to prepare proper guidelines for the administration of the program and to establish criteria for the designation of participating scholars.

(c) Funds for the support of this program shall come from private sources, and grants shall be made for as many suitable recipients as can be found within budget limitations. (1985, c. 757, s. 81(c).)

Article 29.

The North Carolina School of Science and Mathematics.

§ 116-230.1. Policy.

It is hereby declared to be the policy of the State to foster, encourage, promote, and provide assistance in the development of skills and careers in science and mathematics among the people of the State.(1985, c. 757, s. 206(b); 2006-66, s. 9.11(j).)

§ 116-231. Reestablishment of the North Carolina School of Science and Mathematics as a Constituent High School of The University of North Carolina.

The North Carolina School of Science and Mathematics is hereby reestablished, as a constituent high school of The University of North Carolina, and shall be governed by the Board of Governors as prescribed in this Chapter and a Board of Trustees as prescribed in this Article.(1985, c. 757, s. 206(b); 2006-66, s. 9.11(k).)

§ 116-232. Purposes.

The purposes of the School shall be to foster the educational development of North Carolina high school students who are academically talented in the areas of science and mathematics and show promise of exceptional development and global leadership through participation in a residential educational setting emphasizing instruction in the areas of science and mathematics; and to provide instruction, methods, and curricula designed to improve teaching and learning in North Carolina and the nation with an emphasis on distance education and programs that expand pathways for students into careers in science and mathematics.(1985, c. 757, s. 206(b); 2006-66, s. 9.11(l).)

§ 116-233. Board of Trustees; appointment; terms of office.

(a)     Notwithstanding the provisions of G.S. 116-31(d), there shall be a Board of Trustees of the School, which shall consist of 27 members as follows:

(1)     Thirteen members who shall be appointed by the Board of Governors of The University of North Carolina, one from each congressional district.

(2)     Four members without regard to residency who shall be appointed by the Board of Governors of The University of North Carolina.

(3)     Three members, ex officio, who shall be the chief academic officers, respectively, of constituent institutions. The Board of Governors shall in 1985 and quadrennially thereafter designate the three constituent institutions whose chief academic officers shall so serve, such designations to expire on June 30, 1989, and quadrennially thereafter.

(4)     The chief academic officer of a college or university in North Carolina other than a constituent institution, ex officio. The Board of Governors shall designate in 1985 and quadrennially thereafter which college or university whose chief academic officer shall so serve, such designation to expire on June 30, 1989, and quadrennially thereafter.

(5)     Two members appointed by the General Assembly upon the recommendation of the President Pro Tempore of the Senate in accordance with G.S. 120-121.

(6)     Two members appointed by the General Assembly upon the recommendation of the Speaker of the House of Representatives in accordance with G.S. 120-121.

(7)     Two members appointed by the Governor.

(b)     Appointed members of the Board of Trustees shall be selected for their interest in and commitment to public education and to the purposes of the School, and they shall be charged with the responsibility of serving the interests of the whole State. In appointing members, the objective shall be to obtain the services of the best qualified persons, taking into consideration the desirability of diversity of membership, including men and women, representatives of different races, and members of different political parties.

(c) No member of the General Assembly or officer or employee of the State, the School, The University of North Carolina, or of any constituent institution of The University of North Carolina, shall be eligible to be appointed to the Board of Trustees except as specified under subdivision (3) of subsection (a) of this section. No spouse of a member of the General Assembly, or of an officer or employee of the school may be a member of the Board of Trustees. Any appointed trustee who is elected or appointed to the General Assembly or who becomes an officer or employee of the State, except as specified under subdivision (3) of subsection (a) of this section, or whose spouse is elected or appointed to the General Assembly or becomes such an officer or employee of the School, shall be deemed thereupon to resign from his or her membership on the Board of Trustees. This subsection does not apply to ex officio members.

(d) Members appointed under subdivisions (1) or (2) of subsection (a) of this section shall serve staggered four-year terms expiring June 30 of odd numbered years.

(d1) Only an ex officio member shall be eligible to serve more than two successive terms.

(d2) Any vacancy in the membership of the Board of Trustees appointed under G.S. 116-233(a)(1) or (2) shall be reported promptly by the Secretary of the Board of Trustees to the Board of Governors of The University of North Carolina, which shall fill any such vacancy by appointment of a replacement member to serve for the balance of the unexpired term. Any vacancy in members appointed under G.S. 116-233(a)(5) or (6) shall be filled in accordance with G.S. 120-122. Any vacancy in members appointed under G.S. 116-233(a)(7) shall be filled by the Governor for the remainder of the unexpired term. Reapportionment of congressional districts does not affect the right of any member to complete the term for which the member was appointed.

(e) Of the initial members appointed under G.S. 116-233(a)(5), one member shall serve a term to expire June 30, 1987, and one member shall serve a term to expire June 30, 1989. Subsequent appointments shall be for four-year terms. The initial members appointed under G.S. 116-233(a)(6), shall be appointed for terms to expire June 30, 1987. Subsequent appointments shall be for two-year terms. The initial members appointed under G.S. 116-233(a)(7) shall be appointed for terms to expire January 15, 1989. Successors shall be appointed for four-year terms.

(f) Whenever an appointed member of the Board of Trustees shall fail, for any reason other than ill health or service in the interest of the State or nation, to be present at three successive regular meetings of the Board, his or her place as a member of the Board shall be deemed vacant. (1985, c. 757, s. 206(b); 1991 (Reg. Sess., 1992), c. 879, ss. 1, 2; 1995, c. 490, s. 45; c. 509, s. 65; 2003-57, ss. 1, 2; 2006-66, s. 9.11(m); 2007-278, s. 4.)

§ 116-234. Board of Trustees; meetings; rules of procedure; officers.

(a) The Board of Trustees shall meet at least three times a year and may hold special meetings at any time, at the call of the chairman or upon petition addressed to the chairman by at least four of the members of the Board.

(b) Notwithstanding the provisions of G.S. 116-32, the Board of Trustees shall elect a chairman and a vice-chairman; no ex officio member may hold such an office.

(c) The Board of Trustees shall determine its own rules of procedure and may delegate to such committees as it may create such of its powers as it deems appropriate.

(d) Members of the Board of Trustees, other than ex officio members under G.S. 116-233(a)(3), shall receive such per diem compensation and necessary travel and subsistence expenses while engaged in the discharge of their official duties as is provided by law for members of State boards and commissions. Ex officio members under G.S. 116-233(a)(3) shall be reimbursed for travel expenses as provided by G.S. 138-6. (1985, c. 757, s. 206(b); 1995, c. 509, s. 66; 2006-66, s. 9.11(n).)

§ 116-235. Board of Trustees; additional powers and duties.

(a) In addition to the powers enumerated in Chapter 116, Article I, Part 3, the Board of Trustees shall have the powers and duties set out in this section.

(a1) Academic Program. -

(1) The Board of Trustees shall establish the standard course of study for the School. This course of study shall set forth the subjects to be taught in each grade and the texts and other educational materials on each subject to be used in each grade.

(2) The Board of Trustees shall adopt regulations governing class size, the instructional calendar, the length of the instructional day, and the number of instructional days in each term.

(b) Students. -

(1) Admission of Students. - The School shall admit students in accordance with criteria, standards, and procedures established by the Board of Trustees. To be eligible to be considered for admission, an applicant must be either a legal resident of the State, as defined by G.S. 116-143.1(a)(1), or a student whose parent is an active duty member of the Armed Forces, as defined by G.S. 116-143.3(2), who is abiding in this State incident to active military duty at the time the application is submitted, provided the student shares the abode of that parent; eligibility to remain enrolled in the School shall terminate at the end of any school year during which a student becomes a nonresident of the State. The Board of Trustees shall ensure, insofar as possible without jeopardizing admission standards, that an equal number of qualified applicants is admitted to the program and to the residential summer institutes in science and mathematics from each of North Carolina's congressional districts. In no event shall the differences in the number of qualified applicants offered admission to the program from each of North Carolina's congressional districts be more than two and one-half percentage points from the average number per district who are offered admission.

(2) School Attendance. - Every parent, guardian, or other person in this State having charge or control of a child who is enrolled in the School and who is less than 16 years of age shall cause such child to attend school continuously for a period equal to the time which the School shall be in session. No person shall encourage, entice, or counsel any child to be unlawfully absent from the School. Any person who aids or abets a student's unlawful absence from the School shall, upon conviction, be guilty of a Class 1 misdemeanor. The Chancellor of the School shall be responsible for implementing such additional policies concerning compulsory attendance as shall be adopted by the Board of Trustees, including regulations concerning lawful and unlawful absences, permissible excuses for temporary absences, maintenance of attendance records, and attendance counseling.

(3) Student Discipline. - Rules of conduct governing students of the School shall be established by the Board of Trustees. The Chancellor, other administrative officers, and all teachers, substitute teachers, voluntary teachers, teacher aides and assistants, and student teachers in the School may use reasonable force in the exercise of lawful authority to restrain or correct pupils and maintain order.

(c) through (h) Repealed by Session Laws 2006-66, s. 9.11(s), effective July 1, 2007.

(i) The Display of the United States and North Carolina Flags and the Recitation of the Pledge of Allegiance. - The Board of Trustees shall adopt policies to require (i) the display of the United States and North Carolina flags in each classroom when available, (ii) the recitation of the Pledge of Allegiance on a daily basis, and (iii) the instruction on the meaning and historical origins of the flag and the Pledge of Allegiance. These policies shall not compel any person to stand, salute the flag, or recite the Pledge of Allegiance. If flags are donated or are otherwise available, flags shall be displayed in each classroom. (1985, c. 757, s. 206(b); 1993, c. 539, ss. 896, 897; 1994, Ex. Sess., c. 24, s. 14(c); 1995, c. 507, s. 15.1; 2002-126, s. 9.12(c); 2005-318, s. 2; 2005-445, s. 8.1; 2006-66, ss. 9.11(o)-9.11(s); 2006-137, s. 5; 2011-183, s. 88.)

§ 116-236: Repealed by Session Laws 2006-66, ss. 9.11(t) through 9.11(v), effective July 1, 2007.

§ 116-237: Repealed by Session Laws 2006-66, ss. 9.11(t) through 9.11(v), effective July 1, 2007.

§ 116-238: Repealed by Session Laws 2006-66, ss. 9.11(t) through 9.11(v), effective July 1, 2007.

§ 116-238.1. (Repealed effective July 1, 2014) Full tuition grant for graduates who attend a State university.

(a) There is granted to each State resident who graduates from the North Carolina School of Science and Mathematics and who enrolls as a full-time student in a constituent institution of The University of North Carolina a sum to be determined by the General Assembly as a tuition grant. The tuition grant shall be for four consecutive academic years and shall cover the tuition cost at the constituent institution in which the student is enrolled. The tuition grant shall be distributed to the student as provided by this section. The grant provided by this section is only available to a student enrolled at the North Carolina School of Science and Mathematics for the 2008-2009 academic year or earlier.

(b)     The tuition grants provided for in this section shall be administered by the State Education Assistance Authority pursuant to rules adopted by the State Education Assistance Authority not inconsistent with this section. The State Education Assistance Authority shall not approve any grant until it receives proper certification from the appropriate constituent institution that the student applying for the grant is an eligible student. Upon receipt of the certification, the State Education Assistance Authority shall remit at the times it prescribes the grant to the constituent institution on behalf, and to the credit, of the student.

(c)     In the event a student on whose behalf a grant has been paid is not enrolled and carrying a minimum academic load as of the tenth classroom day following the beginning of the school term for which the grant was paid, the institution shall refund the full amount of the grant to the State Education Assistance Authority.

(d)     In the event there are not sufficient funds to provide each eligible student with a full grant:

(1)     The Board of Governors of The University of North Carolina, with the approval of the Office of State Budget and Management, may transfer available funds to meet the needs of the programs provided by subsections (a) and (b) of this section; and

(2)     Each eligible student shall receive a pro rata share of funds then available for the remainder of the academic year within the fiscal period covered by the current appropriation.

(e)     Any remaining funds shall revert to the General Fund.

(f)     Notwithstanding any other provision of this section, no tuition grant awarded to a student under this section shall exceed the cost of attendance at the constituent institution at which the student is enrolled. If a student, who is eligible for a tuition grant under this subsection, also receives a scholarship or other grant covering the cost of attendance at the constituent institution for which the tuition grant is awarded, then the amount of the tuition grant shall be reduced by an appropriate amount determined by the State Education

Assistance Authority. The State Education Assistance Authority shall reduce the amount of the tuition grant so that the sum of all grants and scholarship aid covering the cost of attendance received by the student, including the tuition grant under this section, shall not exceed the cost of attendance for the constituent institution at which the student is enrolled. The cost of attendance, as used in this subsection, shall be determined by the State Education Assistance Authority for each constituent institution. (2003-284, s. 9.4(a); 2004-203, s. 47; 2005-276, s. 9.14(a); 2009-451, s. 9.6(a), (b).)

§ 116-238.5: Repealed by Session Laws 2007-484, s. 30, effective August 30, 2007.

§ 116-239. Reserved for future codification purposes.

Article 30.

[Western] North Carolina Arboretum.

§ 116-240. Establishment of Arboretum.

The North Carolina Arboretum is established on land being provided by the United States Forest Service from property presently designated as the Bent Creek Experimental Forest.

The United States Forest Service has committed itself to continuing its work of the land provided to the Arboretum as many of its studies will be compatible with the work of the Arboretum. (1985 (Reg. Sess., 1986), c. 1014, s. 98; 1989, c. 139, s. 1.)

§ 116-241. Purpose and scope of Arboretum.

The Arboretum shall be prepared for viewing and maintaining the necessary plantings that will be added to the present vegetation of the site in order to make the Arboretum fully representative of Western North Carolina. Extensive clearing of underbrush and other debris needed to prepare the area for demonstrations, installation of fencing for security purposes, land modifications and improvement, and plant acquisitions shall be carried out to make the Arboretum both representative and accessible to the public. Roads and pathways shall be constructed as necessary throughout the Arboretum to enable visitors to ride and walk through the area in order to observe and study the various kinds of vegetation. An extensive program of identification of trees, shrubs, and other living material shall be ongoing at the Arboretum. Necessary visitor and educational buildings, greenhouses, and a small lecture hall, with restrooms and other associated requirements, shall be constructed on the property. Machine sheds and service buildings shall also be constructed on the property to house equipment and to provide working space for the personnel employed in developing and operating the Arboretum. (1985 (Reg. Sess., 1986), c. 1014, s. 98.)

§ 116-242. Administration of Arboretum; acceptance of gifts and grants.

The Arboretum shall be administered by The University of North Carolina and through the Board of Directors established in G.S. 116-243. State funds for the administration of the Arboretum shall be appropriated to The University of North Carolina for Western Carolina University to administer on behalf of the arboretum. The North Carolina Arboretum and The University of North Carolina may receive gifts and grants to be used for development or operation of the Arboretum. (1985 (Reg. Sess., 1986), c. 1014, s. 98; 2011-145, s. 9.15(a).)

§ 116-243. Board of directors established; appointments.

A board of directors to govern the operation of the Arboretum is established, to be appointed as follows:

(1) Two by the Governor, initially, one for a two-year term, and one for a four-year term. Successors shall be appointed for four-year terms.

(2) Two by the General Assembly, in accordance with G.S. 120-121, upon the recommendation of the President Pro Tempore of the Senate, initially, one for a two-year term, and one for a four-year term. Successors shall be appointed for four-year terms.

(3) Two by the General Assembly, in accordance with G.S. 120-121, upon the recommendation of the Speaker of the House of Representatives, initially,

one for a two-year term, and one for a four-year term. Successors shall be appointed for four-year terms.

(4) The President of The University of North Carolina or the President's designee to serve ex officio.

(4a) Two by the President of The University of North Carolina. Members shall be appointed for four-year terms, except that the initial terms shall be as provided otherwise by law.

(5) Repealed by Session Laws 2011-145, s. 9.15(b), effective July 1, 2011.

(6) Repealed by Session Laws 2011-145, s. 9.15(b), effective July 1, 2011.

(7) Eight by the Board of Governors of The University of North Carolina, Members shall be appointed for four-year terms, except that the initial terms shall be as otherwise provided by law.

(8) The executive director of the Arboretum shall serve ex officio as a nonvoting member of the Board of Directors.

(9) The President of The North Carolina Arboretum Society, Inc., to serve ex officio.

All appointed members may serve two full four-year terms following the initial appointment and then may not be reappointed until they have been absent for at least one year. Members serve until their successors have been appointed. Appointees to fill vacancies serve for the remainder of the unexpired term. Vacancies in appointments made by the General Assembly shall be filled in accordance with G.S. 120-122. Initial terms begin July 1, 2011.

The Chair of the Board of Directors shall be elected biennially by majority vote of the directors.

The Executive Director of the Arboretum shall report to the President of The University of North Carolina or the President's designee and to the Board of Directors. (1985 (Reg. Sess., 1986), c. 1014, s. 98; 1995, c. 490, s. 63; 2003-102, s. 1; 2004-203, s. 48; 2011-145, s. 9.15(b).)

§ 116-244. Duties of board of directors.

The Board of Directors of the Arboretum has the following duties and responsibilities:

(1)     Development of the policies and procedures concerning the use of the land and facilities being developed as part of the Western North Carolina Arboretum, Inc.;

(2)     Approval of plans for any buildings to be constructed on the facility;

(3)     Maintenance and upkeep of buildings and all properties;

(4)     Approval of permanent appointments to the staff of the Arboretum;

(5)     Recommendations to the General Administration of candidates for Executive Director of the Arboretum;

(6)     Recommendations to the General Administration for necessary termination of the Executive Director or other personnel of the Arboretum;

(7)     Ensurance of appropriate liaison between the Arboretum and the U. S. Forest Service, the National Park Service, The North Carolina Arboretum Society, Inc., Bent Creek Institute, Inc., Centers for Environmental and Climatic Interaction, Inc., NOAA Cooperative Institute for Climate and Satellites, and other scientific and economic development agencies and organizations of interest to and involved in the work at the Arboretum;

(8)     Development of various policies and directives, including the duties of the Executive Director, to be prepared jointly by the members of the Board of Directors and the Executive Director;

(9)     Approval of annual expenditures and budget requests to be submitted to The University of North Carolina General Administration.

The Board of Directors shall meet at least twice a year, and more frequently on the call of the Chair or at the request of at least 10 members of the Board. Meetings shall be held at the Arboretum, any campus of a constituent institution of The University of North Carolina, or at other public locations in support of the Arboretum mission and purposes. (1985 (Reg. Sess., 1986), c. 1014, s. 98; 2011-145, s. 9.15(c).)

§§ 116-245 through 116-249.  Reserved for future codification purposes.

Article 31.

Piedmont Triad Research Institute and Graduate Engineering Program.

§ 116-250.  Piedmont Triad Regional Institute; establishment; board of directors; purpose.

(a)     There is established the Piedmont Triad Research Institute as a nonprofit corporation registered and regulated pursuant to Chapter 55A of the General Statutes.

(b)     The Articles of Incorporation of the Institute shall constitute the board of directors of the Institute of individuals representing industrial and business interests in the Triad area, and of representatives of the following universities:

(1)     North Carolina Agricultural and Technical State University;

(2)     North Carolina State University at Raleigh;

(3)     Wake Forest University; and

(4)     Winston-Salem State University.

(c)     The Institute is established to further education and research in engineering, particularly as engineering may be applied to medicine. (1991, c. 316.)


§ 116-251.  Piedmont Triad Regional Institute's Director; funding administration duties.

The Director of the Piedmont Triad Research Institute shall report directly to the board of directors of the Institute.  The Director shall administer the Institute's funds from three primary sources for the general operation of the Institute and the fourth for the operation of the Piedmont Triad Graduate Engineering Program established by G.S. 116-252.  These sources of funds are as follows:

(1) Funds from external research funding agencies such as the National Science Foundation and the National Institutes of Health;

(2) Funds from industries in support of specific research projects;

(3) Funds from block grants from foundations and chambers of commerce; and

(4) Funds appropriated to the Institute from the State in support of the Piedmont Triad Graduate Engineering Program established by G.S. 116-252. (1991, c. 316, s. 1.)


§ 116-252. Piedmont Triad Graduate Engineering Program; establishment; purpose.

There is established the Piedmont Triad Graduate Engineering Program, to be housed in Winston-Salem in facilities provided by the Bowman Gray School of Medicine at Wake Forest University. The program shall support faculty and graduate students involved in engineering at the campuses of The University of North Carolina in order to allow their participation in engineering teaching and research in the Program, which shall provide much-needed university-level engineering education to the Piedmont Triad area.

The Program shall begin to be phased in effective for the academic year 1991-92. (1991, c. 316.)


§ 116-253. Piedmont Triad Graduate Engineering Program; Board of Governors of The University of North Carolina; adoption of rules.

The Board of Governors, pursuant to its authority under G.S. 116-11, shall adopt rules, after consultation with the board of directors of the Piedmont Triad Research Institute, to implement this Article as it affects the ongoing roles of The University of North Carolina and its designated constituent institutions in the Piedmont Triad Graduate Engineering Program and in the education and research projects of the Institute. (1991, c. 316, s. 1.)

§§ 116-254 through 116-259. Reserved for future codification purposes.

Article 32.

Health Information.

§ 116-260. Information on meningococcal disease immunization.

(a) Each public or private educational institution that offers a postsecondary degree as defined in G.S. 116-15 and that has a residential campus shall provide vaccination information on meningococcal disease to each student. The vaccination information shall be contained on student health forms provided to each student by the educational institution and shall include space for the student to indicate whether or not the student has received the vaccination against meningococcal disease. The vaccination information about meningococcal disease shall include any recommendations issued by the national Centers for Disease Control and Prevention regarding the disease.

(b) The vaccination information obtained under this section that is in the possession of the educational institution is confidential and shall not be a public record under G.S. 132-1.

(c) This section shall not be construed to require the educational institution to provide the meningococcal vaccination to students.

(d) This section shall not apply if the national Centers for Disease Control and Prevention no longer recommends the meningococcal vaccine.

(e) This section does not create a private right of action. (2003-194, s. 1; 2004-203, s. 73.)

§ 116-261: Reserved for future codification purposes.

§ 116-262: Reserved for future codification purposes.

§ 116-263: Reserved for future codification purposes.

§ 116-264: Reserved for future codification purposes.

§ 116-265: Reserved for future codification purposes.

§ 116-266: Reserved for future codification purposes.

§ 116-267: Reserved for future codification purposes.

§ 116-268: Reserved for future codification purposes.

§ 116-269: Reserved for future codification purposes.

§ 116-270: Reserved for future codification purposes.

Article 33.

Airport Authorities.

§ 116-271: Repealed by Session Laws 2011-266, s. 1.41(a), effective June 23, 2011.

§ 116-272: Repealed by Session Laws 2011-266, s. 1.41(a), effective June 23, 2011.

§ 116-273: Repealed by Session Laws 2011-266, s. 1.41(a), effective June 23, 2011.

§ 116-274: Repealed by Session Laws 2011-266, s. 1.41(a), effective June 23, 2011.

§ 116-275: Repealed by Session Laws 2011-266, s. 1.41(a), effective June 23, 2011.

§ 116-276: Reserved for future codification purposes.

§ 116-277: Reserved for future codification purposes.

§ 116-278: Reserved for future codification purposes.

§ 116-279: Reserved for future codification purposes.

Article 34.

Need-Based Scholarships for Students Attending Private Institutions of Higher Education.

§ 116-280. Definitions.

The following definitions apply to this Article:

(1) Academic year. - A period of time in which a student is expected to complete the equivalent of at least two semesters' or three quarters' academic work.

(2) Authority. - The State Education Assistance Authority created by Article 23 of Chapter 116 of the General Statutes.

(3) Eligible private postsecondary institution. - A school that is any of the following:

a. A nonprofit postsecondary educational institution with a main permanent campus located in this State that is not owned or operated by the State of North Carolina or by an agency or political subdivision of the State or by any combination thereof that satisfies all of the following:

1. Is accredited by the Southern Association of Colleges and Schools under the standards of the College Delegate Assembly of the Association or by the New England Association of Schools and Colleges through its Commission on Institutions of Higher Education.

2. Awards a postsecondary degree as defined in G.S. 116-15.

b. A postsecondary institution owned or operated by a hospital authority as defined in G.S. 131E-16(14) or school of nursing affiliated with a nonprofit postsecondary educational institution as defined in sub-subdivision a. of this subsection.

(4) Main permanent campus. - A campus owned by the eligible private postsecondary institution that provides permanent on-premises housing, food services, and classrooms with full-time faculty members and administration that engages in postsecondary degree activity as defined in G.S. 116-15.

(5) Matriculated status. - Being recognized as a student in a defined program of study leading to a degree, diploma, or certificate at an eligible private postsecondary institution.

(6) Scholarship. - A scholarship for education awarded under this Article.

(7) Title IV. - Title IV of the Higher Education Act of 1965, as amended, 20 U.S.C. § 1070, et seq. (2011-145, s. 9.18(a).)


§ 116-281. Eligibility requirements for scholarships.

In order to be eligible to receive a scholarship under this Article, a student seeking a degree, diploma, or certificate at an eligible private postsecondary institution must meet all of the following requirements:

(1) Only needy North Carolina students are eligible to receive scholarships. For purposes of this subsection, "needy North Carolina students" are those eligible students whose expected family contribution under the federal methodology does not exceed an amount as set annually by the Authority based upon costs of attendance at The University of North Carolina.

(2) The student must meet all other eligibility requirements for the federal Pell Grant, with the exception of the expected family contribution.

(3) The student must qualify as a legal resident of North Carolina and as a resident for tuition purposes in accordance with definitions of residency that may from time to time be adopted by the Board of Governors and published in the residency manual of the Board of Governors.

(4) The student must meet enrollment standards by being admitted, enrolled, and classified as an undergraduate student in a matriculated status at an eligible private postsecondary institution.

(5) In order to continue to be eligible for a scholarship for the student's second and subsequent academic years, the student must meet achievement standards by maintaining satisfactory academic progress in a course of study in accordance with the standards and practices used for federal Title IV programs by the eligible private postsecondary institution in which the student is enrolled.

(6) (Repealed effective for the 2014-2015 academic year and each subsequent academic year) A student shall not receive a scholarship under this Article for more than nine full-time academic semesters, or the equivalent if enrolled part-time, unless the student is enrolled in a program officially designated by the eligible private postsecondary institution as a five-year degree program. If a student is enrolled in such a five-year degree program, then the student shall not receive a scholarship under this Article for more than 11 full-time academic semesters or the equivalent if enrolled part-time. (2011-145, s. 9.18(a); 2013-360, s. 11.15(e).)

§ 116-281.1. Semester limitation on eligibility for scholarship.

(a) A student shall not receive a scholarship under this Article for more than 10 full-time academic semesters, or the equivalent if enrolled part-time, unless the student is enrolled in a program officially designated by the eligible private postsecondary institution as a five-year degree program. If a student is enrolled in such a five-year degree program, then the student shall not receive a scholarship under this Article for more than 12 full-time academic semesters or the equivalent if enrolled part-time.

(b) Upon application by a student, the eligible private postsecondary institution may grant a waiver to the student who may then receive a scholarship for the equivalent of one additional full-time academic semester if the student demonstrates that any of the following have substantially disrupted or interrupted the student's pursuit of a baccalaureate degree: (i) a military service obligation, (ii) serious medical debilitation, (iii) a short-term or long-term disability, or (iv) other extraordinary hardship. The eligible private postsecondary institution shall establish policies and procedures to implement the waiver provided by this subsection. (2013-360, s. 11.15(f).)

§ 116-282. Scholarship amounts; amounts dependent on availability of funds.

(a) Subject to the sum appropriated by the General Assembly for an academic year to be awarded as scholarships under this Article, a scholarship awarded under this Article to a student at an eligible private postsecondary institution shall be determined annually by the Authority based upon the enrollment status and expected family contribution of the student, consistent with the methodology for the federal Title IV programs.

(b)     The Authority shall have the power to determine the actual scholarship amounts disbursed to students in any given year based on the sum appropriated for purposes of this Article by the General Assembly for that academic year and any unexpended funds that may be available pursuant to G.S. 116-283.

(c)     The minimum award of a scholarship under this Article shall be five hundred dollars ($500.00). (2011-145, s. 9.18(a).)


§ 116-283. Administration; unexpended scholarship funds do not revert.

(a)     The scholarships provided for in this Article shall be administered by the Authority under rules adopted by the Authority in accordance with the provisions of this Article.

(b)     The Authority may use up to one and one-half percent (1.5%) of the funds appropriated for scholarships under this Article for administrative purposes.

(c)     Scholarship funds unexpended shall remain available for future scholarships to be awarded under this Article. (2011-145, s. 9.18(a).)


§§ 116A-1 through 116A-11: Repealed by Session Laws 1979, 2nd Session, c. 1311, s. 1.


Chapter 116B.

Escheats and Abandoned Property.

Article 1.

Escheats.

§ 116B-1. Escheats to Escheat Fund.

All real estate which has accrued to the State since June 30, 1971, or shall hereafter accrue from escheats, shall be vested in the Escheat Fund. Title to any such real property which has escheated to the Escheat Fund shall be conveyed by deed in the manner now provided by G.S. 146-74 through G.S. 146-78, except as is otherwise provided herein: Provided, that in any action in the superior court of North Carolina wherein the State Treasurer is a party, and wherein said court enters a judgment of escheat for any real property, then, upon petition of the State Treasurer in said action, said court shall have the authority to appoint the State Treasurer or his designated agent as a commissioner for the purpose of selling said real property at a public sale, for cash, at the courthouse door in the county in which the property is located, after properly advertising the sale according to law. The said commissioner, when appointed by the court, shall have the right to convey a valid title to the purchaser of the property at public sale. The funds derived from the sale of any such escheated real property by the commissioner so appointed shall thereafter be paid by him into the Escheat Fund. (Const., art. 9, s. 7; 1789, c. 306, s. 2; P.R.; R.C., c. 113, s. 11; Code, s. 2626; Rev., s. 4282; C.S., s. 5784; 1947, c. 494; 1961, c. 257; 1971, c. 1135, s. 2; 1979, 2nd Sess., c. 1311, s. 1.)


§ 116B-2. Unclaimed real and personal property escheats to the Escheat Fund.

Whenever the owner of any real or personal property situated or located within this State dies intestate, or dies testate but did not dispose of all real or personal property by will, without leaving surviving any heirs, as defined in G.S. 29-2(3), to inherit said property under the laws of this State, such real and personal property shall escheat. The State Treasurer shall have the right to institute a civil action in the superior court of any county in which such real or personal property is situated, against any administrator, executor, and unknown heirs or unknown claimants as party defendants, which unknown heirs or unknown claimants may be served with summons and notice of such action by publication as is now provided by the laws of this State. If an administrator or executor has been appointed, he shall make a determination that there are no known heirs or unknown claimants and shall inform the State Treasurer of that determination. The superior court in which such civil action is instituted shall have the authority to enter a judgment therein declaring the real and personal property unclaimed as having escheated, and the real property may be sold according to the provisions of G.S. 116B-1. A default final judgment may be entered by the clerk of the superior court in such cases when no answer is filed by the administrator, executor, unknown heirs or unknown claimants to the complaint, or if any answer is filed, the allegations of the complaint are either admitted or not denied by such party defendants, and no claim is made in the answer to the property left by said deceased person. The funds derived from such sale shall be paid into the Escheat Fund where said funds, together with all other escheated funds, shall be held without liability for profit or interest, subject to any just claims therefor. (1957, c. 1105, s. 1; 1971, c. 1135, s. 2; 1979, 2nd Sess., c. 1311, s. 1.)

§ 116B-3. Unclaimed personalty on settlements of decedents' estates to the Escheat Fund.

All sums of money or other personal estate of whatever kind which shall remain in the hands of any administrator, executor, administrator c.t.a., or personal representative when the administration of an estate of a person dying intestate, or partially intestate, without leaving any known heirs to inherit same, is ready to be closed, unrecovered or unclaimed by suit, by creditors, heirs, or others entitled thereto, shall, prior to the closing of the administration of the estate, be paid or delivered by such administrator or executor to the State Treasurer as an escheat and shall be included in the disbursements in the final account of such estate. In such cases as above described, the State Treasurer is authorized to demand, sue for, recover, and collect such unclaimed moneys or other personal estate of whatever kind from any administrator or executor after the estate is ready to be closed, or from the clerk of the superior court if the unclaimed assets have been paid over to him, and the State Treasurer shall hold the same without liability for profit or interest, subject to any just claims therefor. The provisions of this section and G.S. 116B-2 shall apply to the estate of a person missing for 30 days or more and the State Treasurer may bring an action to have a receiver appointed in such case under the provisions of Chapter 28C, Estates of Missing Persons. (1957, c. 1105, ss. 2, 2 1/2; 1971, c. 1135, s. 2; 1979, 2nd Sess., c. 1311, s. 1; 1981, c. 531, s. 1.)

§ 116B-4. Claim for escheated property.

Any escheated property or proceeds from the sale of escheated property held by the Escheat Fund pursuant to G.S. 116B-5 may be claimed by an heir of the decedent or by a creditor of the decedent who is not barred from presenting a claim under the provisions of Article 19 of Chapter 28A of the General Statutes. The provisions of G.S. 116B-67(a), (c), (d), and (e) and G.S. 116B-68 shall apply to a claim under this section. (1979, 2nd Sess., c. 1311, s. 1; 1999-460, s. 1.)

§ 116B-5.  Escheat Fund.

All property escheated or abandoned under the provisions of this Chapter and all property escheated or abandoned since June 30, 1971, under the provisions of former Chapter 116A, as amended, shall be paid into a fund to be administered by the Treasurer, which fund shall be designated the Escheat Fund. No escheated or abandoned property heretofore paid or delivered to the University of North Carolina pursuant to any constitutional provision or statute of this State shall be subject to the provisions of this Chapter. (1979, 2nd Sess., c. 1311, s. 1; 1999-460, s. 3(b).)

§ 116B-6.  Administration of Escheat Fund; Escheat Account.

(a)     Escheat Account. - All funds received by the Treasurer as escheated or abandoned property and which were transferred prior to January 1, 1980, to the trust fund created under G.S. 116-209 shall remain in that trust fund and shall be placed in a special fund, designated the "Escheat Account."

(b)     Investment and Transfer of Assets; Income. - The Treasurer is the trustee of the Escheat Account and has full power to invest and reinvest the assets of the Escheat Account and the Escheat Fund. Subject to the Treasurer's withholding an amount necessary to accomplish the Treasurer's duties as set out in this Chapter, including subsections (e), (f) and (g) of this section, the Treasurer shall transfer, at least annually, to the Escheat Account all moneys then in the Treasurer's custody received as, or derived from the disposition of, escheated and abandoned property and shall disburse to the State Education Assistance Authority, as provided in G.S. 116B-7, the income derived from the investment of the Escheat Account and the Escheat Fund. All moneys transferred to the Escheat Account under this section shall be accounted for and administered separately from other assets and money in the trust fund created under G.S. 116-209.

(c) Security Interest in Escheat Account. - The State Education Assistance Authority, in addition to other powers vested under G.S. 116-201 to G.S. 116-209.23, inclusive, is authorized to pledge and vest a security interest in all or any part of the Escheat Account, by resolution adopted or trust agreement approved by it, as security for or insurance respecting the payment of bonds or other obligations, as defined in G.S. 116-201, including principal, interest and redemption premium, if any; provided, that such pledge and security interest in the Escheat Account shall, in the determination of the Authority, constitute a use of the Escheat Fund to aid worthy and needy students who are residents of this State and are enrolled in public institutions of higher education in this State. The Authority may submit to the Treasurer, from time to time as it deems necessary, requisitions for transfers of money in the Escheat Account to pay such bonds and other obligations to the extent necessary under such pledge of, or security interest in, the Escheat Account, or any part thereof, and the Treasurer is authorized and directed to pay such money so requisitioned to the Authority for such purposes.

(d) Limitation on Amount of Obligations Secured. - The principal amount of bonds and other obligations insured or secured by the Escheat Account shall not exceed 10 times the amount held for the credit of the Escheat Account, as certified from time to time by the Treasurer, and, in no event, shall exceed three hundred fifty million dollars ($350,000,000). If the amount held for the credit of the Escheat Account, as certified by the Treasurer, shall be ten percent (10%) or less of the principal amount of the bonds and other obligations so insured or secured, the Authority shall not issue any additional bonds or cause additional obligations to be insured or secured by the Escheat Account until such time as the amount held for the credit of the Escheat Account exceeds ten percent (10%) of the principal amount of the bonds and other obligations secured or insured by the Escheat Account.

(e) Use of Excess Funds. - If the amount held for the credit of the Escheat Account at any time shall exceed the sum of thirty-five million dollars ($35,000,000), such excess may be used by the State Education Assistance Authority, with the written approval of the Treasurer, for the purpose of either (i) making student loans or (ii) refunding outstanding bonds or other obligations issued by the Authority and secured by a pledge of, or a security interest in, the Escheat Account. Any excess so used shall be repaid by the Authority to the Escheat Account in the manner agreed between the Authority and the Treasurer.

(f) Refund Reserve. - The Treasurer shall retain in the Escheat Fund, as a permanent refund reserve, either the sum of five million dollars ($5,000,000) or a sum equal to the total value of escheated or abandoned property received in the preceding fiscal year, whichever is greater, for the purpose of payment of refunds of escheated or abandoned property to persons entitled thereto.

(g) Additional Funds for Refunds. - If at any time the amount of the refund reserve shall be insufficient to make refunds required to be made, the Treasurer, in addition, may use all current receipts derived from escheated or abandoned property, exclusive of earnings and profits on investments of the Escheat Fund and the Escheat Account, for the purpose of making such refunds; and if all such funds shall be inadequate for such refunds, the Treasurer may apply to the Council of State, pursuant to the Executive Budget Act, to the limit of funds available from the Contingency and Emergency Fund, for a loan, without interest, to supply any deficiencies, in whole or in part. No receipts derived from escheated or abandoned property, other than earnings or profits on investments, shall be paid to the Authority until: (i) all valid claims for refund have been paid; (ii) the reserve for refund shall equal five million dollars ($5,000,000); and (iii) the amount loaned from the Contingency and Emergency Fund shall have been repaid by the Escheat Fund.

(h) Expenditures. - The Treasurer may expend the funds in the Escheat Fund, other than funds in the Escheat Account, for the payment of claims for refunds to owners, holders and claimants under G.S. 116B-4; for the payment of costs of maintenance and upkeep of abandoned or escheated property; costs of preparing lists of names of owners of abandoned property to be furnished to clerks of superior court; costs of notice and publication; costs of appraisals; fees of persons employed pursuant to G.S. 116B-8 costs involved in determining whether a decedent died without heirs; fees of persons employed pursuant to G.S. 116B-8 to conduct audits; costs of a title search of real property that has escheated; and costs of auction or sale under this Chapter. All other costs, including salaries of personnel, necessary to carry out the duties of the Treasurer under this Chapter, shall be appropriated from the funds of the Escheat Fund pursuant to the provisions of Article 1, Chapter 143 of the General Statutes.

(i) Records. - The State Treasurer must maintain the records it receives from holders who report unclaimed property in accordance with G.S. 116B-60. To protect the privacy of the owners of unclaimed property, the information that may be subject to public inspection will be limited to the information the State

Treasurer is required to annually submit to the clerks of superior court in accordance with G.S. 116B-62.

(j) Data Sharing. - On or before February 1 of each year, the North Carolina Division of Motor Vehicles, the North Carolina Department of Revenue, and the Division of Employment Security (DES) of the North Carolina Department of Commerce shall provide to the Treasurer, for the Treasurer's confidential use, information to facilitate locating owners of unclaimed property. The Treasurer may not use any information obtained pursuant to this section for any purpose except for locating owners of unclaimed property. (1979, 2nd Sess., c. 1311, s. 1; 1999-460, ss. 3(b), 4(a), (b); 2011-230, s. 1; 2011-401, s. 5.1; 2012-152, s. 3.1; 2012-194, s. 61.5(b); 2013-281, s. 1.)


§ 116B-7. Distribution of fund.

(a) The income derived from the investment or deposit of the Escheat Fund shall be distributed annually on or before August 15 to the State Education Assistance Authority for grants and loans to aid worthy and needy students who are residents of this State and are enrolled in public institutions of higher education in this State. Such grants and loans shall be made upon terms, consistent with the provisions of this Chapter, pursuant to which the State Education Assistance Authority makes grants and loans to other students under G.S. 116-201 to 116-209.23, Article 23 of Chapter 116 of the General Statutes, policies of the Board of Governors of The University of North Carolina regarding need-based grants for students of The University of North Carolina, and policies of the State Board of Community Colleges regarding need-based grants for students of the community colleges.

(b) An amount specified in the Current Operations Appropriations Act shall be transferred annually from the Escheat Fund to the Department of Administration to partially fund the program of Scholarships for Children of War Veterans established by Article 4 of Chapter 165 of the General Statutes. Those funds may be used only for residents of this State who (i) are worthy and needy as determined by the Department of Administration, and (ii) are enrolled in public institutions of higher education of this State. (1979, 2nd Sess., c. 1311, s. 1; 1999-460, s. 3(b); 2002-126, s. 9.19(a); 2003-284, s. 18.5(b); 2013-360, s. 11.1(f).)

§ 116B-8. Employment of persons with specialized skills or knowledge.

The Treasurer may employ the services of such independent consultants, real estate managers and other persons possessing specialized skills or knowledge as the Treasurer deems necessary or appropriate for the administration of this Chapter, including valuation, maintenance, upkeep, management, sale and conveyance of property and determination of sources of unreported abandoned property. The Treasurer may also employ the services of an attorney to perform a title search or to provide an accurate legal description of real property which the Treasurer has reason to believe may have escheated. Persons whose services are employed by the Treasurer pursuant to this section to determine sources and amounts of unreported property are subject to the same policies, including confidentiality and ethics, as employees of the Department of State Treasurer assigned to determine sources and amounts of unreported property. If the Treasurer contracts with any other person to conduct an audit under this Chapter, the audit shall not be performed on a contingent fee basis or any other similar method that may impair an auditor's independence or the perception of the auditor's independence by the public. Notwithstanding the preceding sentence, the Treasurer may contract with any other person on a contingent fee basis to conduct audits of life insurance companies where the audit is being conducted for the purpose of identifying unclaimed death benefits or to conduct audits of holders of unredeemed bond funds. Compensation of persons whose services may be employed pursuant to this section on a contingent fee basis shall be limited to twelve percent (12%) of the final assessment. (1979, 2nd Sess., c. 1311, s. 1; 1999-460, ss. 3(b), 5; 2012-152, s. 3; 2012-194, s. 61.5(a), (b).)


§ 116B-9. Reserved for future codification purposes.


Article 2.

Abandoned Property.

§§ 116B-10 through 116B-26. Repealed by Session Laws 1999-460, s. 2, effective January 1, 2000.

ARTICLE 3.

Administration of Abandoned Property.

§ 116B-27: Recodified as § 116B-5 by Session Laws 1999-460, s. 3(b).

§§ 116B-28 through 116B-35. Repealed by Session Laws 1999-460, s. 3(a), effective January 1, 2000.

§ 116B-36: Recodified as § 116B-6 by Session Laws 1999-460, s. 3(b).

§ 116B-37: Recodified as § 116B-7 by Session Laws 1999-460, s. 3(b).

§§ 116B-38 through 116B-46. Repealed by Session Laws 1999-460, s. 3(a), effective January 1, 2000.

§ 116B-47: Recodified as § 116B-8 by Session Laws 1999-460, s. 3(b).

§§ 116B-48 through 116B-49. Repealed by Session Laws 1999-460, s. 3(a), effective January 1, 2000.

§ 116B-50. Reserved for future codification purposes.

Article 4.

North Carolina Unclaimed Property Act.

§ 116B-51. Short title.

This Article may be cited as the "North Carolina Unclaimed Property Act." (1999-460, s. 6.)

§ 116B-52. Definitions.

In this Chapter:

(1) "Apparent owner" means a person whose name appears on the records of a holder as the person entitled to property held, issued, or owing by the holder.

(2) "Business association" means a corporation, joint stock company, investment company, partnership, unincorporated association, joint venture, limited liability company, business trust, trust company, land bank, safe deposit company, safekeeping depository, financial organization, insurance company, mutual fund, utility, or other business entity consisting of one or more persons, whether or not for profit.

(3) "Domicile" means the state of incorporation of a corporation and the state of the principal place of business of a holder other than a corporation.

(4) "Financial organization" means a savings and loan association, building and loan association, savings bank, industrial bank, bank, banking organization, or credit union.

(5) "Holder" means a person obligated to hold for the account of or deliver or pay to the owner property that is subject to this Chapter.

(6) "Insurance company" means an association, corporation, or fraternal or mutual benefit organization, whether or not for profit, engaged in the business of providing life endowments, annuities, or insurance, including accident, burial, casualty, credit life, contract performance, dental, disability, fidelity, fire, health, hospitalization, illness, life, malpractice, marine, mortgage, surety, wage protection, and workers' compensation insurance.

(7) "Mineral" means gas, oil, coal, other gaseous, liquid, and solid hydrocarbons, oil shale, cement material, sand and gravel, road material, building stone, chemical raw material, gemstone, fissionable and nonfissionable ores, colloidal and other clay, steam and other geothermal resource, or any other substance defined as a mineral by the law of this State.

(8) "Mineral proceeds" means amounts payable for the extraction, production, or sale of minerals, or, upon the abandonment of those payments,

all payments that become payable thereafter. The term includes amounts payable:

a. For the acquisition and retention of a mineral lease, including bonuses, royalties, compensatory royalties, shut-in royalties, minimum royalties, and delay rentals;

b. For the extraction, production, or sale of minerals, including net revenue interests, royalties, overriding royalties, extraction payments, and production payments; and

c. Under an agreement or option, including a joint operating agreement, unit agreement, pooling agreement, and farm-out agreement.

(9) "Owner" means a person who has a legal or equitable interest in property subject to this Chapter or the person's legal representative. The term includes a depositor in the case of a deposit, a beneficiary in the case of a trust other than a deposit in trust, and a creditor, claimant, or payee in the case of other property.

(10) "Person" means an individual, business association, financial organization, estate, trust, government, governmental subdivision, agency, or instrumentality, or any other legal or commercial entity.

(11) "Property" means (i) money or tangible personal property held by a holder that is physically located in a safe deposit box or other safekeeping depository held by a financial institution within this State or (ii) a fixed and certain interest in intangible property that is held, issued, or owed in the course of a holder's business, or by a government, governmental subdivision, agency, or instrumentality, and all income or increments therefrom. The term includes property that is referred to as or evidenced by:

a. Money, a check, draft, deposit, interest, or dividend;

b. Credit balance, customer's overpayment, gift certificate, security deposit, refund, credit memorandum, unpaid wage, unused ticket, mineral proceeds, or unidentified remittance;

c. Stock or other evidence of ownership of an interest in a business association;

d. A bond, debenture, note, or other evidence of indebtedness;

e. Money deposited to redeem stocks, bonds, coupons, or other securities, or to make distributions;

f. An amount due and payable under the terms of an annuity or insurance policy, including policies providing life insurance, property and casualty insurance, workers' compensation insurance, or health and disability insurance; and

g. An amount distributable from a trust or custodial fund established under a plan to provide health, welfare, pension, vacation, severance, retirement, death, stock purchase, profit sharing, employee savings, supplemental unemployment insurance, or similar benefits.

(12) "Record" means information that is inscribed on a tangible medium or that is stored in an electronic or other medium and is retrievable in perceivable form.

(13) "State" means a state of the United States, the District of Columbia, the Commonwealth of Puerto Rico, or any territory or insular possession subject to the jurisdiction of the United States.

(14) "Treasurer" means the Treasurer of the State of North Carolina or the Treasurer's designated agent.

(15) "Utility" means a person who owns or operates for public use any plant, equipment, real property, franchise, or license for the transportation of the public, the transmission of communications, or the production, storage, transmission, sale, delivery, or furnishing of electricity, water, steam, or gas. (1999-460, s. 6; 2011-230, s. 2; 2013-281, s. 2.)

§ 116B-53. Presumptions of abandonment.

(a) Property is unclaimed if the apparent owner has not communicated in writing or by other means reflected in a contemporaneous record prepared by or on behalf of the holder, with the holder concerning the property or the account in which the property is held, and has not otherwise indicated an interest in the property. A communication with an owner by a person (other than the holder or its representative) who has not, in writing, identified the property to the owner is not an indication of interest in the property by the owner.

(b) An indication of an interest in property includes:

(1) The presentment of a check or other instrument of payment of a dividend or other distribution made with respect to an account or underlying stock or other interest in a business association or, in the case of a distribution made by electronic or similar means, evidence that the distribution has been received;

(2) The presentment of a check or other instrument of payment of interest made with respect to debt of a business association or, in the case of an interest payment made by electronic or similar means, evidence that the interest payment has been received;

(3) Owner-directed activity in the account in which the property is held, including a direction by the owner to increase, decrease, or change the amount or type of property held in the account;

(4) The making of a deposit to or withdrawal from an account in a financial organization;

(5) Owner activity in another account with the holder of a deposit described in subdivisions (c)(2) and (c)(6) of this section; and

(6) The payment of a premium with respect to a property interest in an insurance policy; but the application of an automatic premium loan provision or other nonforfeiture provision contained in an insurance policy does not prevent a policy from maturing or terminating if the insured has died or the insured or the beneficiary of the policy has otherwise become entitled to the proceeds before the depletion of the cash surrender value of a policy by the application of those provisions.

(c) Property is presumed abandoned if it is unclaimed by the apparent owner during the time set forth below for the particular property:

(1) Traveler's check, 15 years after issuance.

(2) Time deposit, including a deposit that is automatically renewable, 10 years after the later of initial maturity or the date of the last indication by the owner of interest in the property.

(3) Money order, cashier's check, teller's check, and certified check, seven years after issuance.

(4) Stock or other equity interest in a business association, including a security entitlement under Article 8 of the Uniform Commercial Code, Chapter 25 of the General Statutes, three years after the earlier of:

a. The date of a cash dividend or other distribution unclaimed by the apparent owner.

b. The date a second consecutive mailing, notification, or communication from the holder to the apparent owner is returned to the holder as unclaimed by or undeliverable to the apparent owner.

c. The date the holder discontinued mailings, notifications, or communications to the apparent owner.

This subdivision applies to both the underlying stock, share, or other intangible ownership interest of an owner, and any stock, share, or other intangible interest of which the business association is in possession of the certificate or other evidence or indicia of ownership, and to the stock, share, or other ownership interest of dividend and nondividend paying business associations whether or not the interest is represented by a certificate.

(5) Debt of a business association, including debt evidenced by a matured or called bearer bond or an original issue discount bond, three years after the date of an interest or principal payment unclaimed by the apparent owner.

(5a) Any dividend, profit, distribution, interest, redemption, payment on principal, cash compensation (including amounts from a demutualized insurance company), or other sum held or owing by a business association for or to its shareholder, certificate holder, policyholder, member, bondholder, or other security holder, who has not claimed it, or corresponded in writing with the business association concerning it, within three years after the date prescribed for payment or delivery.

(6)     Demand or savings deposit, five years after the date of the last indication by the owner of interest in the property.

(7)     Money or credits owed to a customer as a result of a retail business transaction, three years after the obligation accrued.

(8)     Any gift certificate or electronic gift card bearing an expiration date and remaining unredeemed or dormant for more than three years after the gift certificate or electronic gift card was sold is deemed abandoned. The amount abandoned is deemed to be sixty percent (60%) of the unredeemed portion of the face value of the gift certificate or the electronic gift card.

(9)     Amount owed by an insurer on a life or endowment insurance policy or an annuity that has matured or terminated, three years after the obligation to pay arose or, in the case of a policy or annuity payable upon proof of death, three years after the insured has attained, or would have attained if living, the limiting age under the mortality table on which the reserve is based.

(10)    Property distributable by a business association in a course of dissolution, one year after the property becomes distributable.

(11)    Property received by a court as proceeds of a class action, and not distributed pursuant to the judgment, one year after the distribution date.

(12)    Property held by a court, government, governmental subdivision, agency, or instrumentality, one year after the property becomes distributable.

(13)    Wages or other compensation for personal services, one year after the compensation becomes payable.

(14)    Deposit or refund owed to a subscriber by a utility, one year after the deposit or refund becomes payable.

(15)    Property in an individual retirement account, defined benefit plan, or other account or plan that is qualified for tax deferral under the income tax laws of the United States, three years after the earliest of the date of the distribution or attempted distribution of the property, the date of the required distribution as stated in the plan or trust agreement governing the plan, or the date, if determinable by the holder, specified in the income tax laws of the United States by which distribution of the property must begin in order to avoid a tax penalty.

(16) All other property, five years after the owner's right to demand the property or after the obligation to pay or distribute the property arises, whichever first occurs.

(d) At the time that an interest in property is presumed abandoned under subsection (c) of this section, any other property right accrued or accruing to the owner as a result of the interest, and not previously presumed abandoned, is also presumed abandoned.

(e) Property is payable or distributable for purposes of this Chapter notwithstanding the owner's failure to make demand or present an instrument or document otherwise required to obtain payment or distribution, except as otherwise provided by the Uniform Commercial Code. (1999-460, s. 6; 2001-226, s. 1; 2005-132, s. 1; 2011-230, s. 3.)

§ 116B-54. Exclusion for forfeited reservation deposits, certain gift certificates or electronic gift cards, prepaid calling cards, certain manufactured home buyer deposits, and certain credit balances.

(a) A forfeited reservation deposit is not abandoned property. For the purposes of this section, the term "reservation deposit" means an amount of money paid to a business association to guarantee that the business association holds a specific service, such as a room accommodation at a hotel, seating at a restaurant, or an appointment with a doctor, for a specified date and place. The term "reservation deposit" does not include an application fee, a utility deposit, or a deposit made toward the purchase of real property.

(b) A gift certificate or electronic gift card is not abandoned property when the gift certificate or electronic gift card:

(1) Conspicuously states that the gift certificate or electronic gift card does not expire;

(2) Bears no expiration date; or

(3) States that a date of expiration printed on the gift certificate or electronic gift card is not applicable in North Carolina.

(c) A prepaid calling card issued by a public utility as defined in G.S. 62-3(23)a.6. is not abandoned property.

(d) A buyer deposit that a dealer is authorized to retain under either G.S. 143-143.21A or G.S. 143-143.21B is not abandoned property and is not subject to this Article.

(e) Credit balances as shown on the records of a business association to or for the benefit of another business association, shall not constitute abandoned property. For purposes of this section, the term "credit balances" means items such as overpayments or underpayments on the sale of goods or services.

(f) A lottery prize that remains unclaimed after the period set by the North Carolina State Lottery Commission for claiming those prizes shall not constitute abandoned property. (1999-460, s. 6; 2005-276, s. 31.1(w1); 2005-344, s. 7.)


§ 116B-55. Contents of safe deposit box or other safekeeping depository.

Contents of a safe deposit box or other safekeeping depository held by a financial organization is presumed abandoned if the apparent owner has not claimed the property within the period established by G.S. 53C-6-13 and shall be delivered to the Treasurer as provided by that section. If the contents include property described in G.S. 116B-53, the Treasurer shall hold the property for the remainder of the applicable period set forth in that section before the property is deemed to be received for purpose of sale under G.S. 116B-65. (1999-460, s. 6; 2012-56, s. 46.)


§ 116B-56. Rules for taking custody.

(a) Except as otherwise provided in this Chapter or by other statute of this State, property that is presumed abandoned, whether located in this or another state, is subject to the custody of this State if:

(1) The last known address of the apparent owner, as shown on the records of the holder, is in this State;

(2) The records of the holder do not reflect the identity of the person entitled to the property, and it is established that the last known address of the person entitled to the property is in this State;

(3) The records of the holder do not reflect the last known address of the apparent owner and it is established that:

a. The last known address of the person entitled to the property is in this State; or

b. The holder is domiciled in this State or is a government or governmental subdivision, agency, or instrumentality of this State and has not previously paid or delivered the property to the state of the last known address of the apparent owner or other person entitled to the property;

(4) The last known address of the apparent owner, as shown on the records of the holder, is in a state that does not provide for the escheat or custodial taking of the property, and the holder is domiciled in this State or is a government or governmental subdivision, agency, or instrumentality of this State;

(5) The last known address of the apparent owner, as shown on the records of the holder, is in a foreign country, and the holder is domiciled in this State or is a government or governmental subdivision, agency, or instrumentality of this State; or

(6) The property is a traveler's check or money order purchased in this State or the issuer of the traveler's check or money order has its principal place of business in this State and the issuer's records show that the instrument was purchased in a state that does not provide for the escheat or custodial taking of the property or do not show the state in which the instrument was purchased.

(b) In the case of an amount payable under the terms of an annuity or insurance policy, the last known address of the person entitled to the property is presumed to be the same as the last known address of the insured or the principal, as shown on the records of the insurance company, if:

(1) A person other than the insured or the principal is entitled to the property; and

(2) Either:

a. No address of the person is known to the insurance company; or

b. The records of the insurance company do not reflect the identity of the person. (1999-460, s. 6.)

§ 116B-57. Dormancy charge; other lawful charges.

(a) A holder may deduct from property presumed abandoned a reasonable charge imposed by reason of the owner's failure to claim the property within a specified time only if there is a valid and enforceable written contract between the holder and the owner under which the holder may impose the charge and the holder regularly imposes the charge, which is not regularly reversed or otherwise canceled.

(b) This Chapter does not prevent a holder from deducting from property presumed abandoned other lawful charges specifically authorized by statute or by a valid and enforceable contract. (1999-460, s. 6.)

§ 116B-58. Burden of proof as to property evidenced by record of check or draft.

A record of the issuance of a check, draft, or similar instrument is prima facie evidence of an obligation. In claiming property from a holder who is also the issuer, the Treasurer's burden of proof as to the existence and amount of the property and its abandonment is satisfied by showing issuance of the instrument and passage of the requisite period of abandonment. Defenses of payment, satisfaction, discharge, and want of consideration are affirmative defenses that must be established by the holder. In asserting these affirmative defenses, a holder who is also the issuer may satisfy the holder's burden of proof by showing a written acknowledgement by the payee of a check, draft, or similar instrument that no obligation is owed the payee. (1999-460, s. 6.)

§ 116B-59. Notice by holders to apparent owners.

(a) A holder of property presumed abandoned shall make a good faith effort to locate an apparent owner.

(b) The holder shall send written notice, by first-class mail, to the apparent owner, not more than 120 days or less than 60 days before filing the report required by G.S. 116B-60, to the last known address of the apparent owner as reflected in the holder's records, if the value of the property is fifty dollars ($50.00) or more.

(c) The notice must contain:

(1) A statement that, according to the records of the holder, property is being held to which the addressee appears entitled and the amount or description of the property;

(2) The name and address of the person holding the property and any necessary information regarding changes of name and address of the holder;

(3) A statement that, if satisfactory proof of claim is not presented by the owner to the holder by the following October 1 or, if the holder is an insurance company, by the following April 1, the property will be placed in the custody of the Treasurer, to whom all further claims shall be directed. (1979, 2nd Sess., c. 1311, s. 1; 1981, c. 531, ss. 4-6; 1993, c. 539, s. 898; c. 541, s. 5; 1994, Ex. Sess., c. 24, s. 14(c); 1999-460, s. 6.)


§ 116B-60. Report of abandoned property; certification by holders with tax return.

(a) A holder of property presumed abandoned shall make a report to the Treasurer concerning the property. Holders reporting 50 or more property owner records shall file the report in an electronic format prescribed by the Treasurer. Holders reporting less than 50 property owner records may file the report electronically. Holders reporting electronically may file an electronic certification and verification in order to comply with subsection (f) of this section.

(b) For amounts due to the apparent owner of property of the value of fifty dollars ($50.00) or more, the report must be verified and must contain the following, if known by the holder:

(1) Except with respect to a traveler's check or money order, full name, last known address, social security number or taxpayer identification number, date of birth, drivers license or state identification number, and e-mail address of each person who, from the records of the holder of the property, appears to be the apparent owner of the property.

(2) A description of the property, the identification number, if any, and the property amount.

(3) Repealed by Session Laws 2011-230, s. 4, effective October 1, 2011.

(4) In the case of an amount held or owing under an annuity or a life or endowment insurance policy, the full name and last known address, social security number or taxpayer identification number, date of birth, drivers license or state identification number, and e-mail address of the annuitant or insured and of the beneficiary.

(5) The date, if any, on which the property became payable, demandable, or returnable, and the date of the last transaction or communication with the apparent owner with respect to the property.

(6) Other information that the Treasurer by rule prescribes as necessary for the administration of this Chapter.

(b1) Amounts due an apparent owner less than fifty dollars ($50.00) may be reported in an aggregate amount without furnishing any of the information required by subsection (b) of this section.

(c) If a holder of property presumed abandoned is a successor to another person who previously held the property for the apparent owner or the holder has changed its name while holding the property, the holder shall file with the report its former names, if any, and the known names and addresses of all previous holders of the property.

(d) The report must be filed before November 1 of each year and cover the 12 months next preceding July 1 of that year, but a report with respect to a life insurance company must be filed before May 1 of each year for the calendar year next preceding.

(e) Before the date for filing the report, the holder of property presumed abandoned may request the Treasurer to extend the time for filing the report.

The Treasurer may grant the extension for good cause. The holder, upon receipt of the extension, may make an interim payment on the amount the holder estimates will ultimately be due, which terminates the accrual of additional interest on the amount paid.

(f) The holder of property presumed abandoned shall file with the report a certification and verification that the holder has complied with G.S. 116B-59.

(f1) Any holder who has intangible property due to be reported with a cumulative value of two hundred fifty dollars ($250.00) or less in a single reporting year shall not be required to report the property in that year but shall report the property in any year when the value or aggregate value exceeds two hundred fifty dollars ($250.00).

(g) Every business association holding property presumed abandoned under this Chapter shall certify the holding in the income tax return required by Chapter 105 of the General Statutes. The certification shall be a part of the tax return with which it is filed. If the business association is not required to file an income tax return under Chapter 105, the certification shall be made in the form and manner required by the Secretary of Revenue. The information appearing on the certification is not privileged or confidential, and this information shall be furnished by the Secretary of Revenue to the Escheat Fund on October 1 of each year, or if this date shall fall on a weekend or holiday, on the next regular business day. (1979, 2nd Sess., c. 1311, s. 1; 1981, c. 531, ss. 7, 8; 1983, c. 204, s. 3; 1985, c. 215, ss. 2, 3; 1987, c. 163, ss. 1-3; 1993, c. 541, s. 6; 1999-460, s. 6; 2009-177, s. 1; 2011-230, s. 4; 2013-281, s. 3.)


§ 116B-61. Payment or delivery of abandoned property.

(a) Upon filing the report required by G.S. 116B-60, the holder of property presumed abandoned shall pay, deliver, or cause to be paid or delivered to the Treasurer the property described in the report, but if the property is an automatically renewable deposit, and a penalty or forfeiture in the payment of interest would result, the time for compliance is extended to the next filing and delivery date at which a penalty or forfeiture would no longer result.

(b) If the property reported to the Treasurer is a security or security entitlement under Article 8 of Chapter 25 of the General Statutes, the Treasurer is an appropriate person to make an indorsement, instruction, or entitlement order on behalf of the apparent owner to invoke the duty of the issuer or its transfer agent or the securities intermediary to transfer or dispose of the security or the security entitlement in accordance with Article 8 of Chapter 25 of the General Statutes.

(c) If the holder of property reported to the Treasurer is the issuer of a certificated security, the Treasurer has the right to obtain a replacement certificate pursuant to G.S. 25-8-405, but an indemnity bond is not required.

(d) An issuer, the holder, and any transfer agent or other person acting pursuant to the instructions of and on behalf of the issuer or holder in accordance with this section is not liable to the apparent owner and must be indemnified against claims of any person in accordance with G.S. 116B-63. (1979, 2nd Sess., c. 1311, s. 1; 1981, c. 531, s. 14; 1987, c. 163, s. 6; 1993, c. 541, s. 7; 1999-460, s. 6.)

§ 116B-62. Preparation of list of owners by Treasurer.

(a) There shall be delivered annually in an electronic format to the Administrative Office of the Courts to be distributed to the clerk of superior court of each county a list prepared by the Treasurer of escheated and abandoned property reported to the Treasurer. The list shall contain all of the following:

(1) The names, if known, in alphabetical order of surname, and last known addresses, if any, of apparent owners of escheated and abandoned property as of June 30 of that year.

(2) The names and addresses of the holders of the abandoned property.

(3) A statement that claim and proof of legal entitlement to escheated or abandoned property shall be presented by the owner to the Treasurer, which statement shall set forth where further information may be obtained.

The Treasurer shall send the list to the Administrative Office of the Courts as soon as possible after June 30 of each year but no later than July 31, and the Administrative Office of the Courts shall distribute the list to each clerk of superior court as soon as possible after receiving it but no later than August 31.

(b) At the time the lists are distributed to the clerks of superior court, but no later than August 31 of each year, the Treasurer shall cause to be published once each week for two consecutive weeks, in at least two newspapers having general circulation in this State, a notice stating the nature of the lists and that the lists are available for inspection at the offices of the respective clerks of superior court, together with any other information the Treasurer deems appropriate to appear in the notice.

(c) The Treasurer is not required to include in any list any item of a value, as determined by the Treasurer, in the Treasurer's discretion, of less than fifty dollars ($50.00), unless the Treasurer deems inclusion of items of lesser amounts to be in the public interest.

(d) The clerks of superior court shall make the lists available for public inspection.

(e) The lists prepared by the Treasurer shall include only escheated and abandoned property reported for the current reporting date and are not required to be cumulative lists of escheated and abandoned property previously reported.

(f) Notwithstanding the provisions of Chapter 132 of the General Statutes, any supporting data, including aging reports, or lists of apparent owners of unclaimed property held by a clerk of superior court or any other office of State or local government may be confidential but shall be disclosed to the Treasurer in accordance with the reporting of escheated and abandoned property. The supporting data and lists of apparent owners of escheated and abandoned property held by the Treasurer may be confidential until 12 months after the list to the clerks of superior court required by subsection (b) of this section has been distributed. This subsection shall not apply to owners of reported property making inquiries about their property to the Escheat Fund. (1979, 2nd Sess., c. 1311, s. 1; 1981, c. 531, ss. 9-13; 1983, c. 204, ss. 4-7; 1985, c. 215, s. 4; 1987, c. 163, ss. 4, 5; 1999-460, s. 6; 2009-312, s. 1; 2010-97, s. 10.)


§ 116B-63. Custody by State; recovery by holder; defense of holder.

(a) In this section, payment or delivery is made in "good faith" if:

(1) Payment or delivery was made in a reasonable attempt to comply with this Chapter;

(2) The holder was not then in breach of a fiduciary obligation with respect to the property and had a reasonable basis for believing, based on the facts then known, that the property was presumed abandoned; and

(3) There is no showing that the records under which the payment or delivery was made did not meet reasonable commercial standards of practice.

(b) Upon payment or delivery of property to the Treasurer, the State assumes custody and responsibility for the safekeeping of the property. A holder who pays or delivers property to the Treasurer in good faith is relieved of all liability arising thereafter with respect to the property.

(c) A holder who has paid money to the Treasurer pursuant to this Chapter may subsequently make payment to a person reasonably appearing to the holder to be entitled to payment. Upon a filing by the holder of proof of payment and proof that the payee was entitled to the payment, the Treasurer shall promptly reimburse the holder for the payment without imposing a fee or other charge. If reimbursement is sought for a payment made on a negotiable instrument, including a traveler's check or money order, the holder must be reimbursed upon filing proof that the instrument was duly presented and that payment was made to a person who reasonably appeared to be entitled to payment. The holder must be reimbursed for payment made even if the payment was made to a person whose claim was barred under G.S. 116B-71(a).

(d) A holder who has delivered property other than money to the Treasurer pursuant to this Chapter may reclaim the property if it is still in the possession of the Treasurer, without paying any fee or other charge, upon filing proof that the apparent owner has claimed the property from the holder.

(e) The Treasurer may accept a holder's affidavit as sufficient proof of the holder's right to recover money and property under this section.

(f) If a holder pays or delivers property to the Treasurer in good faith and thereafter another person claims the property from the holder or another state claims the money or property under its laws relating to escheat or abandoned or unclaimed property, the Treasurer, upon written notice of the claim, shall defend the holder against the claim and indemnify the holder against any liability on the claim resulting from payment or delivery of the property to the Treasurer. (1979, 2nd Sess., c. 1311, s. 1; 1989, c. 114, s. 3; 1999-460, s. 6.)

§ 116B-64. Income or gain accruing after payment or delivery.

If property other than money is delivered to the Treasurer under this Chapter, the owner is entitled to receive from the Treasurer any income or gain realized or accruing on the property at or before liquidation or conversion of the property into money. If the property is interest-bearing or pays dividends, the interest or dividends shall be paid until the date on which the amount of the deposits, accounts, or funds, or the shares must be remitted or delivered to the Treasurer under G.S. 116B-61. Otherwise, when property is delivered or paid to the Treasurer, the Treasurer shall hold the property without liability for income or gain. (1979, 2nd Sess., c. 1311, s. 1; 1999-460, s. 6.)


§ 116B-65. Public sale of abandoned property.

(a) Except as otherwise provided in this section, the Treasurer, within three years after the receipt of abandoned property, shall sell it to the highest bidder at public sale at a location in the State which in the judgment of the Treasurer affords the most favorable market for the property. The Treasurer may decline the highest bid and reoffer the property for sale if the Treasurer considers the bid to be insufficient. The Treasurer need not offer the property for sale if the Treasurer considers that the probable cost of sale will exceed the proceeds of the sale. The Treasurer shall give reasonable notice of the sale as he or she deems appropriate and cost-effective, but, at a minimum, notice must be published at least two times a year in a major newspaper in the State's major media markets. The Treasurer is not required to sell money unless it is a collector's species having value greater than the face value of the money as cash.

(b) Securities listed on an established stock exchange must be sold at prices prevailing on the exchange at the time of sale. Other securities may be sold over the counter at prices prevailing at the time of sale or by any reasonable method selected by the Treasurer. If securities are sold by the Treasurer before the expiration of three years after their delivery to the Treasurer, a person making a claim under this Chapter before the end of the three-year period is entitled to the proceeds of the sale of the securities or the market value of the securities at the time the claim is made, whichever is greater, less any deduction for expenses of sale. A person making a claim under this Chapter after the expiration of the three-year period is entitled to receive the securities delivered to the Treasurer by the holder, if they still remain in the custody of the Treasurer, or the net proceeds received from sale, and is not entitled to receive any appreciation in the value of the property occurring after delivery to the Treasurer, except in a case of intentional misconduct by the Treasurer.

(c)     A purchaser of property at a sale conducted by the Treasurer pursuant to this Chapter takes the property free of all claims of the owner or previous holder and of all persons claiming through or under them. The Treasurer shall execute all documents necessary to complete the transfer of ownership. (1979, 2nd Sess., c. 1311, s. 1; 1999-460, s. 6; 2011-230, s. 5.)


§ 116B-66. Claim of another state to recover property.

(a)     After property has been paid or delivered to the Treasurer under this Article, another state may recover the property if:

(1)     The property was paid or delivered to the custody of this State because the records of the holder did not reflect a last known location of the apparent owner within the borders of the other state, and the other state establishes that the apparent owner or other person entitled to the property was last known to be located within the borders of that state and under the laws of that state the property has escheated or become subject to a claim of abandonment by that state;

(2)     The property was paid or delivered to the custody of this State because the laws of the other state did not provide for the escheat or custodial taking of the property, and under the laws of that state subsequently enacted, the property has escheated or become subject to a claim of abandonment by that state;

(3)     The records of the holder were erroneous in that they did not accurately identify the owner of the property and the last known location of the owner within the borders of another state, and under the laws of that state the property has escheated or become subject to a claim of abandonment by that state; or

(4)     Repealed by Session Laws 2000, c. 140, s. 27.

(5)     The property is a sum payable on a traveler's check, money order, or similar instrument that was purchased in the other state and delivered into the

custody of this State under G.S. 116B-56(a)(6), and under the laws of the other state, the property has escheated or become subject to a claim of abandonment by that state.

(b) A claim of another state to recover escheated or abandoned property must be presented in a form prescribed by the Treasurer, who shall decide the claim within 90 days after it is presented. The Treasurer shall allow the claim upon determining that the other state is entitled to the abandoned property under subsection (a) of this section.

(c) The Treasurer shall require another state, before recovering property under this section, to agree to indemnify this State and its officers and employees against any liability on a claim to the property. (1999-460, s. 6; 2000-140, s. 27.)


§ 116B-67. Claim for property paid or delivered to the Treasurer.

(a) A person, excluding another state, claiming property paid or delivered to the Treasurer may file a claim on a form prescribed by the Treasurer and verified by the claimant.

(b) At the discretion of the Treasurer, the claim shall be made to the holder or to the holder's successor. If the holder is satisfied that the claim is valid and that the claimant is the owner of the property, the holder shall so certify to the Treasurer by written statement attested by the holder under oath, or in the case of a corporation, by two principal officers, or one principal officer and an authorized employee of the corporation. The determination of the holder that the claimant is the owner shall, in the absence of fraud, be binding upon the Treasurer and upon receipt of the certificate of the holder to this effect, the Treasurer shall forthwith authorize and make payment of the claim or return of the property, or if the property has been sold, the amount received from the sale, to the owner, or to the holder in the event the owner has assigned the claim to the holder and the certificate of the holder is accompanied by an assignment. In the event the holder rejects the claim, the claimant may appeal to the Treasurer.

If the holder, or the holder's successor, is not available, the owner may file a claim with the Treasurer on a form prescribed by the Treasurer. In addition to any other information, the claim shall state the facts surrounding the unavailability of the holder and the lack of a successor.

(c)     Within 90 days after a claim is filed, the Treasurer shall allow or deny the claim and give written notice of the decision to the claimant. If the claim is denied, the Treasurer shall inform the claimant of the reasons for the denial and specify what additional evidence is required before the claim will be allowed. The claimant may then file a new claim with the Treasurer or maintain an action under G.S. 116B-68.

(d)     Within 30 days after a claim is allowed, the property or the net proceeds of a sale of the property must be delivered or paid by the Treasurer to the claimant.

(e)     The claimant or claimants and the holder, if the holder either certifies that the claimant is the owner under subsection (b) of this section or recovers money and property from the Treasurer under G.S. 116B-63, shall agree to indemnify, save harmless, and defend the State, the Treasurer, and the Escheat Fund from any claim arising out of or in connection with refund of the property claimed. In like manner, the claimant shall also agree to indemnify, save harmless, and defend the holder, if the holder certifies the claim under subsection (b) of this section or pays or delivers property to the claimant under G.S. 116B-63. (1979, 2nd Sess., c. 1311, s. 1; 1987, c. 163, s. 8; c. 827, s. 18; 1999-460, s. 6.)


§ 116B-68.  Action to establish claim.

A person aggrieved by a decision of the Treasurer or whose claim has not been acted upon within 90 days after its filing may maintain an original action to establish the claim in the Superior Court of Wake County, naming the Treasurer as a defendant. (1999-460, s. 6.)


§ 116B-69.  Election to take payment or delivery.

(a)     The Treasurer may decline to receive property reported under this Chapter which the Treasurer considers to have a value less than the expenses of notice and sale.

(b) A holder, with the written consent of the Treasurer and upon conditions and terms prescribed by the Treasurer, may report and deliver property before the property is presumed abandoned. Property so delivered must be held by the Treasurer and is not presumed abandoned until it otherwise would be presumed abandoned under this Article. (1979, 2nd Sess., c. 1311, s. 1; 1981, c. 531, s. 14; 1987, c. 163, ss. 6, 7; 1993, c. 541, s. 7; 1999-460, s. 6.)


§ 116B-70. Destruction or disposition of property having no substantial commercial value; immunity from liability; property of historical significance.

(a) If the Treasurer determines after investigation that property delivered under this Chapter has no substantial commercial value, the Treasurer may destroy or otherwise dispose of the property at any time. An action or proceeding may not be maintained against the State or any officer, employee, or agent of the State, both past and present, in the person's individual and official capacity, or against the holder for or on account of an act of the Treasurer under this subsection, except for intentional misconduct.

(b) Notwithstanding the provisions of G.S. 116B-65, the Treasurer may retain any tangible property delivered to the Treasurer, if the property has recognized historic significance. The historic significance shall be certified by the Treasurer, with the advice of the Secretary of Cultural Resources; and a statement of the appraised value of the property shall be filed with the certification. Historic property retained under this subsection may be stored and displayed at any suitable location. (1979, 2nd Sess., c. 1311, s. 1; 1999-460, s. 6.)


§ 116B-71. Periods of limitation.

(a) The expiration, before or after the effective date of this Article, of a period of limitation on the owner's right to receive or recover property, whether specified by contract, statute, or court order, does not preclude the property from being presumed abandoned or affect a duty of a holder to file a report or to pay or deliver or transfer property to the Treasurer as required by this Article.

(b) An action or proceeding may not be maintained by the Treasurer to enforce this Article in regard to the reporting, delivery, or payment of property more than five years after the holder filed a report with the Treasurer in which the holder specifically identified property, should have but failed to identify property, or gave express notice to the Treasurer of a dispute regarding property. In the absence of such a report or other express notice, the period of limitation is tolled. The period of limitation is also tolled by the filing of a report that is fraudulent. (1979, 2nd Sess., c. 1311, s. 1; 1993, c. 541, s. 8; 1999-460, s. 6.)


§ 116B-72. Requests for reports and examination of records.

(a) The Treasurer may require a person who has not filed a report, or a person who the Treasurer believes has filed an inaccurate, incomplete, or false report, to file a verified report in a form specified by the Treasurer. The report must state whether the person is holding property reportable under this Chapter, describe property not previously reported or as to which the Treasurer has made inquiry, and specifically identify and state the value of property that may be in issue.

(b) The Treasurer, at reasonable times and upon reasonable notice, may examine the records of any person to determine whether the person has complied with this Chapter. The Treasurer may conduct the examination even if the person believes it is not in possession of any property that must be reported, paid, or delivered under this Chapter. The Treasurer may contract with any other person to conduct the examination on behalf of the Treasurer.

(c) The Treasurer at reasonable times may examine the records of an agent, including a dividend disbursing agent or transfer agent, of a business association that is the holder of property presumed abandoned if the Treasurer has given the notice required by subsection (b) of this section to both the association and the agent at least 90 days before the examination.

(d) Documents and working papers obtained or compiled by the Treasurer, or the Treasurer's agents, employees, or designated representatives, in the course of conducting an examination are confidential, but the documents and papers may be:

(1) Used by the Treasurer in the course of an action to collect unclaimed property or otherwise enforce this Chapter;

(2) Used in joint examinations conducted with or pursuant to an agreement with another state, the federal government, or any other governmental subdivision, agency, or instrumentality;

(3) Produced pursuant to subpoena or court order; or

(4) Disclosed to the abandoned property office of another state for that state's use in circumstances equivalent to those described in this subsection, if the other state is bound to keep the documents and papers confidential.

(e) If an examination results in the disclosure of property reportable under this Chapter, the Treasurer may assess, against a holder who made a fraudulent report, the cost of the examination at the rate of two hundred dollars ($200.00) a day for each examiner, or a greater amount that is reasonable and was incurred, but the assessment may not exceed the value of the property found to be reportable. The cost of an examination made pursuant to subsection (c) of this section may be assessed only against the business association.

(f) If a holder does not maintain the records required by G.S. 116B-73 and the records of the holder available for the periods subject to this Chapter are insufficient to permit the preparation of a report, the Treasurer may require the holder to report and pay to the Treasurer the amount the Treasurer reasonably estimates, on the basis of any available records of the holder or by any other reasonable method of estimation, should have been, but was not reported. (1979, 2nd Sess., c. 1311, s. 1; 1981, c. 671, s. 18; 1999-460, s. 6.)


§ 116B-73. Retention of records.

(a) Except as otherwise provided in subsection (b) of this section, a holder required to file a report under G.S. 116B-60 shall maintain the records containing the information required to be included in the report for five years after the holder files the report, unless a shorter period is provided by rule of the Treasurer.

(b) A business association that sells, issues, or provides to others for sale or issue in this State, traveler's checks, money orders, or similar instruments other than third-party bank checks, on which the business association is directly liable, shall maintain a record of the instruments while they remain outstanding, indicating the state and date of issue, for three years after the holder files the report. (1999-460, s. 6; 2012-187, s. 9.)

§ 116B-74. Discretionary precompliance review.

A holder may request the Treasurer to conduct a precompliance review of the holder's compliance program to educate the holder's employees on the unclaimed property laws and filing procedures and to recommend ways to facilitate the holder's compliance with the law. Subject to the availability of staff, the Treasurer may conduct a precompliance review upon request. The Treasurer may charge the holder a precompliance review fee of up to five hundred dollars ($500.00) per day for conducting this review. (1999-460, s. 6.)

§ 116B-75. Enforcement.

(a)     The Treasurer may maintain an action in this or another state to enforce this Chapter.

(b)     The Treasurer may order a person required to report, pay, or deliver property under this Chapter, or an officer or employee of the person, or a person having possession, custody, care, or control of records relevant to the matter under inquiry, or any other person having knowledge of the property or records, to appear before the Treasurer, at a time and place named in the order, and to produce the records and to give such testimony under oath or affirmation relevant to the inquiry. For purposes of this subsection, the Treasurer may administer oaths or affirmations. If a person refuses to obey an order of the Treasurer, the Treasurer may apply to the Superior Court of Wake County for an order requiring the person to obey the order of the Treasurer. Failure to comply with the court order is punishable for contempt. (1999-460, s. 6.)

§ 116B-76. Interstate agreements and cooperation; joint and reciprocal actions with other states.

(a)     The Treasurer may enter into an agreement with another state to exchange information relating to abandoned property or its possible existence.

The agreement may permit the other state, or another person acting on behalf of a state, to examine records as authorized in G.S. 116B-72. The Treasurer by rule may require the reporting of information needed to enable compliance with an agreement made under this section and prescribe the form.

(b) The Treasurer may join with another state to seek enforcement of this Chapter against any person who is or may be holding property reportable under this Chapter.

(c) At the request of another state, the Attorney General of this State may maintain an action on behalf of the other state to enforce, in this State, the unclaimed property laws of the other state against a holder of property subject to escheat or a claim of abandonment by the other state, if the other state has agreed to pay expenses incurred by the Attorney General in maintaining the action.

(d) The Treasurer may request that the attorney general of another state or another attorney commence an action in the other state on behalf of the Treasurer. With the approval of the Attorney General of this State, the Treasurer may retain any other attorney to commence an action in this State on behalf of the Treasurer. This State shall pay all expenses, including attorneys' fees, in maintaining an action under this subsection. With the Treasurer's approval, the expenses and attorneys' fees may be paid from money received under this Chapter. The Treasurer may agree to pay expenses and attorneys' fees based in whole or in part on a percentage of the value of any property recovered in the action. Any expenses or attorneys' fees paid under this subsection may not be deducted from the amount that is subject to the claim by the owner under this Chapter.

(e) The Treasurer is authorized to make such expenditures from the funds of the Escheat Fund as may be necessary to effectuate the provisions of this section. (1979, 2nd Sess., c. 1311, s. 1; 1999-460, s. 6.)

§ 116B-77. Interest and penalties; waiver.

(a) A holder who fails to report, pay, or deliver property within the time prescribed by this Chapter shall pay to the Treasurer interest at the rate established pursuant to this subsection on the property or value of the property from the date the property should have been reported, paid, or delivered. On or before June 1 and December 1 of each year, the Treasurer shall establish the interest rate to be in effect during the six-month period beginning on the next succeeding July 1 and January 1, respectively, after giving due consideration to current market conditions. If no new rate is established, the rate in effect during the preceding six-month period shall continue in effect. The rate established by the Treasurer may not be less than five percent (5%) per year and may not exceed sixteen percent (16%) per year.

(b) A holder who willfully fails to report, pay, or deliver property within the time prescribed by this Chapter, or willfully fails to perform other duties imposed by this Chapter, shall pay to the Treasurer, in addition to interest as provided in subsection (a) of this section, a civil penalty of one thousand dollars ($1,000) for each day the report, payment, or delivery is withheld, or the duty is not performed, up to a maximum of twenty-five thousand dollars ($25,000), plus twenty-five percent (25%) of the value of any property that should have been but was not reported.

(c) A holder who makes a fraudulent report shall pay to the Treasurer, in addition to interest as provided in subsection (a) of this section, a civil penalty of one thousand dollars ($1,000) for each day from the date a report under this Chapter was due, up to a maximum of twenty-five thousand dollars ($25,000), plus twenty-five percent (25%) of the value of any property that should have been but was not reported.

(d) The Treasurer for good cause may waive, in whole or in part, interest under subsection (a) of this section and penalties under subsection (b) of this section. (1979, 2nd Sess., c. 1311, s. 1; 1989, c. 114, s. 4; 1999-460, s. 6.)


§ 116B-78. Agreement to locate property.

(a) Repealed by Session Laws 2009-312, s. 2, effective October 1, 2009, and applicable to agreements entered into on or after that date.

(a1) Agreements Covered. - An agreement by an owner is covered by this section if its primary purpose is to locate, deliver, recover, or assist in the recovery of property that is distributable to the owner or presumed abandoned.

(a2) Void Agreements. - An agreement covered by this section is void and unenforceable if it was entered into during the period commencing on the date the property was distributable to the owner and extending to a time that is 24 months after the date the property is paid or delivered to the Treasurer. This subsection does not apply to an owner's agreement with an attorney to file a claim or special proceeding as to identified property or contest the Treasurer's denial of a claim or a clerk's denial of a petition.

(b) Criteria for Agreements. - An agreement covered by this section is enforceable only if it meets all of the following criteria:

(1) Is in writing and clearly sets forth the nature of the property and the services to be rendered.

(2) Is signed by the owner, with signature notarized.

(3) Describes the property, which includes the type of property, the property ID held by the State Treasurer, and the name of the holder.

(4) States that there may be other claims to the property that may reduce the share of the owner.

(5) States the value of the property, to the extent known, before and after the fee or other compensation has been deducted.

(6) States clearly the fees and costs for services. Total fees and costs shall be limited as follows:

a. For an agreement covered by this section other than one covered by G.S. 28A-22-11, total fees and costs shall not exceed one thousand dollars ($1,000) or twenty percent (20%) of the value of the property recovered, whichever is less.

b. For an agreement subject to G.S. 28A-22-11 by an heir, unknown or known but unlocated, the primary purpose of which is to locate or recover, or assist in the recovery, of a share in a decedent's estate, or surplus funds in a special proceeding, total fees and costs shall not exceed twenty percent (20%) of the value of the property recovered.

(7) Discloses that the property is being held by the North Carolina Department of State Treasurer's Unclaimed Property Program.

(c) Mineral Proceeds. - If an agreement covered by this section applies to mineral proceeds and the agreement contains a provision to pay compensation that includes a portion of the underlying minerals or any mineral proceeds not then presumed abandoned, the provision is void and unenforceable.

(d) Means of Payment. - Any person who enters into an agreement covered by this section with an owner shall be allowed to receive cash property, but not tangible property or securities, on behalf of the owner but shall not be authorized to negotiate the check made payable to the owner. Tangible property shall be delivered to the owner by the Treasurer, and securities will be reregistered into the owner's name.

(e) Other Remedies. - This section does not preclude an owner from asserting that an agreement covered by this section is invalid on grounds other than as provided in subsection (b) of this section.

(f) Registration. - Any person who enters into an agreement covered by this section with an owner shall register each calendar year with the Treasurer. The information to be required under this subsection shall include the person's name, address, telephone number, state of incorporation or residence, as applicable, and the person's social security or federal identification number. A registration fee of one hundred dollars ($100.00) shall be paid to the Treasurer at the time of the filing of the registration information. Fees received under this subsection shall be credited to the General Fund.

(g) Unfair Trade Practice. - In addition to rendering an agreement void and unenforceable, a failure to comply with the provisions of this section constitutes an unfair or deceptive trade practice under G.S. 75-1.1. (1979, 2nd Sess., c. 1311, s. 1; 1989, c. 114, s. 6; 1999-460, s. 6; 2009-312, s. 2.)


§ 116B-79. Transitional provisions.

(a) An initial report filed under this Article for property that was not required to be reported before the effective date of this Article but which is subject to this Article must include all items of property that would have been presumed abandoned during the 10-year period next preceding the effective date of this Article as if this Article had been in effect during that period.

(b) This Article does not relieve a holder of a duty that arose before the effective date of this Article to report, pay, or deliver property. Except as otherwise provided in G.S 116B-71(b) and G.S. 116B-77(d), a holder who did not comply with the law in effect before the effective date of this Article is subject to the applicable provisions for enforcement and penalties which then existed, which are continued in effect for the purpose of this section. (1999-460, s. 6.)

§ 116B-80. Rules.

The Treasurer may adopt rules necessary to carry out this Chapter. (1979, 2nd Sess., c. 1311, s. 1; 1987, c. 827, s. 19; 1989, c. 114, s. 5; 1999-460, s. 6.)

Chapter 116C.

Continuum of Education Programs.

§ 116C-1. Education Cabinet created.

(a) The Education Cabinet is created. The Education Cabinet shall be located administratively within, and shall exercise its powers within existing resources of, the Office of the Governor. However, the Education Cabinet shall exercise its statutory powers independently of the Office of the Governor.

(b) The Education Cabinet shall consist of the Governor, who shall serve as chair, the President of The University of North Carolina, the State Superintendent of Public Instruction, the Chairman of the State Board of Education, the President of the North Carolina Community Colleges System, the Secretary of Health and Human Services, and the President of the North Carolina Independent Colleges and Universities. The Education Cabinet may invite other representatives of education to participate in its deliberations as adjunct members.

(c) The Education Cabinet shall be a nonvoting body that:

(1) Works to resolve issues between existing providers of education.

(2) Sets the agenda for the State Education Commission.

(3) Develops a strategic design for a continuum of education programs, in accordance with G.S. 116C-3.

(4) Studies other issues referred to it by the Governor or the General Assembly.

(d) The Office of the Governor, in coordination with the staffs of The University of North Carolina, the North Carolina Community College System, and the Department of Public Instruction, shall provide staff to the Education Cabinet. (1993, c. 393, s. 1; 1995, c. 324, s. 15.12(b); 2001-123, s. 1; 2005-276, s. 7.38(a).)

§ 116C-2. State Education Commission.

The State Education Commission shall consist of the Board of Governors of The University of North Carolina, the State Community College Board, and the State Board of Education. The Governor shall call the meetings of the State Education Commission.

The Commission shall be a forum for airing proposals and engaging in board-to-board dialogue about issues the Education Cabinet is addressing. The agenda for Commission meetings shall be set by the Education Cabinet. (1993, c. 393, s. 1.)

§ 116C-3. Strategic design for a continuum of education programs.

The Education Cabinet shall develop a strategic design for a continuum of education programs. A continuum of education programs is the complement of programs delivered by the State to learners at all levels.

The new design shall take into account issues raised by the Government Performance Audit Committee of the Legislative Research Commission.

The design process shall:

(1) Include vigorous examination of all programs as if they were being created for the first time.

(2) Compare the existing structures, funding levels, and responsibilities of each system to the new design.

(3) Focus on issues concerning coursework articulation and plan for how to improve coursework articulation among existing providers of education.

The Education Cabinet shall report to the Joint Legislative Education Oversight Committee on the strategic design it develops prior to January 1, 1995. (1993, c. 393, s. 1; 1993 (Reg. Sess., 1994), c. 677, s. 12.1.)


§ 116C-4. First in America Innovative Education Initiatives Act.

(a) The General Assembly strongly endorses the Governor's goal of making North Carolina's system of education first in America by 2010. With that as the goal, the Education Cabinet shall set as a priority cooperative efforts between secondary schools and institutions of higher education so as to reduce the high school dropout rate, increase high school and college graduation rates, decrease the need for remediation in institutions of higher education, and raise certificate, associate, and bachelor degree completion rates. The Cabinet shall identify and support efforts that achieve the following purposes:

(1) Support cooperative innovative high school programs developed under Part 9 of Article 16 of Chapter 115C of the General Statutes.

(2) Improve high school completion rates and reduce high school dropout rates.

(3) Close the achievement gap.

(4) Create redesigned middle schools or high schools.

(5) Provide flexible, customized programs of learning for high school students who would benefit from accelerated, higher level coursework or early graduation.

(6) Establish high quality alternative learning programs.

(7) Establish a virtual high school.

(8) Implement other innovative education initiatives designed to advance the State's system of education.

(b) The Education Cabinet shall identify federal, State, and local funds that may be used to support these initiatives. In addition, the Cabinet is strongly encouraged to pursue private funds that could be used to support these initiatives.

(c) The Cabinet shall report by January 15, 2004, and annually thereafter, to the Joint Legislative Education Oversight Committee on its activities under this section. The annual reports may include recommendations for statutory changes needed to support cooperative innovative initiatives, including programs approved under Part 9 of Article 16 of Chapter 115C of the General Statutes. (2003-277, s. 1.)

§ 116C-5. STEM education priorities.

(a) The Education Cabinet shall set as a priority an increase in the number of students earning postsecondary credentials in the fields of science, technology, engineering, and mathematics to reduce the gap between needed credentialed workers and available jobs in those fields by 2015.

(b) The Education Cabinet shall encourage cooperative efforts between secondary schools and institutions of higher education to prepare students for postsecondary study in science, technology, engineering, and mathematics, and shall identify and support efforts at institutions of higher education to increase the number of students seeking and successfully completing postsecondary certificates or degrees in those fields. The Education Cabinet shall monitor progress of those efforts.

(c) The Education Cabinet shall determine measurements for assessing the number of available jobs in the fields of science, technology, engineering, and mathematics in the State, and the number of students earning postsecondary credentials in the fields of science, technology, engineering, and mathematics at all institutions of higher education in the State, including community colleges and both public and private colleges and universities.

(d) The Education Cabinet shall identify federal, State, and local funds that may be used to support this priority. In addition, the Education Cabinet is strongly encouraged to pursue private funds that could be used to support this priority.

(e) The Education Cabinet shall report by November 1, 2011, and annually thereafter, on its activities under this section to the Joint Legislative Education Oversight Committee. (2010-41, s. 1.)

Chapter 116D.

Higher Education Bonds.

Article 1.

General Provisions.

§ 116D-1. Definitions.

The following definitions apply in this Chapter:

(1) Board of Governors. - The Board of Governors of the University.

(2) Capital facility. - Any one or more of the following for the University or for a community college:

a. One or more buildings, utilities, structures, or other facilities or property developments, including streets and landscaping, and the acquisition of equipment and furnishings in connection therewith.

b. Additions, extensions, enlargements, renovations, and improvements to existing buildings, utilities, structures, or other facilities or property developments, including streets and landscaping.

c. Land or an interest in land.

d. Other infrastructure.

The term includes, without limitation, classroom buildings, laboratory buildings, research facilities, libraries, physical education facilities, continuing education centers, student cafeterias, and activity facilities, including sports facilities, student and faculty housing facilities, and administrative office facilities.

(3) Cost. - Any of the following in financing the cost of capital facilities and special obligation bond projects, as authorized by this Chapter:

a. The cost of constructing, reconstructing, renovating, repairing, enlarging, acquiring, and improving capital facilities and special obligation bond projects, including the acquisition of land, rights-of-way, easements, franchises, equipment, furnishings, and other interests in real or personal property acquired or used in connection with a capital facility or special obligation bond project.

b. The cost of engineering, architectural, and other consulting services as may be required.

c. The cost of providing personnel to ensure effective project management.

d. Finance charges, reserves for debt service, and interest prior to and during construction.

e. Administrative expenses and charges incurred by the State in connection with the administration of a bond program created under this Chapter.

f. The cost of bond insurance, investment contracts, credit enhancement, and liquidity facilities, interest-rate swap agreements or other derivative products, financial and legal consultants, and related costs of bond and note issuance.

g. The cost of reimbursing the State for any payments made for any cost described in this subdivision.

h. Any other costs and expenses necessary or incidental to the purposes of this Chapter.

(4) Credit facility. - An agreement entered into by the State Treasurer on behalf of the State with a bank, savings and loan association or other banking institution, an insurance company, reinsurance company, surety company or other insurance institution, a corporation, investment banking firm or other investment institution, or any financial institution or other similar provider of a credit facility, which provider may be located within or without the United States,

and providing for prompt payment of all or any part of the principal or purchase price (whether at maturity, presentment or tender for purchase, redemption or acceleration), redemption premium, if any, and interest on any bonds or notes payable on demand or tender by the owner, in consideration of the State's agreeing to repay the provider of the credit facility in accordance with the terms and provisions of the agreement.

(5)    Fiscal period. - A fiscal biennium or a fiscal year of the fiscal biennium.

(6)    Fiscal year. - The fiscal year of the State beginning on July 1 of one calendar year and ending on June 30 of the next calendar year.

(7)    Par formula. - A provision or formula adopted by the State to provide for the adjustment, from time to time, of the interest rate or rates borne or provided for by any bonds or notes, including:

a.    A provision providing for an adjustment so that the purchase price of bonds or notes in the open market would be as close to par as possible.

b.    A provision providing for an adjustment based upon a percentage or percentages of a prime rate or base rate, which percentages may vary or be applied for different periods of time.

c.    A provision that the State Treasurer determines is consistent with this Chapter and will not materially and adversely affect the financial position of the State and the marketing of bonds or notes at a reasonable interest cost to the State.

(8)    Securities issued under this Chapter. - Any of the following:

a.    University improvement general obligation bonds, refunding bonds, notes, and refunding notes issued under Article 2 of this Chapter.

b.    Special obligation bonds, bond anticipation notes, and refunding bonds issued under Article 3 of this Chapter.

c.    Community college general obligation bonds, refunding bonds, notes, and refunding notes issued under Article 4 of this Chapter.

(9)    State. - The State of North Carolina.

(10) State Treasurer. - The incumbent Treasurer, from time to time, of the State.

(11) University. - The University of North Carolina and its constituent and affiliated institutions, including, without limitation, the University of North Carolina Center for Public Television, the University of North Carolina Health Care System, the North Carolina School of Science and Mathematics, and the North Carolina Arboretum. (2000-3, s. 1.2.)

§ 116D-2. General provisions.

(a) Signatures. - Should any officer whose signature or facsimile signature appears on securities issued under this Chapter cease to be that officer before the delivery of the securities, the signature or facsimile signature shall nevertheless have the same validity for all purposes as if the officer had remained in office until delivery of the securities. Securities issued under this Chapter may bear the facsimile signatures of persons, who at the actual time of the execution of the securities were the proper officers to sign any security although at the date of the security those persons may not have been officers.

(b) Tax Exemption. - Securities issued under this Chapter shall at all times be free from taxation by the State or any political subdivision or any of their agencies, excepting estate, inheritance, or gift taxes, income taxes on the gain from the transfer of the securities, and franchise taxes. The interest on the securities is not subject to taxation as income.

(c) Investment Eligibility. - Securities issued under this Chapter are securities in which all of the following may invest, including capital in their control or belonging to them: public officers, agencies, and public bodies of the State and its political subdivisions, insurance companies, trust companies, investment companies, banks, savings banks, savings and loan associations, credit unions, pension or retirement funds, other financial institutions engaged in business in the State, executors, administrators, trustees, and other fiduciaries. Securities issued under this Chapter are securities which may properly and legally be deposited with and received by any officer or agency of the State or a political subdivision of the State for any purpose for which the deposit of bonds or notes of the State or any political subdivision is now or may later be authorized by law.

(d) Inconsistent Laws. - All general, special, or local laws that are inconsistent with this Chapter do not apply to this Chapter. (2000-3, s. 1.2.)

§ 116D-3. Reports.

(a) Board of Governors. - The Board of Governors shall report to the Joint Legislative Commission on Governmental Operations by September 15 of each year, and more frequently as the Commission requests, on the following:

(1) Repealed by Session Laws 2012-142, s. 9.4(c), effective July 1, 2012.

(2) Special Obligation Bonds. - The Board of Governors shall report on special obligation bonds issued under Article 3 of this Chapter, including the amount of debt, itemized for each institution of the University, by bond issue, and by project. The report shall include schedules of debt service requirements and actual payments, as well as evidence of compliance with additional financial covenants required by bond documents. The report shall identify the trends and current revenue streams of the sources of obligated resources pledged for each bond issue.

(b) Treasurer. - Upon issuance of university improvement general obligation bonds under Article 2 of this Chapter or community college general obligation bonds under Article 4 of this Chapter, the Treasurer shall forward a schedule of required payments of principal and interest over the life of the bonds to the Director of the Budget, with copies to the Joint Legislative Commission on Governmental Operations and the Fiscal Research Division. The Treasurer shall report to the Joint Legislative Commission on Governmental Operations by September 15 of each year, and more frequently as the Commission requests, on the university improvement general obligation bonds issued under Article 2 of this Chapter and community college general obligation bonds issued under Article 4 of this Chapter, including the annual debt service requirements over the remainder of the life of the bonds.

(c) Repealed by Session Laws 2012-142, s. 8.3(b), effective July 1, 2012. (2000-3, s. 1.2; 2012-142, ss. 8.3(b), 9.4(c).)

§ 116D -4. Minority and historically underutilized business participation.

(a) Minority Business Participation. - The goals set by G.S. 143-128 for participation in projects by minority businesses apply to projects funded by the proceeds of bonds or notes issued under this section. The following State agencies shall monitor compliance with this requirement and shall report to the General Assembly by January 1 of each year on the participation by minority businesses in these projects. The State Construction Office, Department of Administration, shall monitor compliance with regard to projects funded by the proceeds of university improvement general obligation bonds and notes and special obligation bonds and notes; the Board of Governors of The University of North Carolina shall provide the State Construction Office any information required by the State Construction Office to monitor compliance. The Community Colleges System Office shall monitor compliance with regard to projects funded by the proceeds of community college general obligation bonds and notes.

(b) Participation in Providing Professional Services. - The Department of State Treasurer shall provide contracting opportunities for historically underutilized businesses in providing professional services in connection with the issuance of bonds and notes authorized by this section. As used in this subsection, the term "historically underutilized business" means a business described in G.S. 143-48. The Department of State Treasurer shall strive to increase the amount of legal, financial, and other professional services acquired by it from historically underutilized businesses. With the assistance of the Office for Historically Underutilized Businesses in the Department of Administration, the Department of State Treasurer shall set objectives for contracting with these businesses, identify and eliminate barriers or constraints that may restrict these businesses from contracting with the Department, and develop a plan for meeting its objectives. The Department of State Treasurer shall report quarterly to the Office for Historically Underutilized Businesses on its progress in carrying out the requirements of this subsection.(2000-3, s. 7(a), (b); 2001-487, s. 26.)


§ 116D-5: Repealed by Session Laws 2011-43, s. 1, effective April 19, 2011.


Article 2.

General Obligation Bonds for Financing Capital Facilities for The University of North Carolina.

§ 116D-6. Short title.

This Article may be cited as the University Improvement General Obligation Bonds Finance Act. (2000-3, s. 1.2.)


§ 116D-7. Definitions.

The following definitions apply in this Article:

(1) Bonds. - Bonds authorized to be issued under this Article, including refunding bonds.

(2) Notes. - Notes issued under this Article.

(3) University improvement general obligation bonds. - Bonds authorized to be issued under this Article, including refunding bonds. (2000-3, s. 1.2.)


§ 116D-8. Authorization of bonds and notes.

Subject to a favorable vote of a majority of the qualified voters of the State who vote on the question of issuing university improvement general obligation bonds in the election held as provided by law, the State Treasurer may, by and with the consent of the Council of State, issue and sell, at one time or from time to time, university improvement general obligation bonds of the State to be designated "State of North Carolina University Improvement General Obligation Bonds", with any additional designations as may be determined to indicate the issuance of bonds from time to time, or notes of the State. Except as otherwise provided by this Article, the aggregate amount of bonds and notes issued pursuant to this Article shall not exceed two billion five hundred million dollars ($2,500,000,000). The bonds and notes shall be issued in the following years up to the following amounts:

| Fiscal Year | Aggregate Amount |
|---|---|
| 2000-2001 | $ 201,600,000 |

| | |
|---|---|
| 2001-2002 | 241,900,000 |
| 2002-2003 | 483,900,000 |
| 2003-2004 | 483,900,000 |
| 2004-2005 | 564,500,000 |
| 2005-2006 | 524,200,000 |

If less than the aggregate amount of bonds or notes authorized to be issued in a fiscal year is issued in that fiscal year, the balance for that fiscal year may be issued in any subsequent fiscal year. Refunding bonds and notes issued pursuant to G.S. 116D-11(f) shall not be included in the limitation on the aggregate amount of bonds and notes that may be issued pursuant to this Article.

The proceeds of bonds or notes issued under this Article shall be applied to finance the cost of improvement, construction, and acquisition of capital facilities for the University or to refund any outstanding bonds or notes issued under this Article. The capital facilities to be improved, constructed, or acquired with the proceeds of bonds or notes shall be determined as provided in G.S. 116D-9. (2000-3, s. 1.2.)

§ 116D-9. Designation of capital facilities and preconditions to bond issuance.

The capital facilities to be financed in whole or in part with the proceeds of university improvement general obligation bonds shall be set forth in legislation enacted from time to time by the General Assembly. This legislation shall also provide for voter approval of the bonds to finance the capital facilities and shall become effective only upon approval by the voters. The proceeds of university improvement general obligation bonds shall not be expended to pay the costs of any capital facilities other than those set forth in that legislation. (2000-3, s. 1.2.)

§ 116D-10. Faith and credit.

The faith and credit and taxing power of the State are hereby pledged for the payment of the principal of and the interest on bonds and notes. The State retains the right to amend any provision of this Article to the extent it does not impair any contractual right of a bond owner. (2000-3, s. 1.2.)

§ 116D-11. Issuance of bonds and notes.

(a) Terms and Conditions. - Bonds or notes may bear any dates, may be serial or term bonds or notes, or any combination of these, may mature in any amounts and at any times, not exceeding 25 years from their dates, may be payable at any places, either within or without the United States, in any coin or currency of the United States that at the time of payment is legal tender for payment of public and private debts, may bear interest at any rates, which may vary from time to time, and may be made redeemable before maturity, at the option of the State or otherwise as may be provided by the State, at any prices, including a price greater than the face amount of the bonds or notes, and under any terms and conditions, all as may be determined by the State Treasurer, by and with the consent of the Council of State.

(b) Signatures; Form and Denomination; Registration. - Bonds or notes may be issued in certificated or uncertificated form. If issued in certificated form, bonds or notes shall be signed on behalf of the State by the Governor or shall bear the Governor's facsimile signature, shall be signed by the State Treasurer or shall bear the State Treasurer's facsimile signature, and shall bear the Great Seal of the State or a facsimile of the Seal impressed or imprinted on them. If bonds or notes bear the facsimile signatures of the Governor and the State Treasurer, the bonds or notes shall also bear a manual signature which may be that of a bond registrar, trustee, paying agent, or designated assistant of the State Treasurer. The form and denomination of bonds or notes, including the provisions with respect to registration of the bonds or notes and any system for their registration, shall be as the State Treasurer may determine in conformity with this Article.

(c) Manner of Sale; Expenses. - Subject to the approval by the Council of State as to the manner in which bonds or notes shall be offered for sale, whether at public or private sale, whether within or without the United States, and whether by publishing notices in certain newspapers and financial journals, mailing notices, inviting bids by correspondence, negotiating contracts of purchase or otherwise, the State Treasurer is authorized to sell bonds or notes at one time or from time to time at any rates of interest, which may vary from time to time, and at any prices, including a price less than the face amount of the bonds or notes, as the State Treasurer may determine. All expenses incurred in the preparation, sale, and issuance of bonds or notes shall be paid by the State Treasurer from the proceeds of bonds or notes or other available moneys.

(d)     Application of Proceeds. - The proceeds of any bonds or notes shall be used solely for the purposes for which the bonds or notes were issued and shall be disbursed in the manner and under the restrictions, if any, that the Council of State may provide in the resolution authorizing the issuance of, or in any trust agreement securing, the bonds or notes.

Any additional moneys which may be received by means of a grant or grants from the United States or any agency or department thereof or from any other source to aid in financing the cost of a capital facility may be disbursed, to the extent permitted by the terms of the grant or grants, without regard to any limitations imposed by this Article.

(e)     Notes; Repayment. - By and with the consent of the Council of State, the State Treasurer is authorized to borrow money and to execute and issue notes of the State for the same, but only in the following circumstances and under the following conditions:

(1)     For anticipating the sale of bonds, the issuance of which the Council of State has approved, if the State Treasurer considers it advisable to postpone the issuance of the bonds.

(2)     For the payment of interest on or any installment of principal of any bonds then outstanding, if there are not sufficient funds in the State treasury with which to pay the interest or installment or principal as they respectively become due.

(3)     For the renewal of any loan evidenced by notes authorized in this Article.

(4)     For the purposes authorized in this Article.

(5)     For refunding bonds or notes as authorized in this Article.

Funds derived from the sale of bonds or notes may be used in the payment of any bond anticipation notes issued under this Article. Funds provided by the General Assembly for the payment of interest on or principal of bonds shall be used in paying the interest on or principal of any notes and any renewals thereof, the proceeds of which have been used in paying interest on or principal of the bonds.

(f) Refunding Bonds and Notes. - By and with the consent of the Council of State, the State Treasurer is authorized to issue and sell refunding bonds and notes for the purpose of refunding bonds or notes issued pursuant to this Article and to pay the cost of issuance of the refunding bonds or notes. The refunding bonds and notes may be combined with any other issues of State bonds and notes similarly secured. Refunding bonds or notes may be issued at any time prior to the final maturity of the debt or obligation to be refunded. The proceeds from the sale of any refunding bonds or notes shall be applied to the immediate payment and retirement of the bonds or notes being refunded or, if not required for the immediate payment of the bonds or notes being refunded, the proceeds shall be deposited in trust to provide for the payment and retirement of the bonds or notes being refunded and to pay any expenses incurred in connection with the refunding. Money in a trust fund may be invested in (i) direct obligations of the United States government, (ii) obligations the principal of and interest on which are guaranteed by the United States government, (iii) obligations of any agency or instrumentality of the United States government if the timely payment of principal and interest on the obligations is unconditionally guaranteed by the United States government, or (iv) certificates of deposit issued by a bank or trust company located in the State if the certificates are secured by a pledge of any of the obligations described in (i), (ii), or (iii) above having an aggregate market value, exclusive of accrued interest, equal at least to the principal amount of the certificates so secured. This section does not limit the duration of any deposit in trust for the retirement of bonds or notes being refunded but that have not matured and are not presently redeemable, or if presently redeemable, have not been called for redemption.

(g) University Improvement Bonds Fund. - The proceeds of university improvement general obligation bonds and notes, including premium thereon, if any, except the proceeds of bonds the issuance of which has been anticipated by bond anticipation notes or the proceeds of refunding bonds or notes, shall be placed by the State Treasurer in a special fund to be designated "University Improvement Bonds Fund". Moneys in the University Improvement Bonds Fund shall be used for the purposes set forth in this Article.
Any additional moneys that may be received by means of a grant or grants from the United States of America or any agency or department thereof or from any other source to aid in financing the cost of any university improvements authorized by this Article may be placed by the State Treasurer in the University

Improvement Bonds Fund or in a separate account or fund and shall be disbursed, to the extent permitted by the terms of the grant or grants, without regard to any limitations imposed by this Article.

The proceeds of university improvement general obligation bonds and notes may be used with any other moneys made available by the General Assembly for the making of university improvements, including the proceeds of any other State bond issues, whether previously made available or which may be made available after the effective date of this Article. The proceeds of university improvement bonds and notes shall be expended and disbursed under the direction and supervision of the Director of the Budget. The funds provided by this Article for university improvements shall be disbursed for the purposes provided in this Article upon warrants drawn on the State Treasurer by the State Controller, which warrants shall not be drawn until requisition has been approved by the Director of the Budget and which requisition shall be approved only after full compliance with the State Budget Act, Chapter 143C of the General Statutes. (2000-3, s. 1.2; 2001-414, s. 45; 2006-203, s. 56.)

§ 116D-12. Variable rate demand bonds and notes.

(a)     In fixing the details of bonds and notes, the State Treasurer may provide that the bonds and notes may:

(1)     Be made payable from time to time on demand or tender for purchase by the owner, if a credit facility supports the bonds or notes, unless the State Treasurer specifically determines that a credit facility is not required upon a finding and determination by the State Treasurer that the absence of a credit facility will not materially and adversely affect the financial position of the State and the marketing of the bonds or notes at a reasonable interest cost to the State.

(2)     Be additionally supported by a credit facility.

(3)     Be made subject to redemption or a mandatory tender for purchase prior to maturity.

(4)     Bear interest at rates that may vary from any periods of time, as may be provided in the proceedings providing for the issuance of the bonds or notes, including, without limitation, any variations as may be permitted pursuant to a par formula.

(5) Be made the subject of a remarketing agreement whereby an attempt is made to remarket bonds or notes to new purchasers prior to their presentment for payment to the provider of the credit facility or to the State.

(b) If the aggregate principal amount payable by the State under a credit facility is in excess of the aggregate principal amount of bonds or notes secured by the credit facility, whether as a result of the inclusion in the credit facility of a provision for the payment of interest for a limited period of time or the payment of a redemption premium, or for any other reason, then the amount of authorized but unissued bonds or notes during the term of the credit facility shall not be less than the amount of the excess, unless the payment of the excess is otherwise provided for by agreement of the State executed by the State Treasurer. (2000-3, s. 1.2.)

§ 116D-13. Other agreements.

The State Treasurer may authorize, execute, obtain, or otherwise provide for bond insurance, investment contracts, credit and liquidity facilities, interest rate swap agreements and other derivative products, and any other related instruments and matters the State Treasurer determines are desirable in connection with the issuance of bonds or notes. The State Treasurer is authorized to employ and designate any financial consultants, underwriters, and bond attorneys to be associated with any bond issue under this Article as the State Treasurer considers necessary. (2000-3, s. 1.2.)

§§ 116D-14 through 116D-20. Reserved for future codification purposes.

Article 3.

Special Obligation Bonds for Improvements to the Facilities of The University of North Carolina.

§ 116D-21. Purpose.

The purpose of this Article is to authorize the Board of Governors of The University of North Carolina to issue special obligation bonds, payable from obligated resources, but with no pledge of taxes or the faith and credit of the State or any agency or political subdivision of the State, to pay the cost, in whole or in part, of improvements to the facilities of the University. (2000-3, s. 1.2.)

§ 116D-22. Definitions.

The following definitions apply in this Article:

(1) Existing facilities. - Buildings and facilities then existing that generate income or receipts to the Board of Governors that are pledged, under the provisions of a resolution authorizing the issuance of the special obligation bonds under this Article, to the payment of the bonds.

(2) Institution. - Each of the institutions enumerated in G.S. 116-2, and any affiliated institutions of the University, including, without limitation, the University of North Carolina Center for Public Television, the University of North Carolina Health Care System, the North Carolina School of Science and Mathematics, and the North Carolina Arboretum.

(3) Obligated resources. - Any sources of income or receipts of the Board of Governors or the institution at which a special obligation bond project is or will be located that are designated by the Board as the security and source of payment for bonds issued under this Article to finance a special obligation bond project, including, without limitation, any of the following:

a. Rents, charges, or fees to be derived by the Board of Governors or the institution from any activities conducted at the institution.

b. Earnings on the investment of the endowment fund of the institution at which a special obligation project will be located, to the extent that the use of the earnings will not violate any lawful condition placed by the donor upon the part of the endowment fund that generates the investment earnings.

c. Funds to be received under a contract or a grant agreement, including "overhead costs reimbursement" under a grant agreement, entered into by the Board of Governors or the institution to the extent the use of the funds is not restricted by the terms of the contract or grant agreement or the use of the funds as provided in this Article does not violate the restriction.

d. Funds appropriated from the General Fund to the Board of Governors on behalf of a constituent institution for utilities of the institution that constitute energy savings as that term is defined in G.S. 143-64.17.

Except as provided in sub-subdivision d. of this subdivision, obligated resources do not include funds appropriated to the Board of Governors or the institution from the General Fund by the General Assembly from funds derived from general tax and other revenues of the State, and obligated resources do not include tuition payment by students.

(4) Special obligation bonds. - Bonds issued under this Article to finance the cost of a special obligation project, which bonds are secured by and payable from obligated resources designated by the Board of Governors at the time the issuance of the bonds is authorized in accordance with this Article.

(5) Special obligation bond project. - Any capital facilities located or to be located at an institution for the purpose of carrying out the mission of that institution and designated specifically by the Board of Governors as a "special obligation bond project" for purposes of this Article. A special obligation bond project need not necessarily consist of buildings or facilities that are expected to generate "self-liquidating revenues" to the Board of Governors or the institution from direct rentals, charges, or fees from the services provided by the building or facility, and may include facilities such as classroom buildings, administration buildings, research facilities, libraries, and equipment that do not produce direct, or indirect, income to the Board of Governors or the institution. (2000-3, s. 1.2; 2011-145, s. 9.6D(h).)


§ 116D-23. Credit and taxing power of State not pledged; statement on face of bonds.

Special obligation bonds issued under this Article shall not constitute a debt or liability of the State or any political subdivision of the State or a pledge of the faith and credit of the State or of any political subdivision of the State. Special obligation bonds shall be secured solely by the obligated resources pledged to their payment. All of the special obligation bonds shall contain on their face a statement to the effect that neither the State nor the Board of Governors is obligated to pay the bonds or the interest on the bonds except from the obligated resources pledged for payment and that neither the faith and credit nor the taxing power of the State or of any political subdivision or instrumentality of the State is pledged to the payment of the principal of or the interest on the bonds. The issuance of special obligation bonds under this Article does not directly or indirectly or contingently obligate the State or any political subdivision of the State to levy or to pledge any taxes for the bonds. (2000-3, s. 1.2.)

§ 116D-24.  General powers of Board of Governors.

The Board of Governors is authorized, subject to the requirements of this Article, to do all of the following:

(1)     Determine the location and character of any special obligation bond project, to acquire, construct, and provide the project, and to maintain, repair, and operate and enter into contracts for the management, lease, use, or operation of all or any portion of any special obligation bond project and any existing facilities.

(2)     Issue special obligation bonds to pay all or any part of the cost of a special obligation bond project, and to fund or refund any bonds previously issued by the Board of Governors to finance facilities designated as a special obligation bond project.

(3)     Fix and revise from time to time and charge and collect fees, rates, rents, charges, and other income for the use of and for the services furnished by the institution that are designated as obligated resources in connection with a special obligation bond issue.

(4)     Establish and enforce, and to agree through any resolution or trust agreement authorizing or securing bonds under this Article to make and enforce, rules for the use of and services rendered by the institution of the income or receipts to be obtained from the use or services designated as obligated resources in connection with a special obligation bond issue.

(5)     Acquire, hold, lease, and dispose of real and personal property in the exercise of its powers and the performance of its duties and to lease all or any part of a special obligation bond project and any existing facilities for any

periods of years, not exceeding 40 years, upon any terms and conditions as the Board of Governors determines, subject to the provisions of G.S. 143-341.

(6) Employ consulting engineers, attorneys, accountants, construction and financial experts, superintendents, managers, and any other employees and agents as may be necessary in its judgment in connection with a special obligation bond project and existing facilities, and to fix their compensation.

(7) Enter into all contracts and agreements necessary or incidental to the performance of its duties and the execution of its powers under this Article.

(8) Receive and accept from any federal, State, or other public agency and any private agency, person, or other entity donations, loans, grants, aid, or contributions of any money, property, labor, or other things of value for a special obligation bond project or any other services provided by the institution that is designated as the obligated resource in connection with a special obligation bond issue, and to agree to apply and use them in accordance with the terms and conditions under which they are provided.

(9) Do all acts and things necessary or convenient to carry out the powers granted by this Article. (2000-3, s. 1.2.)


§ 116D-25. Consultation with the Joint Legislative Commission on Governmental Operations.

Whenever this Article requires the approval of the Director of the Budget of an action, the Director of the Budget may consult with the Joint Legislative Commission on Governmental Operations before giving approval. (2000-3, s. 1.2.)


§ 116D-26. Issuance of special obligation bonds and bond anticipation notes.
(a) Authority. - The Board of Governors may issue, subject to the approval of the Director of the Budget, at one time or from time to time, special obligation bonds of the Board of Governors for the purpose of paying all or any part of the cost of acquiring, constructing, or providing a special obligation project. Before issuing special obligation bonds, the Board of Governors shall first adopt a resolution (i) setting forth the designation by the Board of Governors that the

buildings or facilities to be financed by the bond issue are the special obligation bond project being financed and (ii) designating the obligated resources that will secure and be the source of payment of the special obligation bonds to be issued. The Board of Governors shall not issue any special obligation bonds unless the Board of Governors finds that sufficient obligated resources are reasonably expected to be available (i) to pay the principal and interest on the special obligation bonds proposed to be issued, (ii) to create and maintain any reserves for the payment of the special obligation bonds, to the extent the Board of Governors is required to maintain reserves for this purpose by the terms of the trust agreement or resolution authorizing the issuance of the special obligation bonds, and (iii) to provide for the maintenance and operation of the facilities that are to generate the obligated resources to the extent the Board of Governors is required to maintain those facilities by the terms of the trust agreement or resolution authorizing the issuance of the special obligation bonds. Notwithstanding any other provision of this Article, the proceeds of special obligation bonds to be secured by obligated resources derived from the operation of or activities at one institution may not be applied to finance a special obligation project to be located at another institution.

(b) Approval Required. - The Board of Governors shall not issue any special obligation bonds for a project at an institution unless the board of trustees of that institution has approved the issuance of bonds for that project. The Board of Governors shall not issue special obligation bonds under this Article until the effective date of legislation enacted by the General Assembly authorizing the undertaking of the special obligation bond project to be financed and fixing the maximum aggregate principal amount of special obligation bonds that shall be issued for that purpose. In submitting proposed special obligation bond projects to the General Assembly for approval, the Board of Governors shall submit information on the need for each project, project costs, estimates of increased operating costs upon completion, estimated debt service requirements, and the sources and amounts of obligated resources to be pledged for the repayment of the bonds. If the obligated resources to repay the bonds or to operate the proposed project potentially involve increased costs to students or to the General Fund, these costs shall be identified in the Board of Governors' submission.

Except as provided in this Article, special obligation bond projects may be undertaken, special obligation bonds may be issued, and other powers vested in the Board of Governors under this Article may be exercised by the Board without obtaining the consent of any department, division, commission, board, bureau, or agency of the State and without any other proceedings or the happening of any other conditions or things other than those proceedings, conditions, or things which are specifically required by this Article.

(c)     Term; Form. - The special obligation bonds of each issue shall be dated, shall mature at any times not exceeding 30 years from their dates, shall bear interest at any rates as may be determined by the Board of Governors, and may be redeemable before maturity at the option of the Board, at any prices and under any terms and conditions as may be fixed by the Board prior to the issuance of the special obligation bonds. The Board of Governors shall determine the form and manner of execution of the special obligation bonds and shall fix the denominations of the special obligation bonds and the places of payment of principal and interest, which may be at any bank or trust company within or without the State. Notwithstanding any of the other provisions of this Article or any recitals in any special obligation bonds issued under the provisions of this Article, all special obligation bonds shall be negotiable instruments under the laws of this State, subject only to the provisions for registration in a resolution authorizing the issuance of the special obligation bonds or a trust agreement securing the bonds. The Board of Governors may sell the special obligation bonds in any manner, at public or private sale, and for any price, as it may determine to be for its best interests.

(d)     Proceeds; Additional Bonds. - The proceeds of the special obligation bonds of each issue shall be used solely for the purpose for which the bonds have been authorized and shall be disbursed in the manner and under such restrictions, if any, as the Board of Governors may provide in the resolution authorizing the issuance of the bonds or in the trust agreement securing them. Unless otherwise provided in the authorizing resolution or in the trust agreement securing the special obligation bonds, if the proceeds of the special obligation bonds, by error of estimates or otherwise, are less than the cost of the special obligation bond project, additional bonds may in like manner be issued to provide the amount of the deficit and shall be deemed to be of the same issue and shall be entitled to payment from the same fund without preference or priority of the bonds first issued for the same purpose.

The resolution providing for the issuance of special obligation bonds, and any trust agreement securing them, may also contain limitations upon the issuance of additional special obligation bonds as the Board of Governors considers proper, and the additional special obligation bonds must be issued under the restrictions and limitations prescribed by the resolution or trust agreement.

(e) Temporary Bonds; Notes. - Before preparing definitive bonds, the Board of Governors may, under like restrictions, issue interim receipts or temporary bonds exchangeable for definitive bonds when the bonds have been executed and are available for delivery. The Board may also provide for the replacement of any bonds which become mutilated, destroyed, or lost.

The Board of Governors may enter into or negotiate a note with an acceptable bank or trust company in lieu of issuing special obligation bonds for the financing of special obligation bond projects covered under this Article. The terms and conditions of any note of this nature shall be in accordance with the terms and conditions surrounding issuance of the special obligation bonds.

(f) Bond Anticipation Notes. - The Board of Governors may issue, subject to the approval of the Director of the Budget, at one time or from time to time, bond anticipation notes of the Board of Governors in anticipation of the issuance of special obligation bonds authorized by this Article. The principal of and the interest on these notes shall be payable solely from the proceeds of special obligation bonds or renewal notes or, in the event bond or renewal note proceeds are not available, from the obligated resources designated for their payment. The notes of each issue shall be dated, shall mature at any times not exceeding 30 years from their dates, shall bear interest at any rates as may be determined by the Board of Governors, and may be redeemable before maturity, at the option of the Board of Governors, at any prices and under any terms and conditions as may be fixed by the Board of Governors prior to the issuance of the notes. If the Board of Governors issues a bond anticipation note for a term in excess of three years, no individual project may be funded from the proceeds of the note for longer than three years. The Board shall determine the form and the manner of execution of the notes and shall fix the denominations of the notes and the places of payment of principal and interest, which may be at any bank or trust company within or without the State. Notwithstanding any of the other provisions of this Article or any recitals in any notes issued under the provisions of this Article, all notes shall be negotiable instruments under the laws of this State, subject only to the provisions for registration in a resolution authorizing the issuance of the notes or any trust agreement securing the bonds in anticipation of which the notes are being issued. The Board of Governors may sell the notes in any manner, at public or private sale, and for any price, as it may determine to be for its best interests.
The proceeds of the notes shall be used solely for the purpose for which the special obligation bonds have been authorized, and the note proceeds shall be disbursed in any manner and under any restrictions as the Board of Governors

may provide in the resolution authorizing the issuance of the notes or bonds or in the trust agreement securing the special obligation bonds.

The resolution providing for the issuance of notes, and any trust agreement securing the special obligation bonds in anticipation of which the notes are being authorized, may also contain limitations upon the issuance of additional notes as the Board of Governors considers proper, and such additional notes shall be issued under the restrictions and limitations prescribed by the resolution or trust agreement. The Board may also provide for the replacement of any notes which shall become mutilated, destroyed, or lost.

Except as provided in this Article, notes may be issued under this Article and other powers vested in the Board of Governors under this Article may be exercised by the Board without obtaining the consent of any department, division, commission, board, bureau, or agency of the State and without any other proceedings or the happening of any other conditions or things than those proceedings, conditions, or things which are specifically required by this Article.

Unless the context indicates otherwise, the word "bonds", wherever used in this Article, include the words "bond anticipation notes." (2000-3, s. 1.2; 2003-357, s. 1.)


§ 116D-27. Trust agreement; money received deemed trust funds; insurance; remedies.

(a) Trust Agreement Securing Bonds. - In the discretion of the Board of Governors and subject to the approval of the Director of the Budget, any special obligation bonds issued under this Article may be secured by a trust agreement by and between the Board of Governors and a corporate trustee, which may be any trust company or bank having the powers of a trust company within or without the State. The trust agreement or the resolution providing for the issuance of special obligation bonds may pledge or assign the obligated resources designated as security for the special obligation bonds, but shall not convey or mortgage any property of the institution. The trust agreement or resolution providing for the issuance of special obligation bonds may contain provisions for protecting and enforcing the rights and remedies of the holders of the special obligation bonds that are reasonable and proper and not in violation of law, including covenants setting forth the duties of the Board of Governors in relation to the acquisition, construction, or provision of any of the charging and collecting of any rates, fees, or charges that have been designated as obligated resources, the maintenance, repair, operation, and insurance of any property of the institution, and the custody, safeguarding, and application of all moneys. It shall be lawful for any bank or trust company incorporated under the laws of the State which may act as depositary of the proceeds of special obligation bonds or funds securing special obligation bonds to furnish any indemnifying bonds or to pledge any securities as may be required by the Board of Governors. A trust agreement or resolution may set forth the rights and remedies of the holders of the special obligation bonds and the rights, remedies, and immunities of the trustee or trustees, if any, and may restrict the individual right of action by the holders. In addition to the foregoing, a trust agreement or resolution may contain other provisions the Board of Governors considers reasonable and proper for the security of the holders. All expenses incurred in carrying out the provisions of the trust agreement or resolution may be treated as a part of the cost of the special obligation bond projects for which the special obligation bonds are issued or as an expense of operation of the special obligation bond project.

(b)     Trust Funds. - All moneys received pursuant to the authority of this Article, whether as proceeds from the sale of bonds, or as obligated resources, are trust funds to be held and applied solely as provided in this Article. The Board of Governors may provide for the payment of all or part of the proceeds of the sale of the special obligation bonds and the obligated resources to any officer, board, or depositary that it may designate for their custody, and may provide for their method of disbursement, with any safeguards and restrictions it may determine. Any officer with whom, or any bank or trust company with which, moneys are deposited shall act as trustee of the moneys and shall hold and apply them for the purposes of this Article, subject to any requirements provided in this Article and in the resolution or trust agreement, authorizing or securing the special obligation bonds.

(c)     Insurance. - Notwithstanding the provisions of any other law, the Board of Governors may carry insurance on any special obligation bond projects and any existing facilities in any amounts and covering any risks it considers advisable.

(d)     Remedies. - Any holder of special obligation bonds issued under this Article and the trustees under a trust agreement, except to the extent the rights given in this section may be restricted by the trust agreement or the resolution authorizing the issuance of the special obligation bonds, may, either at law or in equity, by suit, action, mandamus, or other proceedings, protect and enforce any and all rights under the laws of the State or granted under this Article or under the trust agreement or resolution, and may enforce and compel the performance of all duties required by this Article or by the trust agreement or resolution to be performed by the Board of Governors or by any of its officers, including the fixing, charging, and collecting of obligated resources. (2000-3, s. 1.2.)

§ 116D-28. Fixing and collecting obligated resources.

(a) Board to Provide Sufficient Resources. - For the purpose of aiding in the financing of a special obligation bond project and to provide security to the owners of the special obligation bonds issued to finance the special obligation bond project, the Board of Governors is authorized, to the extent the generation of the obligated resources is in the control of the Board, to fix, revise from time to time, charge, and collect the rents, charges, fees, or other revenues constituting the obligated resources. Fees and other revenue sources constituting obligated resources may be imposed or increased only with the approval of the Board of Governors. As long as any special obligation bonds issued under this Article and payable from those obligated resources are outstanding, the obligated resources, to the extent within the control of the Board of Governors, shall be so fixed and adjusted, with relation to other funds available, as to provide funds pursuant to the requirements of the resolution or trust agreement authorizing or securing the special obligation bonds and at least sufficient to pay the principal of and the interest on the special obligation bonds as they become due and payable, to assure the continued collection of the obligated resources, and to create and maintain reserves for these purposes. A sufficient amount of the obligated resources, except any part that may be necessary to pay the cost of maintenance, repair, and operation, and to provide reserves for these purposes and for renewals, replacements, extensions, enlargements, and improvements as may be provided for in the resolution authorizing the issuance of the special obligation bonds or in the trust agreement securing the same, shall be set aside at regular intervals as may be provided in the resolution or trust agreement authorizing the issuance of the special obligation bonds in a sinking fund which is hereby pledged to, and charged with, the payment of the principal of and the interest on the special obligation bonds as they become due and the redemption price or the purchase price of special obligation bonds retired by call or purchase as provided in the resolution or trust agreement. This pledge shall be valid and binding from the time it is made, the obligated resources so pledged and thereafter received by the Board of Governors shall immediately be subject to the lien of the pledge without any physical delivery of the pledge or further act, and the lien of the pledge shall be valid and binding as against all parties having claims of any kind in tort, contract, or otherwise against the Board of Governors, irrespective of whether the parties have notice of the pledge. Neither the resolution nor any trust agreement by which a pledge is created need be filed or recorded except in the records of the Board of Governors. The use and disposition of moneys to the credit of the sinking fund shall be subject to the provisions of the resolution authorizing the issuance of the special obligation bonds or of the trust agreement securing the bonds.

(b)     State Pledge. - The State pledges to, and agrees with, the holders of any special obligation bonds or notes issued by the Board of Governors pursuant to this Article that as long as any of the special obligation bonds or notes are outstanding and unpaid, the State will not limit or alter the rights vested in the Board of Governors at the time of issuance of the special obligation bonds or notes to set the terms and conditions of the special obligation bonds or notes and to fulfill the terms of any agreements made with the bondholders or noteholders. The State shall in no way impair the rights and remedies of the bondholders or noteholders until the special obligation bonds or notes and all costs and expenses in connection with any action or proceedings by or on behalf of the bondholders or noteholders are fully paid, met, and discharged. (2000-3, s. 1.2.)

§ 116D-29.  Vesting powers in committee.

The Board of Governors may authorize its budget and finance committee to sell any special obligation bonds which the Board has, with the approval of the Director of the Budget, authorized to be issued under this Article in any manner and under any limitations or conditions as the Board prescribes and to perform other functions under this Article the Board determines. (2000-3, s. 1.2.)

§ 116D-30.  Refunding bonds.

The Board of Governors may, subject to the approval of the Director of the Budget, issue from time to time refunding bonds for the purpose of refunding any bonds by the Board under this Article or under any Article of Chapter 116 of the General Statutes, including the payment of any redemption premium on them and any interest accrued or to accrue to the date of redemption of the bonds refunded. The Board of Governors is further authorized, subject to the approval of the Director of the Budget, to issue from time to time refunding bonds for the combined purpose of (i) refunding any bonds issued by the Board under this Article or under any Article of Chapter 116 of the General Statutes, including the payment of any redemption premium on them and any interest accrued or to accrue to the date of redemption of the bonds, and (ii) paying all or any part of the cost of acquiring or constructing any additional special obligation bond projects.

This Article, as applicable, governs the issuance of refunding bonds, their maturities and other details, the rights and remedies of their holders, and the rights, powers, privileges, duties, and obligations of the Board of Governors with respect to them. (2000-3, s. 1.2.)

§ 116D-31. Additional and alternative method.

This Article provides an additional and alternative method for the doing of the things authorized and is supplemental and additional to powers conferred by other laws, including G.S. 116-175 to G.S. 116-185, inclusive and G.S. 116-197 and G.S. 116-198, and is not in derogation of or repealing any powers now existing under any other law, whether general, special, or local. The issuance of special obligation bonds or refunding bonds under this Article, however, need not comply with the requirements of any other law applicable to the issuance of bonds. (2000-3, s. 1.2.)

§§ 116D-32 through 116D-40. Reserved for future codification purposes.

Article 4.

Community Colleges Facilities General Obligation Finance Act.

§ 116D-41. Short title.
This Article may be cited as the Community College Facilities General Obligation Finance Act. (2000-3, s. 1.2.)

§ 116D-42. Definitions.

The following definitions apply in this Article:

(1)     Bonds. - Bonds authorized to be issued under this Article, including refunding bonds.

(2)     Community college. - Defined in G.S. 115D-2.

(3)     Community college general obligation bonds. - Bonds authorized to be issued under this Article, including refunding bonds.

(4)     Community Colleges System Office. - The North Carolina Community Colleges System Office, created by Article 1 of Chapter 115D of the General Statutes, or if the Community Colleges System Office is abolished or otherwise divested of its functions under this Article, the public body succeeding it in its principal functions, or upon which are conferred by law the rights, powers, and duties given by this Article to the Community Colleges System Office.

(5)     Notes. - Notes issued under this Article. (2000-3, s. 1.2.)


§ 116D-43. Authorization of bonds and notes.

Subject to a favorable vote of a majority of the qualified voters of the State who vote on the question of issuing community college general obligation bonds in the election held as provided by law, and upon the application of the Community Colleges System Office, the State Treasurer may, by and with the consent of the Council of State, issue and sell, at one time or from time to time, community college general obligation bonds of the State to be designated "State of North Carolina Community College General Obligation Bonds", with any additional designations as may be determined to indicate the issuance of bonds from time to time, or notes of the State. Except as otherwise provided by this Article, the aggregate amount of bonds and notes issued pursuant to this Article shall not exceed six hundred million dollars ($600,000,000). The bonds and notes shall be issued in the following years up to the following amounts:

| Fiscal Year | Aggregate Amount |
| --- | --- |
| 2000-2001 | $48,400,000 |
| 2001-2002 | 58,100,000 |
| 2002-2003 | 116,100,000 |
| 2003-2004 | 116,100,000 |
| 2004-2005 | 135,500,000 |
| 2005-2006 | 125,800,000 |

If less than the aggregate amount of bonds or notes authorized to be issued in a fiscal year is issued in that fiscal year, the balance for that fiscal year may be issued in any subsequent fiscal year. Refunding bonds and notes issued pursuant to G.S. 116D-46(f) shall not be included in the limitation on the aggregate amount of bonds and notes that may be issued pursuant to this Article.

The proceeds of bonds or notes issued under this Article shall be applied to finance the cost of grants to be made by the State to community colleges to finance the cost of capital facilities for the community college or to refund any outstanding bonds or notes issued under this Article. The capital facilities to be improved, constructed, or acquired with the proceeds of bonds or notes shall be determined as provided in G.S. 116D-44. (2000-3, s. 1.2.)

§ 116D-44. Designation of capital facilities and preconditions to bond issuance.

The capital facilities to be financed in whole or in part with the proceeds of community college general obligation bonds shall be described in legislation enacted from time to time by the General Assembly. This legislation shall also provide for voter approval of the bonds to finance the capital facilities and shall become effective only upon approval by the voters. The proceeds of community college general obligation bonds shall not be expended to pay the costs of any capital facilities other than those described in that legislation. (2000-3, s. 1.2.)

§ 116D-45. Faith and credit.

The faith and credit and taxing power of the State are hereby pledged for the payment of the principal of and the interest on bonds and notes. The State retains the right to amend any provision of this Article to the extent it does not impair any contractual right of a bond owner. (2000-3, s. 1.2.)

§ 116D-46. Issuance of bonds and notes.

(a) Terms and Conditions. - Bonds or notes may bear any dates, may be serial or term bonds or notes, or any combination of these, may mature in any amounts and at any times, not exceeding 25 years from their dates, may be payable at any places, either within or without the United States, in any coin or currency of the United States that at the time of payment is legal tender for payment of public and private debts, may bear interest at any rates, which may vary from time to time, and may be made redeemable before maturity, at the option of the State or otherwise as may be provided by the State, at any prices, including a price greater than the face amount of the bonds or notes, and under any terms and conditions, all as may be determined by the State Treasurer, by and with the consent of the Council of State.

(b) Signatures; Form and Denomination; Registration. - Bonds or notes may be issued in certificated or uncertificated form. If issued in certificated form, bonds or notes shall be signed on behalf of the State by the Governor or shall bear the Governor's facsimile signature, shall be signed by the State Treasurer or shall bear the State Treasurer's facsimile signature, and shall bear the Great Seal of the State or a facsimile of the Seal impressed or imprinted on them. If bonds or notes bear the facsimile signatures of the Governor and the State Treasurer, the bonds or notes shall also bear a manual signature which may be that of a bond registrar, trustee, paying agent, or designated assistant of the State Treasurer. The form and denomination of bonds or notes, including the provisions with respect to registration of the bonds or notes and any system for their registration, shall be as the State Treasurer may determine in conformity with this Article.

(c) Manner of Sale; Expenses. - Subject to the approval by the Council of State as to the manner in which bonds or notes shall be offered for sale, whether at public or private sale, whether within or without the United States, and whether by publishing notices in certain newspapers and financial journals, mailing notices, inviting bids by correspondence, negotiating contracts of purchase or otherwise, the State Treasurer is authorized to sell bonds or notes at one time or from time to time at any rates of interest, which may vary from time to time, and at any prices, including a price less than the face amount of the bonds or notes, as the State Treasurer may determine. All expenses incurred in the preparation, sale, and issuance of bonds or notes shall be paid by the State Treasurer from the proceeds of bonds or notes or other available moneys.

(d) Application of Proceeds. - The proceeds of any bonds or notes shall be used solely for the purposes for which the bonds or notes were issued and shall be disbursed in the manner and under the restrictions, if any, that the Council of State may provide in the resolution authorizing the issuance of, or in any trust agreement securing, the bonds or notes.

Any additional moneys which may be received by means of a grant or grants from the United States or any agency or department thereof or from any other source to aid in financing the cost of a capital facility may be disbursed, to the extent permitted by the terms of the grant or grants, without regard to any limitations imposed by this Article.

(e) Notes; Repayment. - By and with the consent of the Council of State, the State Treasurer is authorized to borrow money and to execute and issue notes of the State for the same, but only in the following circumstances and under the following conditions:

(1) For anticipating the sale of bonds the issuance of which the Council of State has approved, if the State Treasurer considers it advisable to postpone the issuance of the bonds.

(2) For the payment of interest on or any installment of principal of any bonds then outstanding, if there are not sufficient funds in the State treasury with which to pay the interest or installment or principal as they respectively become due.

(3) For the renewal of any loan evidenced by notes authorized in this Article.
(4) For the purposes authorized in this Article.

(5) For refunding bonds or notes as authorized in this Article.

Funds derived from the sale of bonds or notes may be used in the payment of any bond anticipation notes issued under this Article. Funds provided by the General Assembly for the payment of interest on or principal of bonds shall be used in paying the interest on or principal of any notes and any renewals thereof, the proceeds of which have been used in paying interest on or principal of the bonds.

(f) Refunding Bonds and Notes. - By and with the consent of the Council of State, the State Treasurer is authorized to issue and sell refunding bonds and notes for the purpose of refunding bonds or notes issued pursuant to this Article and to pay the cost of issuance of the refunding bonds or notes. The refunding bonds and notes may be combined with any other issues of State bonds and notes similarly secured. Refunding bonds or notes may be issued at any time prior to the final maturity of the debt or obligation to be refunded. The proceeds from the sale of any refunding bonds or notes shall be applied to the immediate payment and retirement of the bonds or notes being refunded or, if not required for the immediate payment of the bonds or notes being refunded, the proceeds shall be deposited in trust to provide for the payment and retirement of the bonds or notes being refunded and to pay any expenses incurred in connection with the refunding. Money in a trust fund may be invested in (i) direct obligations of the United States government, (ii) obligations the principal of and interest on which are guaranteed by the United States government, (iii) obligations of any agency or instrumentality of the United States government if the timely payment of principal and interest on the obligations is unconditionally guaranteed by the United States government, or (iv) certificates of deposit issued by a bank or trust company located in the State if the certificates are secured by a pledge of any of the obligations described in (i), (ii), or (iii) above having an aggregate market value, exclusive of accrued interest, equal at least to the principal amount of the certificates so secured. This section does not limit the duration of any deposit in trust for the retirement of bonds or notes being refunded but that have not matured and are not presently redeemable, or if presently redeemable, have not been called for redemption.

(g) Community College Bonds Fund. - The proceeds of community college general obligation bonds and notes, including premium thereon, if any, except the proceeds of bonds the issuance of which has been anticipated by bond anticipation notes or the proceeds of refunding bonds or notes, shall be placed by the State Treasurer in a special fund to be designated "Community College Bonds Fund". Moneys in the Community College Bonds Fund shall be used for the purposes set forth in this Article.

Any additional moneys that may be received by means of a grant or grants from the United States of America or any agency or department thereof or from any other source to aid in financing the cost of any community college capital facilities authorized by this Article may be placed by the State Treasurer in the Community College Bonds Fund or in a separate account or fund and shall be disbursed, to the extent permitted by the terms of the grant or grants, without regard to any limitations imposed by this Article.

The proceeds of community college general obligation bonds and notes may be used with any other moneys made available by the General Assembly for the making of grants to community colleges for capital facilities, including the proceeds of any other State bond issues, whether previously made available or which may be made available after the effective date of this Article. The proceeds of community college bonds and notes shall be expended and disbursed under the direction and supervision of the Director of the Budget. The funds provided by this Article for grants to community colleges shall be disbursed for the purposes provided in this Article upon warrants drawn on the State Treasurer by the State Controller, which warrants shall not be drawn until requisition has been approved by the Director of the Budget and which requisition shall be approved only after full compliance with the State Budget Act, Chapter 143C of the General Statutes. (2000-3, s. 1.2; 2001-414, s. 46; 2006-203, s. 57.)

§ 116D-47. Variable rate demand bonds and notes.

(a) In fixing the details of bonds and notes, the State Treasurer may provide that the bonds and notes may:

(1) Be made payable from time to time on demand or tender for purchase by the owner, if a credit facility supports the bonds or notes, unless the State Treasurer specifically determines that a credit facility is not required upon a finding and determination by the State Treasurer that the absence of a credit facility will not materially and adversely affect the financial position of the State and the marketing of the bonds or notes at a reasonable interest cost to the State.
(2) Be additionally supported by a credit facility.

(3) Be made subject to redemption or a mandatory tender for purchase prior to maturity.

(4) Bear interest at rates that may vary from any periods of time, as may be provided in the proceedings providing for the issuance of the bonds or notes, including, without limitation, any variations as may be permitted pursuant to a par formula.

(5) Be made the subject of a remarketing agreement whereby an attempt is made to remarket bonds or notes to new purchasers prior to their presentment for payment to the provider of the credit facility or to the State.

(b) If the aggregate principal amount payable by the State under a credit facility is in excess of the aggregate principal amount of bonds or notes secured by the credit facility, whether as a result of the inclusion in the credit facility of a provision for the payment of interest for a limited period of time or the payment of a redemption premium, or for any other reason, then the amount of authorized but unissued bonds or notes during the term of the credit facility shall not be less than the amount of the excess, unless the payment of the excess is otherwise provided for by agreement of the State executed by the State Treasurer. (2000-3, s. 1.2.)

§ 116D-48. Other agreements.

The State Treasurer may authorize, execute, obtain, or otherwise provide for bond insurance, investment contracts, credit and liquidity facilities, interest rate swap agreements and other derivative products, and any other related instruments and matters the State Treasurer determines are desirable in connection with the issuance of bonds or notes. The State Treasurer is authorized to employ and designate any financial consultants, underwriters, and bond attorneys to be associated with any bond issue under this Article as the State Treasurer considers necessary. (2000-3, s. 1.2.)

§ 116D-49. Procurement of capital facilities.

Any laws, rules, or regulations of the State that relate to the acquisition and construction of capital facilities shall apply to the capital facilities financed pursuant to this Article. (2000-3, s. 1.2.)

Chapter 116E.

Education Longitudinal Data System.

§ 116E-1. Definitions.

(1) "Board" means the governing board of the North Carolina Longitudinal Data System.

(2) "De-identified data" means a data set in which parent and student identity information, including the unique student identifier and student social security number, has been removed.

(3) "FERPA" means the federal Family Educational Rights and Privacy Act, 20 U.S.C. § 1232g.

(4) "Student data" means data relating to student performance. Student data includes State and national assessments, course enrollment and completion, grade point average, remediation, retention, degree, diploma or credential attainment, enrollment, discipline records, and demographic data. Student data does not include juvenile delinquency records, criminal records, and medical and health records.

(5) "System" means the North Carolina Longitudinal Data System.

(6) "Unique Student Identifier" or "UID" means the identifier assigned to each student by one of the following:

a. A local school administrative unit based on the identifier system developed by the Department of Public Instruction.

b. An institution of higher education, nonpublic school, or other State agency operating or overseeing an educational program, if the student has not been assigned an identifier by a local school administrative unit.

(7) "Workforce data" means data relating to employment status, wage information, geographic location of employment, and employer information. (2012-133, s. 1(a).)

§ 116E-2. Purpose of the North Carolina Longitudinal Data System.

(a) The North Carolina Longitudinal Data System is a statewide data system that contains individual-level student data and workforce data from all levels of education and the State's workforce. The purpose of the System is to do the following:

(1) Facilitate and enable the exchange of student data among agencies and institutions within the State.

(2) Generate timely and accurate information about student performance that can be used to improve the State's education system and guide decision makers at all levels.

(3) Facilitate and enable the linkage of student data and workforce data.

(b) The linkage of student data and workforce data for the purposes of the System shall be limited to no longer than five years from the later of the date of the student's completion of secondary education or the date of the student's latest attendance at an institution of higher education in the State. (2012-133, s. 1(a).)


§ 116E-3. North Carolina Longitudinal Data System Board.

(a) There is established the North Carolina Longitudinal Data System Board which shall consist of the following 18 members:

(1) The Superintendent of Public Instruction, or the Superintendent's designee.

(2) The President of The University of North Carolina, or the President's designee.

(3) The President of the North Carolina Community College System, or the President's designee.

(4) The Secretary of the Department of Health and Human Services, or the Secretary's designee.

(5) The Assistant Secretary of the Department of Commerce, Division of Employment Security, or the Assistant Secretary's designee.

(6) The Secretary of the Department of Revenue, or the Secretary's designee.

(7) The Commissioner of Labor, or the Commissioner's designee.

(8) The President of the North Carolina Independent Colleges and Universities, Inc., or the President's designee.

(9) The Commissioner of Motor Vehicles, Department of Transportation, or the Commissioner's designee.

(10) The State Chief Information Officer.

(11) The State Controller, or the Controller's designee.

(12) Three members appointed by the General Assembly upon the recommendation of the President Pro Tempore of the Senate.

(13) Three members appointed by the General Assembly upon the recommendation of the Speaker of the House of Representatives.

(14) One member appointed by the Governor, to serve at the Governor's pleasure.

(b) Appointed members of the Board shall serve terms of four years. Terms of appointed members shall begin May 1, 2013, and every four years thereafter. Appointed members may be reappointed but shall not serve more than two consecutive terms. Vacancies among appointed members shall be filled by the appointing entity and shall be for the remainder of the vacant term.

(c) The chair of the Board shall be the State Chief Information Officer. The Board shall elect from the appointed members a vice-chair for a term of two years.

(d) Members of the Board shall receive such per diem compensation and necessary travel and subsistence expenses while engaged in the official discharge of the official duties as is provided by law for members of State boards and commissions.

(e) The Board shall hold an initial meeting upon appointment of a majority of the appointed members. The Board shall meet at least quarterly, but may meet more frequently upon the call of the chair. (2012-133, s. 1(a); 2013-80, ss. 1-4.)

§ 116E-4. Powers and duties of the Board.

(a) The Board shall have the following powers and duties:

(1) Develop an implementation plan to phase in the establishment and operation of the System.

(2) Provide general oversight and direction to the System.

(3) Approve the annual budget for the System.

(4) Before the use of any individual data in the System, the Board shall do the following:

a. Create an inventory of the individual student data proposed to be accessible in the System and required to be reported by State and federal education mandates.

b. Develop and implement policies to comply with FERPA and any other privacy measures, as required by law or the Board.

c. Develop a detailed data security and safeguarding plan that includes the following:

1. Authorized access and authentication for authorized access.

2. Privacy compliance standards.

3. Privacy and security audits.

4. Breach notification and procedures.

5. Data retention and disposition policies.

(5) Oversee routine and ongoing compliance with FERPA and other relevant privacy laws and policies.

(6) Ensure that any contracts that govern databases that are outsourced to private vendors include express provisions that safeguard privacy and security and include penalties for noncompliance.

(7) Designate a standard and compliance time line for electronic transcripts that includes the use of UID to ensure the uniform and efficient transfer of student data between local school administrative units and institutions of higher education.

(8) Review research requirements and set policies for the approval of data requests from State and local agencies, the General Assembly, and the public.

(9) Establish an advisory committee on data quality to advise the Board on issues related to data auditing and tracking to ensure data validity.

(b) The Board shall adopt rules according to Chapter 150B of the General Statutes as provided in G.S. 116E-6 to implement the provisions of this Article.

(c) The Board shall report quarterly to the Joint Legislative Education Oversight Committee, the Joint Legislative Commission on Governmental Operations, and the Joint Legislative Oversight Committee on Information Technology beginning September 30, 2013. The report shall include the following:

(1) An update on the implementation of the System's activities.

(2) Any proposed or planned expansion of System data.

(3) Any other recommendations made by the Board, including the most effective and efficient configuration for the System. (2012-133, s. 1(a); 2013-80, s. 5; 2013-410, s. 22.)


§ 116E-5. North Carolina Longitudinal Data System.

(a) There is created the North Carolina Longitudinal Data System. The System shall be located administratively within the Department of Public

Instruction but shall exercise its powers and duties independently of the Department of Public Instruction and the State Board of Education.

(b) The System shall allow users to do the following:

(1) Effectively organize, manage, disaggregate, and analyze individual student and workforce data.

(2) Examine student progress and outcomes over time, including preparation for postsecondary education and the workforce.

(c) The System shall be considered an authorized representative of the Department of Public Instruction, The University of North Carolina, and the North Carolina System of Community Colleges under applicable federal and State statutes for purposes of accessing and compiling student record data for research purposes.

(d) The System shall perform the following functions and duties:

(1) Serve as a data broker for the System, including data maintained by the following:

a. The Department of Public Instruction.

b. Local boards of education, local school administrative units, and charter schools.

c. The University of North Carolina and its constituent institutions.

d. The Community Colleges System Office and local community colleges.

e. The North Carolina Independent College and Universities, Inc., and private colleges or universities.

f. Nonpublic schools serving elementary and secondary students.

g. The Department of Commerce, Division of Employment Security.

h. The Department of Revenue.

i. The Department of Health and Human Services.

j. The Department of Labor.

(2) Ensure routine and ongoing compliance with FERPA, the Internal Revenue Code, and other relevant privacy laws and policies, including the following:

a. The required use of de-identified data in data research and reporting.

b. The required disposition of information that is no longer needed.

c. Providing data security, including the capacity for audit trails.

d. Providing for performance of regular audits for compliance with data privacy and security standards.

e. Implementing guidelines and policies that prevent the reporting of other potentially identifying data.

(3) Facilitate information and data requests for State and federal education reporting with existing State agencies as appropriate.

(4) Facilitate approved public information requests.

(5) Develop a process for obtaining information and data requested by the General Assembly and Governor of current de-identified data and research.

(e) Use of data accessible through the System shall be regulated in the following ways:

(1) Direct access to data shall be restricted to authorized staff of the System.

(2) Only de-identified data shall be used in the analysis, research, and reporting conducted by the System.

(3) The System shall only use aggregate data in the release of data in reports and in response to data requests.

(4) Data that may be identifiable based on the size or uniqueness of the population under consideration shall not be reported in any form by the System.

(5) The System shall not release information that may not be disclosed under FERPA, the Internal Revenue Code, and other relevant privacy laws and policies.

(6) Individual or personally identifiable data accessed through the System shall not be a public record under G.S. 132-1.

(f) The System may receive funding from the following sources:

(1) State appropriations.

(2) Grants or other assistance from local school administrative units, community colleges, constituent institutions of The University of North Carolina, or private colleges and universities.

(3) Federal grants.

(4) Any other grants or contributions from public or private entities received by the System. (2012-133, s. 1(a).)


§ 116E-6. Data sharing.

(a) Local school administrative units, charter schools, community colleges, constituent institutions of The University of North Carolina, and State agencies shall do all of the following:

(1) Comply with the data requirements and implementation schedule for the System as set forth by the Board.

(2) Transfer student data and workforce data to the System in accordance with the data security and safeguarding plan developed by the Board under G.S. 116E-5.

(b) Private colleges and universities, the North Carolina Independent Colleges and Universities, Inc., and nonpublic schools may transfer student data and workforce data to the System in accordance with the data security and safeguarding plan developed by the Board under G.S. 116E-5. (2012-133, s. 1(a).)

Chapter 117.

Electrification.

Article 1.

Rural Electrification Authority.

§ 117-1. Rural Electrification Authority created; appointments; terms of members.

An agency to be known as the North Carolina Rural Electrification Authority is hereby created as an agency of the State of North Carolina, such agency to consist of five members to be appointed by the Governor of North Carolina. Current members of the North Carolina Rural Electrification Authority shall complete their respective terms of office. On or after June 5, 1975, the Governor shall appoint two members to replace those members whose terms expire on said date. All appointments made by the Governor shall be made for terms of four years. (1935, c. 288, s. 1; 1975, c. 709, s. 7.)


§ 117-2. Powers.

The purpose of said North Carolina Rural Electrification Authority is to secure electrical service for the rural districts of the State where service is not now being rendered, and it is hereby empowered to do the following in order to accomplish that purpose:

(1)     To investigate all applications from communities unserved, or inadequately served, with electrical energy in North Carolina, and to determine the feasibility of obtaining such service therefor.

(2)     To employ such personnel as shall be necessary to conduct surveys, assist the several communities to organize and finance extensions of rural distribution lines; to negotiate with power companies and other agencies for the supply of electric energy for and on behalf of the rural communities that desire service.

(3)     To contact the power companies and other agencies contiguous to the area and areas desiring service, for the purpose of arranging for the extension

by said companies, or other agencies, of service in that community for such extension as may be feasible for the power company, or other agency, contiguous to the area to finance itself.

(4) To make estimates of costs of extension which the power company would not be willing to finance and report such findings to the citizens of the community desiring service or to the corporations organized under this Chapter, to be known as "electric membership corporations."

(5) To estimate the service charges which said community would have to set up in addition to the rates for energy as may be found necessary in order to make extension self-liquidating.

(6) To have authority to call upon the Utilities Commission of the State to fix such rates and service charges as will be necessary to accomplish the purpose, and the right to petition the Utilities Commission to require extension of lines by the power companies when, in its opinion, it is proper and feasible.

(7) To have the power of eminent domain for the purpose of condemning rights-of-way for the erection of transmission and distribution lines, either in its own name, or in its own name on behalf of the electric membership corporations to be formed as provided by law. For the purposes of exercising the powers of eminent domain the North Carolina Rural Electrification Authority shall be deemed a private condemnor and shall follow the procedures of Chapter 40A for a private condemnor.

(8) To have such right and authority to secure for said local communities or electric membership corporations as may be set up assistance from any agency of the United States government, either by gift or loan, as may be possible to aid said local community in securing electric energy for said community.

(9) To investigate all applications from communities for the formation of electric membership corporations and determine and pass upon the question of granting the authority to form such corporations; to provide forms for making such applications; and to do all things necessary to a proper determination of the question of establishment of the local electric membership corporations.

(10) To act as agent for any electric membership corporations formed under direction or permission of the North Carolina Rural Electrification Authority in securing loans or grants from any agency of the United States government.

(11) To prescribe rules and regulations and the necessary blanks for the electric membership corporations in making applications for grant or loan from any agency of the United States government.

(11a) To receive and investigate complaints from members of electric membership corporations.

(12) To do all other acts and things which may be necessary to aid the rural communities in North Carolina to secure electric energy. (1935, c. 288, s. 2; 1981, c. 919, s. 12; 2013-187, s. 3.)


§ 117-2.1. Additional powers.

In addition to the powers provided in G.S. 117-2, the Authority is empowered, authorized and directed to make, promulgate and implement plans and programs whereby the electric membership corporations organized or domesticated under this Chapter shall promote and foster methods of conserving electric energy in accordance with provisions of the National Energy Act as delegated to the states. (1979, c. 285, s. 1.)


§ 117-3. Authority not granted power to fix rates or order line extensions; right of suggestion and petition.
The Authority itself shall not be a rate-making body, and shall have no power to fix the rates or service charges, or to order the extension of lines by the power companies. The function of making rates and service charges and orders for the extension of lines shall remain in the Utilities Commission of North Carolina, and the Authority shall only have the right of suggestion and petition to the Utilities Commission of its opinion as to the proper rates and service charges and line extensions, and no rate recommended or suggested by the Authority shall be effective until approved by the Utilities Commission: Provided, that if the Utilities Commission of North Carolina does not have the right under the existing law to fix service charges in addition to the rates prescribed for electrical energy, and the power to order line extensions, such power and authority is hereby granted the Utilities Commission of North Carolina to fix and promulgate service charges in addition to rates in any community which avails itself of this Article, and form a corporation authorized hereunder to be known as electric membership

corporation, and to order line extensions when it shall determine that the same is proper and feasible. (1935, c. 288, s. 3.)

§ 117-3.1. Regulatory fee.

(a) Fee imposed. - It is the policy of the State of North Carolina to provide fair regulation of electric and telephone membership corporations in the interest of the public. The cost of regulating electric and telephone membership corporations is a burden incident to the privilege of operating as an electric or telephone membership corporation. Therefore, for the purpose of defraying the cost of regulating electric and telephone membership corporations, every electric and telephone membership corporation subject to the jurisdiction of the Authority shall pay a quarterly regulatory fee, in addition to all other fees and taxes, as provided in this section. The fees collected shall be used only to pay the expenses of the Authority in regulating electric and telephone membership corporations in the interest of the public.

(b) Rate. - For each fiscal year, the regulatory fee shall be the greater of the following:

(1) The rate established by the General Assembly for that year for each electric membership corporation's North Carolina meter connected for service and each telephone membership corporation's North Carolina access line connected for service for each quarter of the year.

(2) Four cents (4¢) for each electric membership corporation's North Carolina meter connected for service and for each telephone membership corporation's North Carolina access line connected for service for each quarter of the year.

When the Authority prepares its budget request for the upcoming fiscal year, the Authority shall propose a rate for the regulatory fee. For fiscal years beginning in an odd-numbered year, that proposed rate shall be included in the budget message the Governor submits to the General Assembly pursuant to G.S. 143C-3-5. For fiscal years beginning in an even-numbered year, that proposed rate shall be included in a special budget message the Governor shall submit to the General Assembly. If the General Assembly decides to set the regulatory fee at a rate higher than the rate in subdivision (2) of this subsection, it shall set the regulatory fee by law.

The regulatory fee may not exceed the amount necessary to generate funds sufficient to defray the estimated cost of the operations of the Authority for the upcoming fiscal year, including a reasonable margin for a reserve fund. The amount of the reserve may not exceed the estimated cost of operating the Authority for the upcoming fiscal year. In calculating the amount of the reserve, the General Assembly shall consider all relevant factors that may affect the cost of operating the Authority or a possible unanticipated increase or decrease in North Carolina electric meters and North Carolina telephone access lines.

(c) When Due. - The regulatory fee imposed under this section is due and payable to the Authority on or before the 15th day of the second month following the end of each quarter. Every electric and telephone membership corporation subject to the regulatory fee shall, on or before the date the fee is due for each quarter, prepare and render a report on a form prescribed by the Authority. The report shall state the electric or telephone membership corporation's total North Carolina electric meters or North Carolina telephone access lines connected for service for the preceding quarter and shall be accompanied by any supporting documentation that the Authority may by rule require.

(d) Use of Proceeds. - A special fund in the office of the State Treasurer, the North Carolina Rural Electrification Authority Fund (NCREA Fund), is created. The fees collected pursuant to this section and all other funds received by the Authority shall be deposited in the NCREA Fund. The NCREA Fund shall be placed in an interest bearing account and any interest or other income derived from the NCREA Fund shall be credited to the NCREA Fund. Moneys in the NCREA Fund shall only be spent pursuant to an appropriation by the General Assembly.

The NCREA Fund shall be subject to the provisions of the State Budget Act except that no unexpended surplus of the NCREA Fund shall revert to the General Fund. All funds credited to the NCREA Fund shall be used only to pay the expenses of the Authority in regulating electric and telephone membership corporations in the interest of the public as provided by this Chapter.(1991, c. 473, s. 1; 1991 (Reg. Sess., 1992), c. 803, s. 1; 2006-203, s. 58.)

§ 117-4. Organization meeting of Authority; chairman and secretary.

Promptly after their appointment the Authority shall meet and organize at such meeting, and at the first meeting of each year thereafter, the members shall choose from their number a chairman. They shall also choose a secretary, who shall be a competent engineer and shall fix his salary subject to the approval as provided in G.S. 143-35 to 143-47. (1935, c. 288, s. 4.)

§ 117-5. Compensation and expenses.

All members of the Authority, except the secretary, shall receive as compensation for their services per diem and actual expenses incurred while in the performance of their duties in accordance with the provisions of G.S. 138-5. (1935, c. 288, s. 5; 1939, c. 97; 1975, c. 709, s. 8.)

Article 2.

Electric Membership Corporations.

§ 117-6. Title of Article.

This Article may be cited as the "Electric Membership Corporation Act." (1935, c. 291, s. 1.)

§ 117-7. Definitions.

The following terms, whenever used or referred to in this Article, shall have the following meanings, unless a different meaning clearly appears from the context:

(1) "Acquire" shall mean acquire by purchase, lease, devise, gift or other mode of acquisition.

(2) "Board" shall mean the board of directors of a corporation formed under this Article.

(3) "Corporation" shall mean a corporation formed under this Article.

(4) "Federal agency" shall mean and include the United States of America, the President of the United States of America, the Federal Emergency Administrator of Public Works and any and all other authorities, agencies, and instrumentalities of the United States of America, heretofore or hereafter created.

(5) "Law" shall mean any act or statute, general, special or local of this State.

(6) "Person" shall mean and include natural persons, firms, associations, corporations, business trusts, partnerships and bodies politic. (1935, c. 291, s. 2.)

§ 117-8. Formation in unserved communities; filing application with Rural Electrification Authority.

When any number of persons residing in the community not served, or inadequately served, with electrical energy desire to secure electrical energy for their community and desire to form corporations to be known as electric membership corporations for said purpose, they shall file application with the North Carolina Rural Electrification Authority for permission to form such corporation. (1935, c. 291, s. 3.)

§ 117-9. Issuance of privilege for formation of such corporation.

Whenever any such application is made by as many as five members of the community, the North Carolina Rural Electrification Authority shall cause a survey of said territory to be made and if, in its opinion, the proposal is feasible, shall issue to said community a privilege for the formation of a corporation as hereinafter set out. Whenever an application has been filed by any community with the North Carolina Rural Electrification Authority, and its application for formation of an electric membership corporation has been approved, the same may be formed as hereinafter provided. (1935, c. 291, s. 4.)

§ 117-10. Formation authorized.

Any number of natural persons not less than three may, by executing, filing and recording a certificate as hereinafter provided, form a corporation not organized for pecuniary profit for the purpose of promoting and encouraging the fullest possible use of electric energy in the rural section of the State by making electric energy available to inhabitants of the State at the lowest cost consistent with sound economy and prudent management of the business of such corporations. (1935, c. 291, s. 5.)

§ 117-10.1. Municipal franchises.

An electric membership corporation shall be eligible to receive a franchise pursuant to G.S. 160-2(6) from any city or town:

(1) In which such electric membership corporation is on April 20, 1965 furnishing electric service at retail to a majority of the electric meters; or

(2) To which such electric membership corporation is on April 20, 1965 furnishing the entire supply of electricity at wholesale; or

(3) Which is newly incorporated subsequent to April 20, 1965, and in which on the effective date of such incorporation the electric membership corporation is furnishing electric service at retail to a majority of the meters. (1965, c. 287, s. 9.)

§ 117-10.2. Restriction on municipal service.

Except as otherwise provided in this section, no electric membership corporation shall furnish electric service to, or within the limits of, any incorporated city or town, except pursuant to a franchise that may be granted under the provisions of G.S. 117-10.1, or as permitted under G.S. 160A-331, 160A-331.2, 160A-332, and 160A-333. In addition, an electric membership corporation may furnish electric service to, or within the limits of, any incorporated city or town if the city or town and all electric suppliers, including public utilities, other electric membership corporations and other cities or towns, then furnishing electric service to or within such city or town consent thereto in writing. (1965, c. 287, s. 10; 1997-346, s. 3; 1999-111, s. 1; 2005-150, s. 6; 2007-419, s. 2.)

§ 117-10.3: Repealed by Session Laws 2007-419, s. 3, effective August 21, 2007.

§ 117-11. Contents of certificate of incorporation.

(a) Required Provisions. - The certificate of incorporation shall be entitled and endorsed "Certificate of Incorporation of _____ Electric Membership Corporation" (the blank space being filled in with the name of the corporation), and shall state:

(1) The name of the corporation, which name shall be such as to distinguish it from any other corporation.

(2) A reasonable description of the territory in which its operations are principally to be conducted.

(3) The location of its principal office and the post-office address thereof.

(4) The maximum number of directors, not less than three.

(5) The names and post-office addresses of the directors, not less than three, who are to manage the affairs of the corporation for the first year of its existence, or until their successors are chosen.
(6) The period, if any, limited for the duration of the corporation. If the duration of the corporation is to be perpetual, this fact should be stated.

(7) The terms and conditions upon which members of the corporation shall be admitted.

(b) Permissible Provisions. - The certificate of incorporation of a corporation may also contain any provision not contrary to law which the incorporators may choose to insert for the regulation of its business, and for the conduct of the affairs of the corporation; and any provisions, creating, defining, limiting or regulating the powers of the corporation, its directors and members. (1935, c. 291, s. 6.)

§ 117-12. Execution and filing of certificate of incorporation by residents of territory to be served.

The natural persons executing the certificate of incorporation shall be residents of the territory in which the principal operations of the corporation are to be conducted who are desirous of using electric energy to be furnished by the corporation. The certificate of incorporation shall be acknowledged by the subscribers before an officer qualified to administer oaths. When so acknowledged, the certificate may be filed in the office of the Secretary of State, who shall forthwith prepare a certified copy or copies thereof and forward one to the register of deeds in each county in which a portion of the territory of the corporation is located, who shall forthwith file such certified copy or copies in their respective offices and record the same as other certificates of incorporation are recorded. As soon as the provisions of this section have been complied with, the proposed corporation described in the certificate so filed, under its designated name, shall be and constitute a body corporate. (1935, c. 291, s. 7; 1967, c. 823, s. 32.)


§ 117-13. Board of directors; compensation; president and secretary.

Each corporation formed under this Article shall have a board of directors, in which management of the affairs of the corporation is vested. The directors of the corporation, other than those named in its certificate of incorporation, shall be elected annually by the members entitled to vote, but if the bylaws so provide the directors may be elected on a staggered-term basis: Provided, that the total number of directors on a board shall be so divided that not less than one third of them, or as nearly thereto as their division for that purpose will permit, shall be elected annually, and no term shall be longer than for three years; and provided further that, except as may be necessary in inaugurating such a plan, all directors shall be elected for terms of equal duration. The directors shall be entitled to receive for their services only such compensation as is provided in the bylaws. The board shall elect annually from its own number a president and a secretary. The directors must be members of the corporation, except that for those corporations whose principal purpose is to furnish bulk electric wholesale power supplies and whose membership consists of other electric membership corporations, the directors may be members, directors, officers or managers of the member corporations, and shall be elected by the member corporation's board of directors. (1935, c. 291, s. 8; 1959, c. 387, s. 1; 1969, c. 760; 1975, c. 314; 1979, c. 285, s. 2; 1981, c. 478.)

§ 117-14. Powers of board.

The board shall have power to do all things necessary or convenient in conducting the business of a corporation, including, but not limited to:

(1) The power to adopt and amend bylaws for the management and regulation of the affairs of the corporation: Provided however, that the certificate of incorporation may reserve to the members of the corporation the power to amend the bylaws. The bylaws of a corporation may make provisions not inconsistent with law or its certificate of incorporation, regulating the admission, withdrawal, suspension or expulsion of members; the transfer of membership; the fees and dues of members and the termination of memberships on nonpayment of dues or otherwise; the number, times and manner of choosing, qualifications, terms of office, official designations, powers, duties, and compensations of its officers; defining a vacancy in the board or in any office and the manner of filling it; the number of members to constitute a quorum at meetings, the date of the annual meeting and the giving of notice thereof, and the holding of special meetings and the giving of notice thereof; the terms and conditions upon which the corporation is to render service to its members; the disposition of the revenues and receipts of the corporation; regular and special meetings of the board and the giving of notice thereof.

(2) To appoint agents and employees and to fix their compensation and the compensation of the officers of the corporation.

(3) To execute instruments.

(4) To delegate to one or more of the directors or to the agents and employees of a corporation such powers and duties as it may deem proper.

(5) To make its own rules and regulations as to its procedure. (1935, c. 291, s. 9; 1941, c. 260.)


§ 117-15. Certificates of membership.

A corporation may issue to its members certificates of membership and each member shall be entitled to only one vote at the meetings of the corporation. (1935, c. 291, s. 10.)

§ 117-16. Corporate purpose; terms and conditions of membership.

The corporate purpose of each corporation formed hereunder shall be to render service to its members only, and no person shall become or remain a member unless such person shall use energy supplied by such corporation and shall have complied with the terms and conditions in respect to membership contained in the bylaws of such corporation: Provided, that such terms and conditions of membership shall be reasonable; and provided further, that no bona fide applicant for membership, who is able and willing to satisfy and abide by all such terms and conditions of membership, shall be denied arbitrarily, or capriciously, or without good cause. With respect to the members of an electric membership corporation whose principal purpose is to furnish or cause to be furnished bulk electric supplies at wholesale, the word "use" as used in this section shall also mean either "use and purchase" or "purchase" solely, as the case may be, and the words "supplied by" shall also mean "supplied for the account of". With respect to an electric membership corporation whose principal purpose is to furnish or cause to be furnished bulk electric supplies at wholesale, it shall be lawful for such corporation to enter into joint arrangements with other power supply entities, including but not limited to investor-owned public utilities and bodies politic, for the purchase and sale of bulk power supplies and bulk power services and for the joint ownership of bulk power supply properties. (1935, c. 291, s. 11; 1959, c. 387, s. 2; 1979, c. 285, s. 3.)


§ 117-16.1. Discrimination prohibited.

No electric membership corporation shall, as to rates or services, make or grant any unreasonable preference or advantage to any member or subject any member to any unreasonable prejudice or disadvantage. No electric membership corporation shall establish or maintain any unreasonable difference as to rates or services either as between localities or as between classes of service. No electric membership corporation shall give, pay, or receive any rebate or bonus, directly or indirectly, or mislead or deceive its members in any manner as to rates charged for the services of such electric membership corporation. (1965, c. 287, s. 11.)


§ 117-17. General grant of powers.

Each corporation formed under this Article is hereby vested with all power necessary or requisite for the accomplishment of its corporate purpose and capable of being delegated by the legislature; and no enumeration of particular powers hereby granted shall be construed to impair any general grant of power herein contained, nor to limit any such grant to a power or powers of the same class as those so enumerated. (1935, c. 291, s. 12.)


§ 117-18. Specific grant of powers.

Subject only to the Constitution of the State, a corporation created under the provisions of this Article shall have power to do any and all acts or things necessary or convenient for carrying out the purpose for which it was formed, including, but not limited to:

(1)     To sue and be sued.

(2)     To have a seal and alter the same at pleasure.

(3)     To acquire, hold and dispose of property, real and personal, tangible and intangible, or interests therein, and to pay therefor in cash or on credit, and to secure and procure payment of all or any part of the purchase price thereof on such terms and conditions as the board shall determine.

(4)     To render service and to acquire, own, operate, maintain and improve a system or systems.

(5)     To pledge all or any part of its revenue or mortgage or otherwise encumber all or any part of its property for the purpose of securing the payment of the principal of and interest on any of its obligations.

(6)     The right to apply to the North Carolina Rural Electrification Authority for permission to construct or place any parts of its system or lines in and along any State highway or over any lands that are now, or may be, the property of this State, or any political subdivision thereof. In all questions involving the right-of-way, or the right of eminent domain, the rulings of the North Carolina Rural Electrification Authority are final. Notwithstanding the foregoing sentence and notwithstanding subdivision (7) of G.S. 117-2, electric membership corporations may, without necessity of the Authority's rulings or participation, exercise the right of eminent domain for the purposes of constructing, operating and

maintaining electric generating, transmission, distribution and related facilities, individually and solely in their own names, pursuant to the provisions of Chapter 40A of the General Statutes; provided, that notwithstanding G.S. 117-30, the foregoing grant of the power of eminent domain to electric membership corporations shall not apply to telephone membership corporations; and, provided further, that the grant of the power of eminent domain is supplementary to the power of eminent domain already devolved upon the Authority.

(7) To accept gifts or grants of money, property, real or personal, from any person or federal agency, and to accept voluntary and uncompensated services.

(8) To make any and all contracts necessary or convenient for the full exercise of the powers in this Article granted, including, but not limited to, contracts with any person or federal agency, for the purchase or sale of energy; for the management and conduct of the business of the corporation, including the regulation of the rates, fees or charges for service rendered by the corporation.

(9) To sell, lease, mortgage or otherwise encumber or dispose of all or any part of its property, as hereinafter provided.

(10) To contract debts, borrow money, and to issue or assume the payment of bonds.

(11) To fix, maintain and collect fees, rents, tolls and other charges for service rendered.

(12) To perform any and all of the foregoing acts and to do any and all of the foregoing things under, through or by means of its own officers, agents and employees, or by contracts with any person or federal agency.

(13) To extend, construct, operate and maintain power lines into adjacent states.

(14) As to electric membership corporations, to conduct the activities permitted by G.S. 117-18.1. (1935, c. 291, s. 13; 1941, c. 335; 1975, c. 141; 1999-180, s. 1; 2001-487, s. 38(f).)

§ 117-18.1. Subsidiary business activities.

(a)     Electric membership corporations may form, organize, acquire, hold, dispose of, and operate any interest up to and including full controlling interest in separate business entities that provide energy services and products, telecommunications services and products, water, and wastewater collection and treatment, so long as those other business entities meet all of the following conditions:

(1)     They are not financed with loans or grants from the Rural Utilities Service (RUS) of the United States Department of Agriculture (USDA) or the USDA or with similar financing from any successor agency. This limitation shall not apply to RUS or USDA loans or grants, or loans or grants from successor agencies, for water or wastewater collection and treatment projects.

(2)     They are subject to all taxes, specifically including federal and State income taxes, levied against business entities of the same structure and engaged in the same activities.

(3)     They fully compensate the electric membership corporation for the use of personnel, services, equipment, or tangible and intangible property, the greater of (i) a competitive price, which is a price comparable with prices generally being charged at the time in arms length transactions in the same market, or (ii) the electric membership corporation's fully distributed costs, which shall include all direct and indirect costs, including cost of capital incurred in providing the personnel, services, equipment, tangible property, or intangible property in question. The value of real property shall include the intangible value of not having to purchase the real property being used, and the value of the identification with the EMC that will exist because of the use of the particular real property. Should the Utilities Commission, upon complaint showing reasonable grounds for investigation, find after investigation, that the charges for those transactions between the electric membership corporation and the other business entity do not conform with the provisions of this subdivision, the Utilities Commission is empowered to direct the electric membership corporation to adjust those charges to comply with the provisions of this subdivision. If the electric membership corporation does not comply with the Utilities Commission's directive, then the Utilities Commission is empowered to direct the electric membership corporation to divest its interest in the other business entity. For purposes of enforcing this subdivision, members of the Utilities Commission, the Utilities Commission staff, and the Public Staff are authorized to inspect the books and records of such other business entities and the electric membership

corporations. The Utilities Commission shall have the authority to adopt rules and reporting requirements to enforce this subdivision. The provisions of G.S. 62-310(a), 62-311, 62-312, 62-313, 62-314, 62-315, 62-316, 62-326, and 62-327 shall apply to electric membership corporations with respect to the application of this subdivision.

(4) They are organized and operated pursuant to Chapter 55 or Chapter 57D of the General Statutes.

(5) They do not receive from an electric membership corporation any investment, loan, guarantee, or pledge of assets in an amount that, in the aggregate, exceeds ten percent (10%) of the assets of that electric membership corporation.

(b) An electric membership corporation may not form or organize a separate business entity to engage in activities involving the distribution, storage, or sale of oil, as defined in G.S. 143-215.77(8), specifically including liquefied petroleum gases, but may acquire, hold, dispose of, and operate any interest in an existing business entity already engaged in these activities, subject to the other provisions of this section.

(c) No director, or spouse of a director, of an electric membership corporation may be employed or have any financial interest in any separate business entity formed, organized, acquired, held, or operated by an electric membership corporation pursuant to the provisions of this section. (1999-180, s. 2; 2013-157, s. 30.)


§ 117-19. Taxes and assessments.

(a) From and after April 20, 1965, no electric membership corporation heretofore or hereafter organized, reorganized, or domesticated under the provisions of this Chapter shall be a public agency; nor shall any such corporation be, or have the rights of, a political subdivision of the State.

(b) With respect to its properties owned and revenues received on and after January 1, 1967, each electric membership corporation operating within the State shall be subject to, and shall pay taxes and assessments under, all laws relative to State, county, municipal and other local taxes and assessments applicable to the electric light and power companies in this State, except income tax.

(c) through (e) Repealed by Session Laws 1997-6, s. 16. (1935, c. 291, s. 14; 1965, c. 287, s. 12; 1997-6, s. 16.)


§ 117-20. Encumbrance, sale, etc., of property.

No corporation may sell, mortgage, lease or otherwise encumber or dispose of any of its property (other than merchandise and property which lie within the limits of an incorporated city or town, or which shall represent not in excess of ten percent (10%) of the total value of the corporation's assets, or which in the judgment of the board are not necessary or useful in operating the corporation) unless

(1) Authorized so to do by the votes cast in person or by proxy by at least two-thirds of its total membership, and
(2) The consent of the holders of seventy-five per centum (75%) in amount of the bonds of such corporation then outstanding is obtained.

Notwithstanding the foregoing provisions of this section, the members of such a corporation may, by the affirmative majority of the votes cast in person or by proxy at any meeting of the members, delegate to the board of directors the power and authority (i) to borrow moneys from any source and in such amounts as the board may from time to time determine, (ii) to mortgage or otherwise pledge or encumber any or all of the corporation's property or assets as security therefor, and (iii) with respect to Electric Membership Corporations only, to sell and lease back any of the corporation's property or assets. (1935, c. 291, s. 15; 1965, c. 287, s. 13; 1969, c. 670, s. 1; 1987, c. 448, s. 1; 1997-346, s. 4; 1999-111, s. 1; 2003-24, s. 1.)


§ 117-21. Issuance of bonds.

A corporation formed hereunder shall have power and is hereby authorized, from time to time, to issue its bonds in anticipation of its revenue for any corporate purpose. Said bonds may be authorized by resolution or resolutions of the board, and may bear such date or dates, mature at such time or times, not exceeding 40 years from their respective dates, bear interest at such rate or rates, be in such denominations, be in such form, either coupon or registered, carry such registration privileges, be executed in such manner, be payable in such medium of payment, at such place or places, and be subject to such terms of redemption, not exceeding par and accrued interest, as such resolution or resolutions may provide. Such bonds may be sold in such manner and upon such terms as the board may determine at not less than par and accrued interest. Any provision of law to the contrary notwithstanding, any bonds and the interest coupons appertaining thereto, if any, issued pursuant to this Article shall possess all of the qualities of negotiable instruments. (1935, c. 291, s. 16; 1969, c. 670, s. 2.)

§ 117-22. Covenants or agreements for security of bonds.

In connection with the issuance of any bonds, a corporation may make covenants or agreements and do any and all acts or things that a business corporation can make or do under the laws of the State in order to secure its obligations or which, in the absolute discretion of the board, tend to make the obligations more marketable, notwithstanding that such covenants, agreements, acts and things may constitute limitations on the exercise of the powers herein granted. (1935, c. 291, s. 17.)

§ 117-23. Purchase and cancellation of bonds.

A corporation shall have power out of any funds available therefor to purchase any bonds issued by it at a price not exceeding the principal amount thereof and accrued interest thereon. All bonds so purchased shall be canceled. (1935, c. 291, s. 18.)

§ 117-24. Dissolution.

Any corporation created hereunder may be dissolved by filing, as hereinafter provided, a certificate which shall be entitled and endorsed "Certificate of Dissolution of _____ " (the blank space being filled in with the name of the corporation) and shall state:

(1)  Name of the corporation, and if such corporation is a corporation resulting from a consolidation as herein provided, the names of the original corporations.

(2)  The date of filing of the certificate of incorporation, and if such corporation is a corporation resulting from a consolidation as herein provided, the dates on which the certificates of incorporation of the original corporations were filed.

(3)  That the corporation elects to dissolve.

(4)  The name and post-office address of each of its directors, and the name, title and post-office address of each of its officers.

Such certificate shall be subscribed and acknowledged in the same manner as an original certificate of incorporation by the president or a vice-president, and the secretary or an assistant secretary, who shall make and annex an affidavit, stating that they have been authorized to execute and file such certificate by the votes cast in person or by proxy by at least two-thirds of its total membership.

A certificate of dissolution and a certified copy or copies thereof shall be filed in the same place as an original certificate of incorporation and thereupon the corporation shall be deemed to be dissolved.

Such corporation shall continue for the purpose of paying, satisfying and discharging any existing liabilities or obligations and collecting or liquidating its assets, and doing all other acts required to adjust and wind up its business and affairs, and may sue and be sued in its corporate name. Any assets remaining after all liabilities or obligations of the corporation have been satisfied or discharged shall be distributed among the members in such manner as is provided for in the corporation's charter or bylaws, and the charter or bylaws may provide for distributions to persons who were members in one or more prior years. (1935, c. 291, s. 19; 1965, c. 287, s. 14; 1987, c. 448, s. 2; 1997-346, s. 5; 1999-111, s. 1; 2003-24, s. 1.)

§ 117-25.  Amendment of certificate of incorporation.

A corporation created hereunder may amend its certificate of incorporation to change its corporate name, to increase or reduce the number of its directors or change any other provision therein: Provided, however, that no corporation shall amend its certificate of incorporation to embody therein any purpose, power or provisions which would not be authorized if its original certificate, including such additional or changed purpose, power or provisions, were offered for filing at the time a certificate under this section is offered. Such amendment may be accomplished by filing a certificate which shall be entitled and endorsed "Certificate of Amendment of _____ Electric Membership Corporation" and state:

(1) The name of the corporation, and if it has been changed, the name under which it was originally incorporated.

(2) The date of filing the certificate of incorporation in each public office where filed.

(3) The purposes, powers, or provisions, if any, to be amended or eliminated, and the purposes, powers or provisions, if any, to be added or substituted.

Such certificate shall be subscribed in the same manner as an original certificate of incorporation hereunder by the president or a vice-president, by the secretary or the assistant secretary, who shall make and annex an affidavit stating that they have been authorized to execute and file such certificate by the votes cast in person or by proxy by a majority of the members of the corporation entitled to vote. Such certificate shall be filed in the same places as an original certificate of incorporation and thereupon the amendment shall be deemed to have been effected. (1935, c. 291, s. 20.)


§ 117-26. Application for grant or loan from governmental agency.

Whenever any corporation organized hereunder desires to secure a grant or loan from any agency of the United States government now in existence or hereafter authorized, they shall apply through the North Carolina Rural Electrification Authority and not direct to the United States agency, and the said North Carolina Rural Electrification Authority alone shall have the authority to make applications for grants or loans to any corporations created hereunder. (1935, c. 291, s. 21.)

§ 117-27. Repealed by Session Laws 1965, c. 287, s. 15.

Article 3.

Miscellaneous Provisions.

§ 117-28. Foreign corporations; domestication; rights and privileges.

Any electric or telephone membership corporation created and existing under and by virtue of the laws of any adjoining state, which corporation desires to extend its lines into this State for the purpose of obtaining its power and energy needs, or an exchange interconnection, or for the purpose of supplying electric or telephone service to citizens and residents of this State, shall be and is hereby granted the right to domesticate in this State as such electric or telephone membership corporation, and, after such domestication, any such corporation shall have and enjoy all the rights, privileges, benefits and immunities granted to electric or telephone membership corporations under the laws of this State and shall be subject to the terms, provisions and conditions of this Chapter, and other applicable laws, to the same extent as such laws are now applicable to membership corporations organized under the laws of this State. (1941, c. 12; 1959, c. 387, s. 3.)

Article 4.

Telephone Service and Telephone Membership Corporations.

§ 117-29. Assistance from Rural Electrification Authority in procuring adequate telephone service.

Any number of persons residing in any rural community who are not provided with telephone service or are inadequately provided with same, may make application to the Rural Electrification Authority, upon such form as may be provided by the Rural Electrification Authority for assistance in securing telephone service, showing the circumstances of such community or communities with regard to telephone service and the need therefor. The Rural Electrification Authority shall make an investigation of the situation with respect to telephone service in such rural community or communities and if, upon investigation, it appears that such community or communities are not served with needed telephones or are inadequately served, the facts with reference thereto shall be collected by the Rural Electrification Authority and the Rural Electrification Authority shall promptly bring these facts to the attention of any telephone company serving the area, and shall make reasonable efforts to get such telephone company to provide the needed telephone service in such community or communities. (1945, c. 853, s. 1.)


§ 117-30.  Telephone membership corporations.

(a) In the event it is ascertained by the Rural Electrification Authority that the community or communities referred to in the foregoing section G.S. 117-29 are in need of telephone service and that there is a sufficient number of persons to be served to justify such services, and the telephone company serving in the area in which the community or communities are located is unwilling to provide such service, a telephone membership corporation may be organized by such community or communities in the same manner that electric membership corporations may be formed under Article 2 of this Chapter, and all of the provisions of said Article shall be applicable to the formation of telephone membership corporations and such corporations shall have all the authority, powers and duties of such a corporation when formed under the provisions of said Article; except that the provisions of G.S. 117-8, 117-9, 117-10.1, 117-10.2, 117-16.1, 117-18(14), 117-18.1, 117-19 and 117-24 shall not be applicable to the organization of a telephone membership corporation, and except that such corporations so formed for the express purpose of providing telephone service necessary to serve the community or communities prescribed in the application may also provide the community or communities prescribed in the application with any communication service for the transmission of voice, sounds, signals, pictures, writing or signs of all kinds through the use of electricity or the electromagnetic spectrum between the transmitting and receiving apparatus, together with any telecommunications service requiring band-width capacity, including, but not limited to community antenna and cable television services, and including all lines, wires, cables, radio, light, electromagnetic impulse and all facilities, systems or other means used in the rendition of such services, but not including message telegram service or radio broadcasting services or facilities within the meaning of section 3(o) of the Federal Communications Act of 1934, as amended (47 USC § 153(o)) and except that such corporation so formed shall have no authority to engage in any other business. Provided, that the references in Article 2 of this Chapter to "power lines" or "energy" as to such telephone membership corporations shall be construed to mean telephone lines, broadband cables and lines, telephone service and broadband communications services. Provided further, that nothing herein shall be construed to authorize any telephone membership corporation organized hereunder to duplicate any line or lines, systems or other means by which adequate telephone service is being furnished; or to build or to construct a telephone line, or telephone lines, or telephone systems, or otherwise to provide facilities or means of furnishing telephone service to any person, community, town or city then being adequately served by a telephone company, corporation or system; or to provide telephone service in an unserved area while any telephone company, corporation or system is acting in good faith and with reasonable diligence in arranging to provide adequate telephone service to such person, community, town or city.

(b) Any telephone membership corporation formed under this Article which now provides or has imminent plans to provide any service which is subject to the requirement of a state or local franchise shall make reasonable efforts to secure any such state or local franchise required for the operation of such service within its service area. Unless otherwise prohibited, any such franchise granted to a telephone membership corporation may be transferred or assigned by that corporation, in its discretion, if such transfer or assignment is reasonably calculated to contribute to the development of any such service within the franchised area. Provided, however, that no telephone membership corporation shall be required to obtain a state or local franchise to provide the types of telephone services being provided on July 1, 1979 by a telephone membership corporation, or the types of telephone services offered by existing telephone membership corporations on July 1, 1979 and proposed to be offered by any telephone membership corporation formed thereafter, without respect to the facilities or methods which are used to provide such services. (1945, c. 853, s. 2; 1965, c. 345, s. 1; 1979, c. 586; 1999-180, s. 3.)


§ 117-31. Power of Rural Electrification Authority to prosecute requested investigations.

In investigating the application filed with the Rural Electrification Authority under the provisions of G.S. 117-30 of this Article, the Rural Electrification Authority shall have the authority to employ such personnel as shall be necessary to conduct surveys; to contact the telephone companies serving the general area for the purpose of arranging for extension of telephone service by such companies to such community or communities; to make estimates of the cost of the extension of telephone service to such community or communities; to call upon the Utilities Commission of the State to fix such rates as will be applicable to such service; to secure for such community or communities any assistance which may be available from the federal government by gift or loan or in any other manner; to investigate all applications for the creation of telephone membership corporations and determine and pass upon the question of granting authority to form such corporation; to provide forms for making such applications, and to do all things necessary to a proper determination of the question of the establishment of such telephone membership corporations in keeping with the provisions of this Article; to act as agent for any such telephone membership corporation in securing loans or grants from any agency of the United States government; to prescribe rules and regulations and the necessary blanks for such membership corporations in making applications for grants or loans from any agency of the United States government; to do all other acts and things which may be necessary to aid the rural communities in North Carolina in securing telephone service. (1945, c. 853, s. 3.)

§ 117-32. Loans from federal agencies; authority of county, etc., to engage in telephone business.

Whenever any corporation organized under the provisions of this Article desires to secure a grant or loan from any agency of the United States government now in existence or hereafter authorized, it shall apply through the North Carolina Rural Electrification Authority and not direct to the United States agency, and the said North Carolina Rural Electrification Authority alone shall have the authority to make application for grants or loans to any such corporation. Nothing in this Article shall be deemed to authorize any county, city or town to engage in the telephone business. (1945, c. 853, s. 4.)

§ 117-33. Declared public agency of State; taxes and assessments.

A telephone membership corporation heretofore or hereafter organized under this Article shall be, and is hereby declared to be a public agency, and shall have within its limits for which it was formed the same rights as any other political subdivision of the State, and all property owned by said telephone membership corporation and used exclusively for the purpose of said corporation shall be held in the same manner and subject to the same taxes and assessments as property owned by any county or municipality of the State so long as said property is owned by said telephone membership corporation and is used for the purposes for which the corporation was formed. Notwithstanding the foregoing, a telephone membership corporation shall not be eligible to receive a permanent registration plate issued under G.S. 20-84. (1965, c. 345, s. 2; 2012-159, s. 2.)

§ 117-34. Dissolution.

Any telephone membership corporation created under this Article may be dissolved by filing, as hereinafter provided, a certificate which shall be entitled and endorsed "Certificate of Dissolution of _____" (the blank space being filled in with the name of the corporation) and shall state:

(1)     Name of the corporation, and if such corporation is a corporation resulting from a consolidation as herein provided, the names of the original corporations.
(2)     The date of filing of the certificate of incorporation, and if such corporation is a corporation resulting from a consolidation as herein provided, the dates on which the certificates of incorporation of the original corporations were filed.

(3)     That the corporation elects to dissolve.

(4)     The name and post-office address of each of its directors, and the name, title and post-office address of each of its officers.

Such certificate shall be subscribed and acknowledged in the same manner as an original certificate of incorporation by the president or a vice-president, and the secretary or an assistant secretary, who shall make and annex an affidavit, stating that they have been authorized to execute and file such certificate by the votes cast in person by at least two-thirds of its total membership, without proxies.

A certificate of dissolution and a certified copy or copies thereof shall be filed in the same place as an original certificate of incorporation and thereupon the corporation shall be deemed to be dissolved.

Such corporation shall continue for the purpose of paying, satisfying and discharging any existing liabilities or obligations and collecting or liquidating its assets, and doing all other acts required to adjust and wind up its business and affairs, and may sue and be sued in its corporate name. Any assets remaining after all liabilities or obligations of the corporation have been satisfied or discharged shall pass to and become the property of the State. (1965, c. 345, s. 2; 1987, c. 448, s. 3.)

§ 117-35. Article complete in itself and controlling.

Article 4 is complete in itself and shall be controlling. The provisions of any other law, general, special, or local except as provided in this Article, shall not apply to a telephone membership corporation formed under this Article. (1965, c. 345, s. 2.)

§§ 117-36 through 117-40. Reserved for future codification purposes.
Article 5.

Consolidation and Merger.

§ 117-41. Consolidation.

(a)     Any two or more electric membership corporations or any two or more telephone membership corporations, organized and operating under this Chapter (each of which is hereinafter designated a "consolidating corporation"), may consolidate into a new corporation (hereinafter designated the "new corporation"), by complying with the provisions of subsections (b) and (c) hereof and of G.S. 117-43.

(b)     The proposition for the consolidation of the consolidating corporations into the new corporation and proposed articles of consolidation to give effect thereto shall be submitted to a meeting of the members of each consolidating corporation, the notice of which shall have attached thereto a copy of the proposed articles of consolidation.

(c)     If the proposed consolidation and the proposed articles of consolidation, with any amendments, are approved by the affirmative vote of not less than two-thirds of those members of each consolidating corporation voting thereon at each such meeting, articles of consolidation in the form approved shall be executed and acknowledged on behalf of each consolidating corporation by its president or vice-president and its seal shall be affixed thereto and attested by its secretary. The articles of consolidation shall recite that they are executed pursuant to this Chapter and shall state:

(1)     The name of each consolidating corporation and the address of its principal office;

(2)     The name of the new corporation and the address of its principal office;

(3)     A statement that each consolidating corporation agrees to the consolidation;

(4)     The names and addresses of the directors of the new corporation; and

(5)     The terms and conditions of the consolidation and the mode of carrying the same into effect, including the manner in which members of the consolidating corporations may or shall become members of the new corporation; and may contain any provisions not inconsistent with this Chapter deemed necessary or advisable for the conduct of the business of the new corporation. The president or vice-president of each consolidating corporation executing such articles of consolidation shall make and annex thereto an affidavit stating that the provisions of this section in respect of such articles were duly complied with by such corporation. (1979, c. 285, s. 4.)

§ 117-42. Merger.

(a)     Any one or more electric membership corporations or any one or more telephone membership corporations, organized and operating under this Chapter (each of which is hereinafter designated a "merging corporation"), may merge into another like corporation (hereinafter designated the "surviving corporation"), by complying with the provision of G.S. 117-42(b) and (c), and G.S. 117-43.

(b)     The proposition for the merger of the merging corporation(s) into the surviving corporation and proposed articles of merger to give effect thereto shall be submitted to a meeting of the members of such merging corporation(s) and of the surviving corporation, the notice of which shall have attached thereto a copy of the proposed articles of merger.

(c) If the proposed merger and the proposed articles of merger, with any amendments, are approved by the affirmative vote of not less than two thirds of those members of each corporation voting thereon at each such meeting, articles of merger in the form approved shall be executed and acknowledged on behalf of each such corporation by its president or vice-president and its seal shall be affixed thereto and attested by its secretary. The articles of merger shall recite that they are executed pursuant to this Chapter and shall state:

(1) The name of each merging corporation and the address of its principal office;

(2) The name of the surviving corporation and the address of its principal office;

(3) A statement that each merging corporation and the surviving corporation agree to the merger;

(4) The names and addresses of the directors of the surviving corporation; and

(5) The terms and conditions of the merger and the mode of carrying the same into effect, including the manner in which members of the merging corporations may or shall become members of the surviving corporation; and may contain any provisions not inconsistent with this Chapter deemed necessary or advisable for the conduct of the business of the surviving corporation. The president or vice-president of each corporation executing such articles of merger shall make and annex thereto an affidavit stating that the provisions of this section in respect of such article were duly complied with by such corporation. (1979, c. 285, s. 4.)


§ 117-43. Filing and recording of articles of consolidation or merger.

Articles of consolidation or merger shall be filed with the Secretary of State, who shall forthwith prepare one or more certified copies thereof and forward one to the register of deeds of each county in which a portion of the territory of the filing corporation is authorized to furnish service, which registers of deeds shall forthwith file such certified copy in their respective offices and record the same as articles of incorporation are recorded. As soon as the provisions of this section have been complied with, the new consolidated corporation or the surviving merged corporation, described and named in the articles so filed, shall become and constitute a body corporate in accordance with the provisions of such articles. (1979, c. 285, s. 4.)

§ 117-44. Effect of consolidation or merger.

Upon compliance with the provisions of G.S. 117-44:

(1)  a.   In the case of a consolidation, the existence of the consolidating corporations shall cease and the articles of consolidation shall be deemed to be the articles of incorporation of the new corporation; and

b.   In the case of a merger, the separate existence of the merging corporations shall cease and the articles of incorporation of the surviving corporation shall be deemed to be amended to the extent, if any, that changes therein are provided for in the articles of merger.

(2)   All the rights, privileges, immunities and franchises and all property, real and personal, including without limitation applications for membership, all debts due on whatever account and all other choses in action, of each of the consolidating or merging corporations shall be deemed to be transferred to and vested in the new or surviving corporation without further act or deed.

(3)   The new or surviving corporation shall be responsible and liable for all the liabilities and obligations of each of the consolidating or merging corporations and any claim existing or action or proceeding pending by or against any of the consolidating or merging corporations may be prosecuted as if the consolidation or merger had not taken place, but the new or surviving corporation may be substituted in its place.

(4)   Neither the rights of creditors nor any liens upon the property of any of such corporations shall be impaired by such consolidation or merger. (1979, c. 285, s. 4.)

§ 117-45. Validation.

No provision of Article 5 nor any provision thereof shall, or shall be construed to, express or imply the invalidity or invalidation of the incorporation or operations of any electric or telephone membership corporation heretofore organized and operating under Chapter 117 of the General Statutes, including but not limited to North Carolina Electric Membership Corporation and any two or more electric or telephone membership corporations which have substantively merged or consolidated; and any such substantive mergers or consolidations are hereby specifically validated. (1979, c. 285, s. 4.)

Article 6.

Indemnification.

§ 117-46. Indemnification of directors, officers, employees, or agents.

The powers, authority and requirements as to indemnification, payment of expenses, and purchase of liability insurance for directors, officers, employees and agents, as set out in G.S. 55A-17.1, 55A-17.2 and G.S. 55A-17.3 shall apply to and may be exercised by any corporation formed under this Chapter. The indemnification of a director, officer, employee or agent of a corporation provided by this section shall not be deemed exclusive of any other rights to which such director, officer, employee or agent may be entitled, under any bylaw, agreement, vote of board of directors or members, or otherwise with respect to any liability or litigation expenses arising out of his activities as director, officer, employee, or agent. (1987, c. 107.)

Chapter 118.

Firemen's and Rescue Squad Workers' Relief and Pension Funds.

§§ 118-1 through 118-66: Recodified as Articles 84 to 88 of Chapter 58.

Chapter 118A.

Firemen's Death Benefit Act.

§§ 118A-1 through 118A-7. Repealed by Session Laws 1973, c. 970, s. 1.

Chapter 118B.

Members of a Rescue Squad Death Benefit Act.

§§ 118B-1 through 118B-7. Repealed by Session Laws 1973, c. 970, s. 2.

Chapter 119.

Gasoline and Oil Inspection and Regulation.

Article 1.

Lubricating Oils.

§ 119-1. Unlawful substitution.

It shall be unlawful for any person, firm or corporation to fill any order for lubricating oil, designated by a trademark or distinctive trade name for an automobile or other internal combustion engine with a spurious or substitute oil unless and until it is explained to the person giving the order that the oil offered is not the oil that he has ordered, and the purchaser shall thereupon elect to take the substitute article that is being offered to him. (1927, c. 174, s. 1.)

§ 119-2. Brand or trade name of lubricating oil to be displayed.

It shall be unlawful for any person, firm or corporation to sell, offer for sale or delivery, or to cause or permit to be sold, offered for sale or delivery, any oil represented as lubricating oil for internal combustion engines unless there shall be firmly attached to or painted at or near the point or outlet from which said oil represented as lubricating oil for internal combustion engines is drawn or poured out for sale or delivery, a sign or label consisting of the word or words in at all times legible letters not less than one-half inch in height comprising the brand or trade name of said lubricating oil: Provided, that if any of said lubricating oil shall have no brand or trade name, the above required sign or label shall consist of the words in letters not less than three inches high, "Lubricating Oil No Brand." (1927, c. 174, s. 2.)

§ 119-3. Misrepresentation of brands for sale.

It shall be unlawful for any person, firm or corporation to display, at the place of sale, any sign, label or other designating mark which describes any lubricating oil for internal combustion engines not actually sold or offered for sale or delivered at the location at which the sign, label or other designating mark is displayed, or to display any label upon any container which label names or describes any lubricating oil for internal combustion engines not actually contained therein, but offered for sale or sold as such: Provided, this section shall not prevent the advertising of such products when no lubricating oil is offered for sale at such place of advertisement. (1927, c. 174, s. 3.)

§ 119-4. Misdemeanor.

Any person, firm or corporation violating any of the provisions of this Article shall for each offense be deemed guilty of a Class 2 misdemeanor. (1927, c. 174, s. 4; 1993, c. 539, s. 899; 1994, Ex. Sess., c. 24, s. 14(c).)

§ 119-5. Person violating or allowing employee to violate Article to forfeit $100.00.

Any person violating this Article, or any person, firm or corporation whose servant, agent or other employee violates this Article in the course of his employment shall forfeit to the manufacturer whose oil was ordered, or to the proprietor of the trademark or trade name by which the oil order was designated by the purchaser, as the case may be, one hundred dollars ($100.00) for each such offense, to be recovered by suit by the person, firm or corporation claiming the penalty against the person, firm or corporation from whom the penalty is claimed. (1927, c. 174, s. 5.)

§ 119-6. Inspection duties devolve upon Commissioner of Agriculture.

The duties of inspection required by G.S. 119-1 through 119-5 shall be performed by the Commissioner of Agriculture. (1933, c. 214, s. 9; 1949, c. 1167.)

Article 2.

Liquid Fuels, Lubricating Oils, Greases, etc.

§ 119-7. Sale of automobile fuels and lubricants by deception as to quality, etc., prohibited.

It shall be unlawful for any person, firm, copartnership, partnership or corporation to store, sell, offer or expose for sale any liquid fuels, lubricating oils, greases or other similar products in any manner whatsoever which may deceive, tend to deceive or have the effect of deceiving the purchaser of said products, as to the nature, quality or quantity of the products so sold, exposed or offered for sale. (1933, c. 108, s. 1.)

§ 119-8. Sale of fuels, etc., different from advertised name prohibited.

No person, firm, partnership, copartnership, or corporation shall keep, expose or offer for sale, or sell any liquid fuels, lubricating oils, greases or other similar products from any container, tank, pump or other distributing device other than those manufactured or distributed by the manufacturer or distributor indicated by the name, trademark, symbol, sign or other distinguishing mark or device appearing upon said tank, container, pump or other distributing device in which said products were sold, offered for sale or distributed. (1933, c. 108, s. 2.)

§ 119-9. Imitation of standard equipment prohibited.

It shall be unlawful for any person, firm or corporation to disguise or camouflage his or their own equipment, by imitating the design, symbol, or trade name of the equipment under which recognized brands of liquid fuels, lubricating oils and similar products are generally marketed. (1933, c. 108, s. 3.)

§ 119-10. Juggling trade names, etc., prohibited.

It shall be unlawful for any person, firm or corporation to expose or offer for sale or sell under any trademark, trade name or name or other distinguishing mark any liquid fuels, lubricating oils, greases or other similar products other than those manufactured or distributed by the manufacturer or distributor marketing such products under such trade name, trademark or name or other distinguishing mark. (1933, c. 108, s. 4.)


§ 119-11. Mixing different brands for sale under standard trade name prohibited.

It shall be unlawful for any person or persons, firm or firms, corporation or corporations or any of their servants, agents or employees, to mix, blend or compound the liquid fuels, lubricating oils, greases or similar products of the manufacturer or distributor with the products of any other manufacturer or distributor, or adulterate the same, and expose or offer for sale or sell such mixed, blended or compounded products under the trade name, trademark or name or other distinguishing mark of either of said manufacturers or distributors, or as the adulterated products of such manufacturer or distributor: Provided, however, that nothing herein shall prevent the lawful owner thereof from applying its own trademark, trade name or symbol to any product or material. (1933, c. 108, s. 5.)


§ 119-12. Aiding and assisting in violation of Article prohibited.

It shall be unlawful, and upon conviction punishable as will hereinafter be stated, for any person or persons, firm or firms, partnership or copartnership, corporation or corporations or any of their agents or employees, to aid or assist any other person in violating any of the provisions of this Article by depositing or delivering into any tank, pump, receptacle or other container any liquid fuels, lubricating oils, greases or other like products other than those intended to be stored, therein, as indicated by the name of the manufacturer or distributor, or the trademark, the trade name, name or other distinguishing mark of the product displayed in the container itself, or on the pump or other distributing device used in connection therewith, or shall by any other means aid or assist another in the violation of any of the provisions of this Article. (1933, c. 108, s. 6.)

§ 119-13. Violation made misdemeanor.

Every person, firm or firms, partnership or copartnership, corporation or corporations, or any of their agents, servants or employees, violating any of the provisions of this Article shall be guilty of a Class 1 misdemeanor. (1933, c. 108, s. 7; 1993, c. 539, s. 900; 1994, Ex. Sess., c. 24, s. 14(c).)

Article 2A.

Regulation of Rerefined or Reprocessed Oil.

§ 119-13.1. Definitions.

As used in this Article:

(1) "Lubricating oil" means any oil classified for the use in an internal combustion engine, hydraulic system, gear box, differential, or wheel bearings.

(1a) "Recycled oil" means any oil prepared from used oil for energy recovery or reuse as a petroleum product by reclaiming, reprocessing, rerefining, or other means that use properly treated used oil as a substitute for petroleum products.

(1b) "Rerefined oil" means used oil that is refined to remove the physical and chemical contaminants acquired through use and that, by itself or when blended with new lubricating oil or additives, meets applicable American Petroleum Institute (A.P.I.) service classifications.

(2) "Specifications" means the minimum chemical properties or analysis as determined by the American Society for Testing Materials (A.S.T.M.) test methods using current ASTM analytical procedures.

(3) "Used oil" means any oil that has been refined from crude or synthetic oil and, as a result of use, storage, or handling becomes unsuitable for its original purpose due to the loss of its original properties or the presence of impurities, but that may be rerefined for further use. (1953, c. 1137; 1979, c. 158, s. 1; 1995, c. 516, s. 1.)


§ 119-13.2. Labels required on sealed containers; oil to meet minimum specifications.

(a) It shall be unlawful to offer for sale or sell or deliver in this State previously used oil that has not been rerefined or recycled oil that has not been rerefined, as defined in G.S. 119-13.1, in a sealed container unless this container be labeled or bear a label on which shall be expressed the brand or trade name of the oil and the words "made from previously used lubricating oil"; the name and address of the person, firm, or corporation that has rerefined or reprocessed said oil or placed it in the container; the Society of Automotive Engineers (S.A.E.) viscosity grade; the net contents of the container expressed in U.S. liquid measure of quarts, gallons, or pints; which label has been registered and approved by the Gasoline and Oil Inspection Division of the Department of Agriculture and Consumer Services; and that the oil in each container shall meet the minimum specifications. The Gasoline and Oil Inspection Board shall adopt minimum quality specifications, the measurement of which shall be accomplished using current A.S.T.M. analytical procedures.

(b) A person may represent a product made in whole or in part from rerefined oil to be substantially equivalent to a product made from virgin oil for a particular end use if the product conforms with the applicable American Petroleum Institute (A.P.I.) service classifications. (1953, c. 1137; 1979, c. 158, s. 2; 1995, c. 516, s. 2; 1997-261, s. 109.)


§ 119-13.3. Violation a misdemeanor.

Any person, firm, or corporation violating any of the provisions of this Article shall for each offense be guilty of a Class 1 misdemeanor. For a second or subsequent offense, the person shall also be enjoined from selling or distributing previously used oil for not less than one year nor more than five years. (1953, c. 1137; 1993, c. 539, s. 901; 1994, Ex. Sess., c. 24, s. 14(c); 1995, c. 516, s. 3.)

Article 3.

Gasoline and Oil Inspection.

§ 119-14. Title of Article.

This Article shall be known as the Gasoline and Oil Inspection Act. (1937, c. 425, s. 1.)

§ 119-15. Definitions that apply to Article.

The following definitions apply in this Article:

(1)  Alternative fuel. - Defined in G.S. 105-449.130.

(2)  Aviation gasoline. - Defined in G.S. 105-449.60.

(3)  Dyed diesel fuel. - Defined in G.S. 105-449.60.

(4)  Dyed diesel fuel distributor. - A person who acquires dyed diesel fuel from either of the following:

a.  A person who is not required to be licensed under Part 2 of Article 36C of Chapter 105 of the General Statutes and who maintains storage facilities for dyed diesel fuel to be used for nonhighway purposes.

b.  Another dyed diesel fuel distributor.

(5)  Gasoline. - Defined in G.S. 105-449.60.

(6)  Jet fuel. - Defined in G.S. 105-449.60.

(7)  Kerosene. - Defined in G.S. 105-449.60.

(8) Kerosene distributor. - A person who acquires kerosene from any of the following for subsequent sale:

a. A supplier licensed under Part 2 of Article 36C of Chapter 105 of the General Statutes.

b. A kerosene supplier.

c. Another kerosene distributor.

(9) Kerosene supplier. - Either of the following:

a. A person who supplies both kerosene and motor fuel and, consequently, is required to be licensed under Part 2 of Article 36C of Chapter 105 of the General Statutes.

b. A person who is not required to be licensed as a supplier under Part 2 of Article 36C of Chapter 105 of the General Statutes and who maintains storage facilities for kerosene to be used to fuel an airplane.

(10) Motor fuel. - Defined in G.S. 105-449.60.

(11) Person. - Defined in G.S. 105-229.90.

(12) Terminal. - Defined in G.S. 105-449.60.

(13) Terminal operator. - Defined in G.S. 105-449.60. (1937, c. 425, s. 2; 1995, c. 390, s. 19; 1995 (Reg. Sess., 1996), c. 647, s. 53; 1997-6, s. 17; 2003-349, s. 10.12; 2005-435, s. 19; 2008-134, s. 59.)


§ 119-15.1. List of persons who must have a license.

(a) License. - A person may not engage in business in this State as any of the following unless the person has a license issued by the Secretary authorizing the person to engage in business:

(1) A kerosene supplier.

(2) A kerosene distributor.

(3) A kerosene terminal operator.

(4) A dyed diesel fuel distributor.

(b) Exception. - A kerosene supplier license is not required if the supplier is licensed as a supplier under Part 2 of Article 36C of Chapter 105 of the General Statutes. A kerosene distributor is required to have a kerosene distributor license only if the distributor imports kerosene. Other kerosene distributors may elect to have a kerosene license. A kerosene terminal operator license is not required if the terminal operator is licensed as a terminal operator under Part 2 of Article 36C of Chapter 105 of the General Statutes. (2003-349, s. 10.14; 2004-170, s. 33; 2004-203, s. 82; 2005-435, s. 20.)

§ 119-15.2. How to apply for a license.

To obtain a license, an applicant must file an application with the Secretary of Revenue on a form provided by the Secretary. An application must include the applicant's name, address, federal employer identification number, and any other information required by the Secretary. An applicant must meet the requirements for obtaining a license set out in G.S. 105-449.69(b) and (c). (2003-349, s. 10.14.)

§ 119-15.3. Bond or letter of credit required as a condition of obtaining and keeping certain licenses.

(a) Initial Bond. - An applicant for a license as a kerosene supplier, kerosene distributor, or kerosene terminal operator must file with the Secretary of Revenue a bond or an irrevocable letter of credit. A bond or irrevocable letter of credit must be conditioned upon compliance with the requirements of this Article, be payable to the State, and be in the form required by the Secretary. The amount of the bond or irrevocable letter of credit may not be less than five hundred dollars ($500.00) and may not be more than twenty thousand dollars ($20,000).

(b) Adjustments to Bond. - When notified by the Secretary of Revenue, a person that has filed a bond or irrevocable letter of credit and that holds a license listed in this Article must file an additional bond or irrevocable letter of credit in the amount requested by the Secretary. The person must file the additional bond or irrevocable letter of credit within 30 days after receiving the notice from the Secretary. The amount of the initial bond or irrevocable letter of credit and the additional bond or irrevocable letter of credit by the license holder, however, may not exceed the limits set in subsection (a) of this section.

(c) Class 1. - A person who fails to comply with this section is guilty of a Class 1 misdemeanor. (2003-349, s. 10.14; 2004-203, s. 82; 2005-435, s. 21.)

§§ 119-16 through 119-16.1: Repealed by Session Laws 1995, c. 390, ss. 20 and 21.

§ 119-16.2: Repealed by Session Laws 2003-349, s. 10.13, effective January 1, 2004.

§ 119-16.3. Certain kerosene sales prohibited.

It shall be a Class 1 misdemeanor for any distributor to sell kerosene dispensed from a pump located on the same island where there are pumps dispensing gasoline or gasohol. An island is a group of two or more dispensing pumps within 15 feet of each other. This section shall apply only to pumps installed after October 1, 1985. (1985, c. 314; 1993, c. 539, s. 903; 1994, Ex. Sess., c. 24, s. 14(c).)

§ 119-17: Repealed by Session Laws 2007-527, s. 20, effective August 31, 2007.

§ 119-18. Inspection tax and distribution of the tax proceeds.

(a) Tax. - An inspection tax of one fourth of one cent (1/4 of 1¢) per gallon is levied upon all of the fuel listed in this subsection regardless of whether the fuel is exempt from the per-gallon excise tax imposed by Article 36C or 36D of

Chapter 105 of the General Statutes. The inspection tax on motor fuel is due and payable to the Secretary of Revenue on the date the per gallon excise tax on motor fuel is due and payable under Article 36C of Chapter 105 of the General Statutes. The inspection tax on alternative fuel is due and payable to the Secretary of Revenue on the date the excise tax on alternative fuel is due and payable under Article 36D of Chapter 105 of the General Statutes. The inspection tax on kerosene is payable monthly to the Secretary by a supplier that is licensed under Part 2 of Article 36C of Chapter 105 of the General Statutes and by a kerosene supplier. A monthly report is due on the date a monthly return is due under G.S. 105-449.90 and applies to kerosene sold during the preceding month by a supplier licensed under that Part and to kerosene received during the preceding month by a kerosene supplier. A kerosene terminal operator must file a return in accordance with the provisions of G.S. 105-449.90. The inspection tax on jet fuel and aviation gasoline is payable as specified by the Secretary of Revenue.

(1) Motor fuel.

(2) Alternative fuel used to operate a highway vehicle.

(3) Kerosene.

(4) Jet fuel.

(5) Aviation gasoline.

(a1) Deferred Payment. - A licensed kerosene distributor that buys kerosene from a supplier licensed under Part 2 of Article 36C of Chapter 105 of the General Statutes has the right to defer payment of the inspection tax until the supplier is required to remit the tax to this State or another state. A licensed kerosene distributor that pays the tax due a supplier licensed under that Part by the date the supplier must pay the tax to the State may deduct from the amount due a discount in the amount set in G.S. 105-449.93.

(b) Proceeds. - The proceeds of the inspection tax levied by this section shall be applied first to the costs of administering this Article and Subchapter V of Chapter 105 of the General Statutes. The remainder of the proceeds shall be credited on a monthly basis to the Highway Fund to be used for system preservation under the Department of Transportation in the highway maintenance program.

(c)     No Local Tax. - No county, city, or town shall impose any inspection charge, tax, or fee, in the nature of the charge prescribed by this section, upon kerosene and motor fuel. (1917, c. 166, s. 4; C.S., s. 4856; 1933, c. 544, s. 5; 1937, c. 425, s. 5; 1967, c. 1110, s. 12; 1973, c. 476, s. 193; 1985, c. 602, s. 2; 1991, c. 636, s. 12; 1991 (Reg. Sess., 1992), c. 913, s. 12; 1993, c. 402, s. 8; 1995, c. 390, s. 23; 1995 (Reg. Sess., 1996), c. 647, s. 55; 2003-349, ss. 10.15, 10.16; 2006-162, s. 15(e); 2008-134, s. 60; 2011-145, s. 28.25A(b).)

§ 119-19.  Authority of Secretary to cancel a license.

The Secretary of Revenue may cancel a license issued under this Article upon the written request of the license holder. The Secretary may summarily cancel a license issued under this Article or under Article 36C or 36D of Chapter 105 of the General Statutes when the Secretary finds that the license holder is incurring liability for the tax imposed by this Article after failing to pay a tax when due under this Article. The Secretary may cancel the license of a license holder who files a false report under this Article or fails to file a report required under this Article after holding a hearing on whether the license should be cancelled.

The Secretary must send a person whose license is summarily cancelled a notice of the cancellation and must give the person an opportunity to have a hearing on the cancellation within 10 days after the cancellation. The Secretary must give a person whose license may be cancelled after a hearing at least 10 days' written notice of the date, time, and place of the hearing. A notice of a summary license cancellation and a notice of hearing must be sent by registered mail to the last known address of the license holder.

When the Secretary cancels a license and the license holder has paid all taxes and penalties due under this Article, the Secretary must either return to the license holder the bond filed by the license holder or notify the person liable on the bond and the license holder that the person is released from liability on the bond. (1933, c. 544, s. 10; 1967, c. 1110, s. 12; 1973, c. 476, s. 193; 1995, c. 390, s. 24; 2004-170, s. 34.)

§ 119-20.  Repealed by Session Laws 1963, c. 1169, s. 6.

§119-21.  On failure to report, Secretary may determine tax.

Whenever any person shall neglect or refuse to make and file any report as required by this Article, or shall file an incorrect or fraudulent report, the Secretary of Revenue shall determine after an investigation the number of gallons of kerosene oil and other motor fuel with respect to which the person has incurred liability under the tax laws of the State of North Carolina, and shall fix the amount of the taxes and penalties payable by the person under this Article accordingly. In any action or proceeding for the collection of the inspection tax for kerosene oil or motor fuel and/or any penalties or interest imposed in connection therewith, an assessment by the Secretary of Revenue of the amount of tax due, and/or interest and/or penalties due to the State, shall constitute prima facie evidence of the claim of the State; and the burden of proof shall be upon the person to show that the assessment was incorrect and contrary to law; and the Secretary of Revenue may institute action therefor in the Superior Court of Wake County, regardless of the residence of such person or the place where the default occurred. (1933, c. 544, s. 12; 1973, c. 476, s. 193.)

§ 119-22: Repealed by Session Laws 1995, c. 390, s. 25.

§ 119-23. Administration by Commissioner of Agriculture; collection of fees by Department of Revenue and payment into State treasury; disposition of moneys by State Treasurer.

Gasoline and oil inspection fees or taxes shall be collected by, and reports relating thereto, shall be made to, the Department of Revenue. The administration of the gasoline and oil inspection law shall otherwise be administered by the Commissioner of Agriculture. Except as provided in G.S. 119-26.1(c) and G.S. 119-39.1, all moneys received under the authority of this Article shall be paid into the State treasury and the State Treasurer shall place to the credit of the "State Highway Fund" that proportion of said funds representing inspection fees collected on highway use motor fuels, as certified monthly to the State Treasurer by the Secretary of Revenue, and the remainder of said funds shall be credited to the general fund. (1937, c. 425, s. 6; 1941, c. 36; 1949, c. 1167; 1963, c. 245; 1973, c. 476, s. 193; 1998-215, s. 23(b).)

§ 119-24: Repealed by Session Laws 1991, c. 10, s. 3.

§ 119-25. Inspectors, clerks and assistants.

The Secretary of Revenue and the Commissioner of Agriculture, respectively, shall appoint and employ such number of inspectors, clerks and assistants as may be necessary to administer and effectively enforce all the provisions of the gasoline and oil inspection law with the administration or enforcement of which each said Commissioner [or Secretary] is charged. All inspectors shall be bonded in the sum of one thousand dollars ($1,000) in the usual manner provided for the bonding of State employees, and the expense of such bonding shall be paid from the Gasoline and Oil Inspection Fund created by this Article. Each inspector, before entering upon his duties, shall take an oath of office before some person authorized to administer oaths. Any inspector who, while in office, shall be interested directly or indirectly in the manufacture or vending of any illuminating oils or gasoline or other motor fuels shall be guilty of a Class 1 misdemeanor. (1937, c. 425, s. 8; 1949, c. 1167; 1973, c. 476, s. 193; 1993, c. 539, s. 904; 1994, Ex. Sess., c. 24, s. 14(c).)

§ 119-26. Gasoline and Oil Inspection Board created; composition, appointment of members, etc.; expenses; powers generally; adoption of standards, etc.; sale of products not complying with standards; renaming, etc., of gasoline.

In order to more fully carry out the provisions of this Article there is hereby created a Gasoline and Oil Inspection Board of five members, to be composed of the Commissioner of Agriculture, the Director of the Gasoline and Oil Inspection Division, and three members to be appointed by the Governor, who shall serve at his will. The Commissioner of Agriculture and the Director of the Gasoline and Oil Inspection Division shall serve without additional compensation. Other members of the Board shall each receive the amount provided by G.S. 138-5 for each day he attends a session of the Board and for each day necessarily spent in traveling to and from his place of residence, and he shall receive five cents (5¢) a mile for the distance to and from Raleigh by the usual direct route for each meeting of the Board which he attends. These expenses shall be paid from the Gasoline and Oil Inspection Fund created by this Article. The duly appointed and acting Gasoline and Oil Inspection Board shall have the power, in its discretion, after public notice and provision for the hearing of all interested parties, to adopt standards for kerosene and one or more grades of gasoline based upon scientific tests and ratings for each of the articles for which inspection is provided; to require the labeling of dispensing pumps or other dispensing devices, and to prescribe the forms therefor; to require that the label, name, or brand under which gasoline is thereafter to be sold be applied at the time of its first purchase within the State and to pass all rules and regulations necessary for enforcing the provisions of the laws relating to the transportation and inspection of petroleum products; provided, however, that the action of said Gasoline and Oil Inspection Board shall be subject to the approval of the Governor of the State; and provided further, that if the Gasoline and Oil Inspection Board should promulgate any regulation which requires that gasoline be labeled, named or branded at the time of its first sale in the State, that such regulation shall provide in addition that any subsequent owner may rename, rebrand, or relabel such gasoline if such subsequent owner first files with the Board a notice of intention to do so, said notice to contain information showing the original brand, name, label, the company or person from whom the gasoline has been or is to be purchased, the minimum specifications registered by the seller, the brand, name, or label that is to be given such gasoline and the minimum specifications of such gasoline as filed with the Board; provided, further, that no labeling, naming or branding of gasoline which may be required by the Gasoline and Oil Inspection Board under the provisions of this Article, shall be construed as permitting gasoline to become the subject of fair trade contracts, as provided in G.S. 66-52. After the adoption and publication of said standards it shall be unlawful to sell or offer for sale or exchange or use in this State any products which do not comply with the standards so adopted. The said Gasoline and Oil Inspection Board shall, from time to time after a public hearing, have the right to amend, alter, or change said standards. Three members of said Board shall constitute a quorum. (1937, c. 425, s. 9; 1941, c. 220; 1949, c. 1167; 1961, c. 961; 1969, c. 445, s. 2.)

§ 119-26.1. Content of motor fuels and reformulated gasoline.

(a) Rules adopted pursuant to G.S. 143-215.107(a)(9) to regulate the content of motor fuels or to require the use of reformulated gasoline shall be implemented by the Department of Agriculture and Consumer Services and the Gasoline and Oil Inspection Board. Such rules shall be implemented within any area specified by the Environmental Management Commission when the Commission certifies to the Commissioner of Agriculture that implementation:

(1) Will improve the ambient air quality within the specified county or counties;

(2) Is necessary to achieve attainment or preclude violations of the National Ambient Air Quality Standards; or

(3) Is otherwise necessary to meet federal requirements.

(b) The Department of Agriculture and Consumer Services and the Gasoline and Oil Inspection Board may adopt rules to implement this section. Rules shall be consistent with the implementation schedule and rules adopted by the Environmental Management Commission.

(c) The Commissioner of Agriculture may assess and collect civil penalties for violations of rules adopted under G.S. 143-215.107(a)(9) or this section in accordance with G.S. 143-215.114A. The Commissioner of Agriculture may institute a civil action for injunctive relief to restrain, abate, or prevent a violation or threatened violation of rules adopted under G.S. 143-215.107(a)(9) or this section in accordance with G.S. 143-215.114C. The assessment of a civil penalty under this section and G.S. 143-215.114A or institution of a civil action under G.S. 143-215.114C and this section shall not relieve any person from any other penalty or remedy authorized under this Article.

(c1) The clear proceeds of civil penalties assessed pursuant to this subsection shall be remitted to the Civil Penalty and Forfeiture Fund in accordance with G.S. 115C-457.2.

(d) The Commissioner of Agriculture may delegate his powers and duties under this subsection to the Director of the Standards Division of the Department of Agriculture and Consumer Services. (1991 (Reg. Sess., 1992), c. 889, s. 4; 1997-261, s. 83; 1998-215, s. 23(a); 1999-328, s. 2.3.)

§ 119-26.2: Repealed by Session Laws 2013-265, s. 16, effective July 17, 2013.

§ 119-26.3. MTBE in motor fuels prohibited.

(a) Definitions. - As used in this section:

(1) "Motor fuel" has the same meaning as in G.S. 105-449.60.

(2) "MTBE" means the fuel additive methyl tertiary butyl ether.

(b) Prohibition; De Minimis Exception. - No person shall knowingly add MTBE to any motor fuel manufactured, distributed, stored, sold, or offered for sale in this State. No person shall manufacture, distribute, store, sell, or offer for sale motor fuel that contains a concentration of MTBE of more than one-half of one percent (0.5%) by volume in this State. The presence of MTBE in a motor fuel caused solely by incidental commingling of the motor fuel with other motor fuel that contains MTBE during transfer or storage of the motor fuel does not constitute a violation of this section.

(c) Transportation Through State Not Prohibited. - This section shall not be construed to prohibit the transport of motor fuel containing MTBE through this State.

(d) Rules. - The Gasoline and Oil Inspection Board shall adopt rules to implement this section. (2005-93, s. 1.)

§ 119-27. Display of grade rating on pumps, etc.; sales from pumps or devices not labeled; sale of gasoline not meeting standard indicated on label.

In the event that the Gasoline and Oil Inspection Board shall adopt standards for grades of gasoline, at all times there shall be firmly attached to or painted on each dispensing pump or other dispensing device used in the retailing of gasoline a label stating that the gasoline contained therein is North Carolina _____ grade. Any person, firm, partnership, or corporation who shall offer or expose for sale gasoline from any dispensing pump or other dispensing device which has not been labeled as required by this section, and/or offer and expose for sale any gasoline which does not meet the required standard for the grade indicated on the label attached to the dispensing pump or other dispensing device, shall be guilty of a Class 2 misdemeanor, and the gasoline offered or exposed for sale shall be confiscated.

The gasoline and oil inspectors shall have the authority to immediately seize and seal, to prevent further sales, any dispensing pump or other dispensing device from which gasoline is offered or exposed for sale in violation of or without complying with the provisions of this Article. Provided, however, that this section shall not be construed to permit the destruction of any gasoline which may be blended or rerefined or offered for sale as complying with the legal specifications of a lower grade except under order of the court in which an indictment is brought for violation of the provisions of this Article. Provided, further, that gasoline that has been confiscated and sealed by the gasoline and oil inspectors for violation of the provisions of this Article shall not be offered or exposed for sale until the Director of the Gasoline and Oil Inspection Division has been fully satisfied that the gasoline offered or exposed for sale has been blended or rerefined or properly labeled to meet the requirements of this Article and the owners of said gasoline have been notified in writing of this fact by said Director and, provided, further, that the permitting of blending, rerefining or properly labeling of confiscated gasoline shall not be construed to in any manner affect any indictment which may be brought for violation of this section. (1937, c. 425, s. 11; 1939, c. 276, s. 1; 1941, c. 220; 1993, c. 539, s. 905; 1994, Ex. Sess., c. 24, s. 14(c).)

§ 119-27.1. Self-service gasoline pumps; display of owner's or operator's name, address and telephone number.

(a)     Every owner of, or other person in control of, a self-service gas pump or station whose equipment permits purchase and physical transfer of gasoline or oil products by insertion of money into some device or machine without the necessity of personal service by the owner or his agent shall clearly affix a sticker to each pump showing his name, address, and telephone number.

(b)     The North Carolina Department of Agriculture and Consumer Services shall have the responsibility for the enforcement of this section. (1973, c. 1324, s. 1; 1997-261, s. 84.)

§ 119-27.2. Labels for dispensing pumps and devices offering ethanol-blended gasoline for retail sale.

(a)     The Gasoline and Oil Inspection Board shall adopt rules to require labels for all dispensing pumps and other dispensing devices that offer ethanol-blended gasoline for retail sale in North Carolina. The Board shall require the use of labels to indicate that the gasoline offered for retail sale contains either of the following:

(1)     Ten percent (10%) or less ethanol by volume.

(2)     Greater than ten percent (10%) ethanol by volume.

(b) Rules adopted pursuant to subsection (a) of this section may include information as to the ethanol content of blended gasoline that is more specific than the information required by subsection (a) of this section. (2011-25, s. 1.)

§ 119-28. Regulations for sale of substitutes.

All materials, fluids, or substances offered or exposed for sale, purporting to be substitutes for or motor fuel improvers, shall, before being sold, exposed or offered for sale, be submitted to the Commissioner of Agriculture for examination and inspection, and shall only be sold or offered for sale when properly labeled with a label, the form and contents of which label has been approved by the said Commissioner of Agriculture in writing. (1937, c. 425, s. 12; 1949, c. 1167.)

§ 119-29. Rules and regulations of Board available to interested parties.

It shall be the duty of the Commissioner of Agriculture to make available for all interested parties the rules and regulations adopted by the Gasoline and Oil Inspection Board for the purpose of carrying into effect the laws relating to the inspection and transportation of petroleum products. (1937, c. 425, s. 13; 1949, c. 1167.)

§ 119-30. Establishment of laboratory for analysis of inspected products.

The Commissioner of Agriculture is authorized to provide for the analysis of samples of inspected articles by establishing a laboratory under the Gasoline and Oil Inspection Division for the analysis of inspected products. (1937, c. 425, s. 14; 1949, c. 1167.)

§ 119-31. Payment for samples taken for inspection.

The gasoline and oil inspectors shall pay at the regular market price, at the time the sample is taken, for each sample obtained for inspection purposes when request for payment is made: Provided, however, that no payment shall be made any retailer or distributor unless said retailer or distributor or his agent shall sign a receipt furnished by the Commissioner of Agriculture showing that payment has been made as requested. (1937, c. 425, s. 15; 1949, c. 1167.)

§ 119-32. Powers and authority of inspectors.

The gasoline and oil inspectors shall have the right of access to the premises and records of any place where petroleum products are stored for the purpose of examination, inspection and/or drawing of samples, and said inspectors are hereby vested with the authority and powers of peace and police officers in the enforcement of motor fuel tax and inspection laws throughout the State, including the authority to arrest, with or without warrants, and take offenders before the several courts of the State for prosecution or other proceedings, and seize or hold or deliver to the sheriff of the proper county all motor or other vehicles and all containers used in transporting motor fuels and/or other liquid petroleum products in violation of or without complying with the provisions of this Article or the rules, regulations or requirements of the Commissioner of Agriculture and/or the Gasoline and Oil Inspection Board and also all motor fuels contained therein. Said inspectors shall have power and authority on the public highways or any other place to stop and detain for inspection and investigation any vehicle containing any motor fuel and/or other liquid petroleum products in excess of 100 gallons or commonly used in the transportation of such fuels and the driver or person in charge thereof, and to require the production by such driver or person in charge of all records, documents and papers required by law to be carried and exhibited by persons in charge of vehicles engaged in transporting such fuels; and whenever said inspectors shall find or see any person engaged in handling, selling, using, or transporting any fuels in violation of any of the provisions of the motor fuel tax or inspection laws of this State, or whenever any such person shall fail or refuse to exhibit to said inspectors, upon demand therefor, any records, documents or papers required by law to be kept subject to inspection or to be exhibited by such person, said person shall be guilty of a Class 1 misdemeanor, and it shall be the duty of said inspectors to immediately arrest such violator and take him before some proper peace officer of the county in which the offense was committed and institute proper prosecution. (1937, c. 425, s. 16; 1949, c. 1167; 1993, c. 539, s. 906; 1994, Ex. Sess., c. 24, s. 14(c).)

§ 119-33. Investigation and inspection of measuring equipment; devices calculated to falsify measures.

(a) The gasoline and oil inspectors shall be required to investigate and inspect the equipment for measuring gasoline, kerosene, lubricating oil, and other liquid petroleum products. The inspectors shall be under the supervision of the Commissioner of Agriculture, and are hereby vested with the same power and authority now given by law to inspectors of weights and measures, in order to effectuate the provisions of this Article. The rules, regulations, specifications and tolerance limits as promulgated by the National Conference on Weights and Measures, and recommended by the National Institute of Standards and Technology, shall be observed by said inspectors insofar as they apply to the inspection of equipment used in measuring gasoline, kerosene, lubricating oil and other petroleum products. Inspectors of weights and measures appointed and maintained by the various counties and cities of the State shall have the same power and authority given by this section to inspectors under the supervision of the Commissioner of Agriculture. In all cases where it is found, after inspection, that the measuring equipment used in connection with the distribution of such products is inaccurate, the inspector shall condemn and seize all incorrect devices which in his best judgment cannot be satisfactorily repaired, but measuring equipment, that in the judgment of the inspector may be repaired, shall be marked or tagged as "condemned for repairs" in a manner prescribed by the Commissioner of Agriculture. After notice in writing the owners or users of such measuring devices which have been condemned for repairs shall have the devices repaired and corrected within 10 days by a registered petroleum device technician, and neither the owners nor the users of the devices shall use or dispose of the measuring devices in any manner, but shall hold the devices at the disposal of the gasoline and oil inspector. The inspector shall confiscate and destroy all measuring devices which have been condemned for repairs and have not been repaired as required by this Article. The gasoline and oil inspectors shall officially seal all dispensing pumps or other dispensing devices found to be accurate on inspection. The finding, upon inspection at a later date, that any pump is inaccurate and the seal broken, shall constitute prima facie evidence of intent to defraud by giving inaccurate measure, and (i) the owner, (ii) the user, or (iii) both of them shall be guilty of a Class 2 misdemeanor. Any person other than a registered petroleum device technician who removes or breaks any seal placed upon a measuring or dispensing device by any oil and gas inspector until the provisions of this section have been complied with shall be guilty of a Class 2 misdemeanor. Any person, firm, or corporation who sells or has in his possession for the purpose of selling or using any measuring device to be used or calculated to be used to falsify any measure shall be guilty of a Class 1 misdemeanor.

(b) The Gasoline and Oil Inspection Board may adopt rules to provide for the registration of petroleum device technicians. The rules may establish qualifications for registration and may also establish grounds for the suspension or revocation of registration. The annual fee for registration of a petroleum device technician shall be twenty dollars ($20.00). (1937, c. 425, s. 17; 1949, c. 1167; 1993, c. 539, s. 907; 1994, Ex. Sess., c. 24, s. 14(c); 2013-344, s. 1.)

§ 119-34. Responsibility of retailers for quality of products.

The retail dealer shall be held responsible for the quality of the petroleum products he sells or offers for sale: Provided, however, that the retail dealer shall be released if the results of analysis of a sealed sample taken in a manner prescribed by the Commissioner of Agriculture at the time of delivery, and in the presence of the distributor or his agent, show that the product delivered by the distributor was of inferior quality. It shall be the duty of the distributor or his agent to assist in sampling the product delivered. (1937, c. 425, s. 18; 1949, c. 1167.)

§ 119-35. Adulteration of products offered for sale.

It shall be unlawful for any person, firm, or corporation who has purchased gasoline or other liquid motor fuel upon which a road tax has been paid to in anywise adulterate the same by the addition thereto of kerosene or any other liquid substance and sell or offer for sale the same. Any person violating the provisions of this section shall be guilty of a Class 1 misdemeanor. (1937, c. 425, s. 19; 1993, c. 539, s. 908; 1994, Ex. Sess., c. 24, s. 14(c).)

§ 119-36. Certified copies of official tests admissible in evidence.

A certified copy of the official test of the analysis of any petroleum product, under the seal of the Commissioner of Agriculture, shall be admissible as evidence of the fact therein stated in any of the courts of this State on the trial of any issue involving the qualities of said product. (1937, c. 425, s. 20; 1949, c. 1167.)

§ 119-37. Retail dealers required to keep copies of invoices and delivery tickets.

Every person, firm, or corporation engaged in the retail business of dispensing gasoline and/or other petroleum products to the public shall keep on the premises of said place of business, for a period of one year, duplicate original copies of invoices or delivery tickets of each delivery received, showing the name and address of the party to whom delivery is made, the date of delivery, the kind and amount of each delivery received, and the name and address of the distributor. Each delivery ticket or invoice shall be signed by the retailer or his agent and the distributor or his agent. Such records shall be subject to inspection at any time by the gasoline and oil inspectors. (1937, c. 425, s. 21.)

§ 119-38. Prosecution of offenders.

All prosecutions for fines and penalties under the provisions of this Article shall be by indictment in a court of competent jurisdiction in the county in which the violation occurred. (1937, c. 425, s. 22.)

§ 119-39. Violation a misdemeanor.

Unless another penalty is provided in this Article, any person violating any of the provisions of this Article or any of the rules and regulations of the Secretary of Revenue or the Commissioner of Agriculture and/or the Gasoline and Oil Inspection Board shall be guilty of a Class 1 misdemeanor. (1937, c. 425, s. 23; 1949, c. 1167; 1973, c. 476, s. 193; 1993, c. 539, s. 909; 1994, Ex. Sess., c. 24, s. 14(c).)

§ 119-39.1. Civil Penalties.

The Commissioner of Agriculture may assess a civil penalty of not more than five thousand dollars ($5,000) against any person who violates a provision of this Article or any rule promulgated thereunder. In determining the amount of the penalty, the Commissioner shall consider the degree and extent of harm caused by the violation.

The clear proceeds of civil penalties assessed pursuant to this section shall be remitted to the Civil Penalty and Forfeiture Fund in accordance with G.S. 115C-457.2. (1995, c. 516, s. 4; 1998-215, s. 24.)

§§ 119-40 through 119-41: Repealed by Session Laws 1995 (Regular Session, 1996), c. 647, s. 56.

§ 119-42. Persons engaged in transporting required to have in possession an invoice, bill of sale or bill of lading.

Every person hauling, transporting or conveying into, out of, or between points in this State any motor fuel and/or any liquid petroleum product that is or may hereafter be made subject to the inspection laws of this State over either the public highways or waterways of this State, shall, during the entire time he is so engaged, have in his possession an invoice, or bill of sale, or bill of lading showing the true name and address of the person from whom he has received the motor fuel and/or other liquid petroleum products, the kind, and the number of gallons so originally received by him, and the true name and address of every person to whom he has made deliveries of said motor fuel and/or other liquid petroleum products or any part thereof and the number of gallons so delivered to each said person. Such person engaged in transporting said motor fuels and/or other petroleum products shall, at the request of any agent of the Commissioner of Agriculture, exhibit for inspection such papers or documents immediately, and if said person fails to produce said papers or documents or if, when produced, they fail to clearly disclose said information, the agent of the Commissioner of Agriculture shall hold for investigation the vehicle and contents thereof. If investigation shows that said motor fuels and/or other petroleum products are being transported in violation of or without compliance with the motor fuel tax and/or inspection laws of this State such fuels and/or other petroleum products and the vehicle used in the transportation thereof are hereby declared common nuisances and contraband, and shall be seized and sold and the proceeds shall go to the common school fund of the State: Provided, however, that this Article shall not be construed to include the carrying of motor fuel in the supply tank of vehicles which is regularly connected with the carburetor of the engine of the vehicle, except when said fuel supply tank shall have a capacity of more than 100 gallons: And, provided further, that this section shall not be construed to include the carrying of motor fuel in the supply tank which is regularly connected with the carburetor of the engine of any vehicle operated by franchise carriers engaged solely in the transportation of passengers to, from and between points in North Carolina. (1937, c. 425, s. 25; 1939, c. 276, s. 3; 1949, c. 1167.)


§119-43. Display required on containers used in making deliveries.

Every person delivering at wholesale or retail any gasoline in this State shall deliver the same to the purchaser only in tanks, barrels, casks, cans, or other containers having the word "Gasoline" or the name of such other like products of petroleum, as the case may be, in English, plainly stenciled or labeled in colors to meet the requirements of the regulations adopted by the Commissioner of Agriculture and/or the Gasoline and Oil Inspection Board. Such dealers shall not deliver kerosene oil in any barrel, cask, can, or other container which has not been stenciled or labeled as hereinbefore provided. Every person purchasing gasoline for use or sale shall procure and keep the same only in tanks, barrels, casks, cans, or other containers stenciled or labeled as hereinbefore provided: Provided, that nothing in this section shall prohibit the delivery of gasoline by hose or pipe from a tank directly into the tank of any automobile or any other motor vehicle: Provided further, that in case gasoline or other inflammable liquid is sold in bottles, cans, or packages of not more than one gallon for cleaning and other similar purposes, the label shall also bear the words "Unsafe when exposed to heat or fire." (1937, c. 425, s. 26; 1939, c. 276, s. 4; 1949, c. 1167.)


§ 119-44: Repealed by Session Laws 1995 (Regular Session, 1996), c. 647, s. 56.


§ 119-45. Certain laws adopted as part of Article.

General Statutes 119-1 through 119-5 and G.S. 119-7 through 119-13 are hereby made a part of this Article. (1937, c. 425, s. 28.)


§ 119-46. Charges for analysis of samples.

The Secretary of Revenue is hereby authorized to fix and collect such charges as he may deem adequate and reasonable for any analysis made by the Gasoline and Oil Inspection Division of any sample submitted by any person, firm, association or corporation other than samples submitted by the gasoline and oil inspectors in the performance of the duties required of said inspectors under this Article: Provided, however, that no charge shall be made for the analysis of any sample submitted by any municipal, county, State or federal official when the results of such analyses are necessary for the performance of his official duties. All moneys collected for such analyses shall be paid into the State treasury to the credit of the Gasoline and Oil Inspection Fund. (1937, c. 425, s. 29; 1973, c. 476, s. 193.)


§ 119-47. Inspection of fuels used by State.

The Gasoline and Oil Inspection Division is hereby authorized, upon request of the proper State authority, to inspect, analyze, and report the result of such analysis of all fuels purchased by the State of North Carolina for the use of all departments and institutions. (1937, c. 153.)
Article 4.

Liquefied Petroleum Gases.

§§ 119-48 through 119-53. Recodified as §§ 119-54 to 119-59.


Article 5.

Liquefied Petroleum Gases.

§ 119-54. Purpose; definitions; scope of Article.

(a)It is the purpose of this Article to provide for the adoption and promulgation of a code of safety, and such rules and regulations setting forth minimum general standards of safety for the design, construction, location, installation, and operation of the equipment used in handling, storing, measuring, transporting, distributing, and utilizing liquefied petroleum gases and to provide for the administration and enforcement of the code and such rules and regulations thereby adopted. Words used in this Article shall be defined as follows:

(1)     "Board" means the North Carolina Board of Agriculture.

(2)     "Commissioner" means the Commissioner of Agriculture or his designated agent.

(3)     "Dealer" means any person, firm, or corporation who is engaged in or desires to engage in:

a.      The business of selling or otherwise dealing in liquefied petroleum gases which require handling, storing, measuring, transporting, or distributing liquefied petroleum gas; or

b.      The business of installing, servicing, repairing, adjusting, connecting, or disconnecting containers, equipment, or appliances which use liquefied gas. A person who engages in any of the aforementioned activities only in connection with his or his employer's use of liquefied petroleum gas and not as a business shall not be deemed to be a "dealer" for the purposes of this Article.

(4)     "Liquefied petroleum gas" means any material which is composed predominantly of any of the following hydrocarbons, or mixtures of the same: propane, propylene, butanes (normal butanes or isobutane), butylenes.

(b)     This Article does not apply to the design, construction, location, installation, or operation of equipment or facilities covered by the Building Code pursuant to Article 9 of Chapter 143 of the General Statutes. (1955, c. 487; 1959, c. 796, s. 1; 1961, c. 1072; 1981, c. 486, s. 1; 1989, c. 25, s. 1.)


§ 119-55. Power of Board of Agriculture to set minimum standards; regulation by political subdivisions.

The Board shall have the power and authority to set minimum standards and promulgate rules and regulations for the design, construction, location, installation, and operation of equipment and facilities used in handling, storing, measuring, transporting, distributing, and utilizing liquefied petroleum gas.

Any municipality or political subdivision may adopt and enforce a safety code dealing with the handling of liquefied petroleum gas which conforms with the regulations adopted by the Board, and the inspection service rendered by such municipality or political subdivision shall conform to the requirements of the inspection service rendered by the Board in the enforcement of this Article. (1955, c. 487; 1959, c. 796, s. 2; 1961, c. 1072; 1963, c. 671; 1967, c. 1231; 1969, c. 1133; 1975, c. 610, s. 1; 1977, c. 410; 1981, c. 486, s. 1.)

§ 119-56. Registration of dealers; liability insurance or substitute required.

A person shall not hold himself out or commence operation as a dealer without first having registered as provided in this section. A dealer shall register with the Commissioner on a form to be furnished by the Commissioner. Such form shall give the name and address of the dealer, the place or places of and type or types of business of such dealer, and such other pertinent information as the Commissioner may deem necessary. Verification of the insurance coverage required by this section or of proof of alternative means of financial responsibility permitted by this section shall be submitted to the Commissioner as a condition of the issuance of any registration or renewal of such registration.

There shall be two classes of dealers:

(1)     A Class A dealer is one who engages in the transportation of liquefied petroleum gas.

(2)     A Class B dealer is one who does not engage in the transportation of liquefied petroleum gas.

A Class A dealer shall obtain and maintain general liability insurance, including product liability, of one million dollars ($1,000,000) and motor vehicle liability insurance of one million dollars ($1,000,000) combined single limit. A Class B dealer shall obtain and maintain general liability insurance, including product liability, of one hundred thousand dollars ($100,000). Verification of said insurance coverage shall be made in a manner satisfactory to the Commissioner. The Commissioner may from time to time request in writing that a dealer provide within 10 days of such request verification of said insurance coverage or proof of alternative means of financial responsibility. In lieu of insurance, the dealer may file and maintain a bond, certificate of deposit or irrevocable letter of credit in a form satisfactory to the Commissioner which provides protection for the public in the same amounts and to the same extent as said insurance.

The provisions of this section shall not apply to a dealer who retails liquefied petroleum gas in containers of less than 50 pounds water capacity and which retailing does not involve the filling or transportation of such containers. (1955, c. 487; 1961, c. 1072; 1981, c. 486, s. 1; 1987, c. 453; 2009-386, s. 1.)

§ 119-57. Administration of Article; rules and regulations given force and effect of law.

It shall be the duty of the Commissioner to administer all the provisions of this Article and all the rules and regulations made and promulgated under this Article; to conduct inspections of liquefied petroleum gas containers and installations; to investigate for violations of this Article and the rules and regulations adopted pursuant to the provisions thereof, and to prosecute violations of this Article or of such rules and regulations adopted pursuant to the provisions thereof. (1955, c. 487; 1961, c. 1072; 1981, c. 486, s. 1; 2009-386, s. 2.)

§ 119-58. Unlawful acts.

(a)     It shall be an unlawful act for any person to:

(1)     Sell any liquefied petroleum gas burning appliance designed or built for domestic use that has not been approved by the American Gas Association, Inc., the Underwriters Laboratory, Inc., or other laboratory approved by the Building Code Council.

(2)     Repealed by Session Laws 1999-344, s. 1, effective July 22, 1999, and applicable to liquefied petroleum gas burning appliances installed on and after that date.

(3)     Repealed by Session Laws 1999-344, s. 1, effective July 22, 1999, and applicable to liquefied petroleum gas burning appliances installed on and after that date.

(4)     Fill a consumer tank or container in excess of 85 percent (85%) of its water capacity, or to fill a tank or container on the premises of a consumer that is not equipped with a fill tube or gauge; provided, the tank or container may be filled by weight if the tank or container is weighed before and after filling.

(5) Disconnect an appliance from a gas supply line without capping or plugging the line before leaving the premises.

(6) Turn on the gas after reestablishing an interrupted service without first having checked and closed all gas outlets.

(7) Violate any provisions of this Article or any rules adopted pursuant to this Article.

(b) Every supply tank or container with its regulating equipment connected in a service system, shall be identified while in service by the supplier with an attached tag, label, or other marking that includes the name of the person supplying liquefied petroleum gas to the system, and it shall be unlawful for any person, other than the supplier or the owner of the system, to disconnect, interrupt or fill the system with liquefied petroleum gas without the consent of the supplier. If another registered supplier is requested by the consumer to connect service and is given permission by the consumer to do so, the new supplier shall notify the former supplier before disconnecting the former service and connecting the new service and shall cap or plug all disconnected equipment outlets and leave the equipment in a condition consistent with this Article and the rules adopted pursuant to this Article. (1955, c. 487; 1959, c. 796, s. 3; 1961, c. 1072; 1981, c. 486, s. 1; 1987, c. 282, s. 17; 1999-344, s. 1.)


§ 119-59. Sanctions for violations.

(a) Criminal. - A dealer who violates a provision of this Article or a rule adopted under it is guilty of a Class 1 misdemeanor.

(b) Injunction. - The Commissioner or an agent of the Commissioner may apply to any superior court judge and the court may temporarily restrain or preliminarily or permanently enjoin any violation of this Article or a rule adopted under it.

(c) Civil Penalty. - The Commissioner may assess a civil penalty against any person who violates a provision of this Article or a rule adopted under it. The penalty may not exceed three hundred dollars ($300.00) for the first violation, five hundred dollars ($500.00) for a second violation, and one thousand dollars ($1,000) for a third or subsequent violation. In determining the amount of a penalty, the Commissioner shall consider the degree and extent of harm or potential harm that has resulted or could have resulted from the violation. The clear proceeds of civil penalties assessed pursuant to this subsection shall be remitted to the Civil Penalty and Forfeiture Fund in accordance with G.S. 115C-457.2.

(d) Registration. - The Commissioner may deny, suspend, or revoke the registration of a dealer who violates a provision of this Article or a rule adopted under it. (1955, c. 487; 1961, c. 1072; 1981, c. 486, s. 1; 1993, c. 356, s. 2; c. 539, s. 911; 1994, Ex. Sess., c. 24, s. 14(c); 1998-215, s. 25; 2009-386, s. 3.)

§ 119-60. Liquefied petroleum gas accidents; liability limitations.

Any person who provides assistance upon request of any police agency, fire department, rescue or emergency squad, or any governmental agency in the event of an accident or other emergency involving the use, handling, transportation, transmission or storage of liquefied petroleum gas, when the reasonably apparent circumstances require prompt decisions and actions, shall not be liable for any civil damages resulting from any act of commission or omission on his part in the course of his rendering such assistance unless such acts or omissions amount to willful or wanton negligence or intentional wrongdoing. Nothing in this section shall be deemed or construed to relieve any person from liability for civil damages (a) where the accident or emergency referred to above involved his own facilities or equipment or (b) resulting from any act of commission or omission on his part in the course of providing care or assistance in the normal and ordinary course of conducting his own business or profession, nor shall this section be construed to relieve from liability for civil damages any other tortfeasor not referred to herein. When the assistance takes the form of rendering first aid or emergency health care treatment, questions of liability shall be governed by G.S. 90-21.14. (1981, c. 660.)

§ 119-61. Replacement data plates for liquefied petroleum gas tanks.

A liquefied petroleum gas tank of 120 gallons or more that is subject to the American Society of Mechanical Engineers (ASME) Code must have a data plate indicating that it was built in accordance with that Code. The Commissioner may issue a data plate to replace a rusting or partially detached data plate on a liquefied petroleum gas tank. The Commissioner shall charge a person to whom a replacement data plate is issued a fee of twenty dollars ($20.00) for the plate. Fees collected under this section shall be credited to the Department of Agriculture and Consumer Services and applied to the cost of issuing replacement data plates. (1993, c. 356, s. 1; 1997-261, s. 109; 2009-386, s. 4.)

§ 119-62. Liquefied petroleum gas dealers and their employees, agents, subcontractors; liability limitations.

(a)     A dealer shall not be liable for any civil damages resulting from any act or failure to act if the alleged injury, damage, or loss claimed in the action was caused by any one or more of the following:

(1)     The installation, alteration, modification, or repair of liquefied petroleum gas equipment or a liquefied petroleum gas appliance by a person, other than the dealer, and the installation, alteration, modification, or repair was done without the knowledge and consent of the dealer.

(2)     The use of liquefied petroleum gas equipment or a liquefied petroleum gas appliance by a person, other than the dealer, in a manner or for a purpose other than that for which the equipment or appliance was intended, and the use of the equipment or appliance in a manner or for a purpose other than that for which the equipment or appliance was intended took place without the knowledge and consent of the dealer.

(3)     The installation of liquefied petroleum gas equipment or a liquefied petroleum gas appliance by a person, other than the dealer, in a manner not in accordance with the instructions of the manufacturer of the equipment or appliance or in a manner not in accordance with rules adopted under this Article, and the installation of the equipment or appliance in a manner not in accordance with the instructions of the manufacturer of the equipment or appliance or in a manner not in accordance with rules adopted under this Article took place without the knowledge and consent of the dealer.

(b)     Nothing in this section alters a dealer's duty to exercise reasonable care.

(c)     As used in this section, "dealer" means dealer as defined in G.S. 119-54 and any employee, agent, and subcontractor of the dealer. (2007-302, s. 1.)

§ 119-63. Reserved for future codification purposes.

Article 5A.

Propane Assessment Act.

§ 119-63.1. Title.

This Article shall be known as the "Propane Assessment Act." (2013-299, s. 1.)

§ 119-63.2. Purpose.

It is in the public interest for the State to enable dealers and distributors of propane to assess the product in order to raise funds for the purposes of promoting the common good, welfare, and advancement of the propane industry. (2013-299, s. 1.)

§ 119-63.3. Definitions.

The following definitions apply in this Article:

(1) Association. - The North Carolina Propane Gas Association, Inc., a North Carolina nonprofit corporation.

(2) Commissioner. - The Commissioner of Agriculture or his or her designee.

(3) Dealer. - Any person who is registered with the Commissioner pursuant to G.S. 119-56 to engage in:

a. The business of selling or otherwise dealing in liquefied petroleum gases requiring handling, storing, measuring, transporting, or distributing liquefied petroleum gas; or

b. The business of installing, servicing, repairing, adjusting, connecting or disconnecting containers, equipment, or appliances using liquefied gas. A person who engages in any of the aforementioned activities only in connection with his or her employer's use of liquefied petroleum gas and not as a business shall not be deemed to be a "dealer" for the purposes of this Article.

Any person who retails liquefied petroleum gas in containers of less than 50 pounds water capacity and whose retail business does not involve the filling or transportation of such containers is not a "dealer" for purposes of this Article.

(4)     Department. - The North Carolina Department of Agriculture and Consumer Services.

(5)     Distributor. - A person whose primary business involves the sale of liquefied petroleum gas to a dealer.

(6)     Foundation. - North Carolina Propane Education & Research Foundation, a North Carolina nonprofit corporation that is tax exempt under section 501(c)(3) of the Internal Revenue Code.

(7)     Liquefied petroleum gas. - Any material which is composed predominantly of any of the following hydrocarbons or mixtures of the same: propane, propylene, butanes (normal butanes or isobutane), and butylenes.

(8)     Person. - An individual, a partnership, a firm, or a corporation.

(9)     Propane. - A liquefied petroleum gas.  (2013-299, s. 1.)


§ 119-63.4.  Referendum.

(a)     The Foundation may from time to time conduct referenda among dealers and distributors in this State upon the question of whether an assessment shall be levied on propane sold in this State.

(b)     The Foundation, upon prior consultation with the Association, shall determine:

(1)     The amount of the proposed assessment.

(2)     The time and place of the referendum.

(3)     Procedures for conducting the referendum and counting of votes.

(4) The proposed effective date for the imposition of the assessment, which shall not be less than 180 days from the date the referendum ballot is required to be returned to the Foundation in order to be considered on the question presented.

(5) Any other matters pertaining to the referendum.

(c) The amount of the proposed assessment shall be stated on the referendum ballot. The amount may not exceed the maximum allowable rate of two-tenths of one cent ($.002) for each gallon of propane sold in this State by distributors to dealers.

(d) All dealers and distributors may vote in the referendum. Each distributor and each dealer shall have one vote regardless of the number of bulk plants or retail sales outlets owned. Any dispute over eligibility to vote or any other matter relating to the referendum shall be resolved by the Foundation. The Foundation shall make reasonable efforts to provide all dealers and distributors with notice of the referendum and an opportunity to vote.

(e) Prior to conducting any referenda, the Foundation shall request a list of dealers and their addresses from the Department, and the Department shall provide such information to the Foundation. In order to be eligible to vote, a distributor shall provide the Foundation with a written statement signed by an authorized individual containing its corporate name, address, and the individual authorized to cast a ballot on its behalf, which statement shall be effective until revoked or modified in like manner.

(f) A proposed assessment shall become effective if more than fifty percent (50%) of the eligible votes cast by dealers in the referendum are cast in favor of the assessment and if more than fifty percent (50%) of the eligible votes cast by distributors in the referendum are cast in favor of the assessment. If the assessment is approved by the referendum, then the Foundation shall notify the Department and the Association of the amount of the assessment and the effective date of the assessment. The Department shall notify all distributors and dealers of the assessment. (2013-299, s. 1.)

§ 119-63.5. Payment and collection of assessment; refunds.

(a) Each distributor, as the owner of propane at the time of odorization, or at the time of import of odorized propane, shall make the assessment based on the volume of odorized propane sold and placed into commerce in this State. Each dealer must pay the assessment on each gallon of propane purchased from a distributor. The assessment charge shall be identified and listed as a separate line item on each distributor's invoice to a dealer for the sale of odorized propane.

(b) Each distributor shall collect the assessment from the dealer to whom the sale is made. Each distributor shall remit to the Foundation the sum of the amount of the assessment multiplied by the number of gallons of propane sold to any dealer during the preceding quarter not later than the 25th day of the month following the end of the prior quarter. The Foundation shall provide forms to the distributors for reporting the assessment. Each distributor shall file the report not later than the 25th day of the month following the end of the prior quarter regardless of the amount due.

(c) A distributor shall keep records of the number of gallons of propane sold to dealers, including number of gallons, name of dealer, and rate of assessment. All documents or records regarding purchases and sales that are made or kept as required by this subsection or subsection (d) of this section shall be made available to the Foundation upon its written request from time to time for the purpose of determining the distributor's compliance with the provisions of this Article. The Foundation shall keep the records confidential and shall not disclose the records except to its accountants, attorneys, or financial advisors without a court order directing it to do so.

(d) The Foundation may bring an action to recover any unpaid assessments plus the reasonable costs, including attorneys' fees, incurred in the action and may use assessment funds to cover all reasonable costs and expenses incurred in connection with recovery of any unpaid assessment.

(e) A dealer may request a refund of the assessment collected from the dealer in the prior month by submitting a written request for a refund to the Foundation no later than 30 days after the end of the month for which the refund is requested. The refund request shall state specifically the period of time for which a refund is requested, the amount of the refund, the distributors to whom the dealer paid assessments, and the amount of each assessment paid and shall be accompanied by proof of payment of the assessment satisfactory to the Foundation. The Foundation shall mail a refund to the dealer within 30 days of receipt of a properly documented refund request, provided that the Foundation shall have no obligation to make a refund to a dealer of assessments that are not yet paid to the Foundation by the distributor. Any dealer who requests and is paid a refund in accordance with this subsection shall not be eligible to receive the benefit of any consumer rebate programs for a period of one year following the date of a refund request under this subsection and shall not be entitled to the payment of any interest by the Foundation on the amount refunded. (2013-299, s. 1.)

§ 119-63.6. Use of assessments; reporting.

(a) The Foundation shall use the funds to promote the common good, welfare, and advancement of the propane industry, including, but not limited to, the following activities and programs: education, training, safety compliance, equipment replacement for low-income customers, marketing, advertising, promotion, and customer rebates to encourage energy-efficient appliance and equipment purchases by residential, commercial, or agricultural consumers. The Foundation shall consult with the Association regarding its proposed use of the funds. In addition, the Foundation shall consult with agricultural industry trade associations and other organizations representing agricultural consumers of propane to ensure that some programs and activities benefit the agriculture industry.

(b) No funds collected pursuant to this Article shall be used in any manner for influencing State or federal legislation or for lobbying.

(c) No more than ten percent (10%) of the funds collected pursuant to this Article shall be used by the Foundation for administrative expenses relating to the expenditure of the funds. The Foundation may advance costs of conducting referenda pursuant to this Article and reimburse those costs from the assessment funds. Costs of conducting referenda, litigation expenses incurred in connection with actions authorized by G.S. 119-63.5, and the cost of the audit required by subsection (e) of this section are not administrative expenses.

(d) All funds received by the Foundation pursuant to this Article shall be kept in separate accounts from other Foundation funds. The Foundation shall keep minutes, books, and records that clearly reflect all of the acts and transactions of the Foundation with respect to use and expenditure of the funds. The Foundation shall submit a written report annually, not later than March 31 of each year, to the Commissioner on the use and expenditure of the funds received pursuant to this Article.

(e) The books and records of the Foundation shall be audited by a certified public accountant each fiscal year with respect to the receipt and use of the funds. Copies of such audit shall be provided to the Commissioner, to the Association, and to any other interested party upon written request. The Foundation may pay for the audit from the assessment funds. (2013-299, s. 1.)

§ 119-63.7. Termination of assessment.

(a) Upon the Commissioner's receipt of a petition signed by at least ten percent (10%) of the dealers requesting a referendum pursuant to this section, or a receipt of a petition signed by at least fifty percent (50%) of the distributors requesting a referendum pursuant to this section, the Department shall notify the Foundation, and the Foundation shall, within six months, conduct a referendum upon the question of continuing the assessment. If a majority of the votes eligible to be cast by dealers in the referendum are cast against continuing the assessment then in effect and a majority of the votes eligible to be cast by distributors in the referendum are cast against continuing the assessment then in effect, or if the Foundation fails to conduct a referendum within the six-month period, the assessment expires at the end of the year that follows the year in which the Commissioner received a petition pursuant to this section. If more than two-thirds of the eligible votes cast by dealers and more than two-thirds of the eligible votes cast by distributors in the referendum conducted pursuant to this section are in favor of continuing the assessment, then no subsequent referendum shall be required to be conducted pursuant to this section for a period of at least three years from the date the petition was received by the Commissioner.

(b) The Foundation may, on its own initiative, conduct a referendum at any time upon the question of continuing the assessment. If a majority of the votes eligible to be cast by dealers in the referendum are cast against continuing the assessment and if a majority of the votes eligible to be cast by distributors in the referendum are cast against continuing the assessment, the assessment then in effect expires at the end of the year that follows the year in which the referendum was conducted.

(c) The Foundation shall certify to the Department the election results of any referendum conducted pursuant to this Article and shall provide the Department, upon written request, with any documents, papers, tallies, or other information related to the conduct of any referendum conducted by the Foundation. (2013-299, s. 1.)

§ 119-63.8. Association activities deemed not in restraint of trade; pricing.

(a) No meeting or activity undertaken by the Association or the Foundation in pursuance of the provisions of this Article shall be considered illegal under antitrust law or a restraint of trade.

(b) In all cases, the price of propane shall be determined by market forces. Neither the Foundation nor the Association may take any action nor shall any provision of this Article be interpreted as establishing an agreement to pass along to consumers the cost of any assessment provided for by this Article. (2013-299, s. 1.)

§ 119-64: Reserved for future codification purposes.


Article 6.

Contract Rights Regarding Tax Reimbursement.

§ 119-65. Timing of reimbursement payments under contract.

(a) Right. - When a contract calls for one party to reimburse a second party for the federal manufacturer's excise taxes levied on petroleum products in Part III of Subchapter A of Chapter 32 of the Internal Revenue Code, whether as a separate item or as part of the price, the party making the reimbursement has the right to choose to tender payment for the taxes no more than one business day before the day the second party is required to remit the taxes to the federal Internal Revenue Service. The party making the reimbursement has the option of exercising this right. Exercise of this right does not relieve the party of the obligation to make the reimbursement as provided for in the contract, but affects only the timing of when that reimbursement must be tendered.

(b) Procedure. - In order to exercise the contractual right established in subsection (a) of this section, the party making the reimbursement must notify the second party in writing of the intent to exercise the payment option and the effective date of the exercise. The effective date must be no earlier than the beginning of the next federal tax quarter or 30 days after the notice of intent is received, whichever is later.

(c) Security. - If the party making the reimbursement exercises the contractual right provided in this section, the second party may require security for the payment of the taxes in proportion to the amount the taxes represent compared to the security required on the contract as a whole. The second party may not, however, change the other payment terms of the contract without a valid business reason other than the exercise of the contractual right, except to require the payment of the taxes under the contractual right to be made by electronic funds transfer. (2002-108, s. 1.)

# Vision Books Order Form

| | |
|---|---|
| Fax Orders: | 1-980-299-5965 |
| Phone Orders: | 1-704-898-0770 |
| E-mail Orders: | www.visionbooks.org |
| Mail Orders: | Vision Books, LLC<br>P.O. Box 42406<br>Charlotte, NC 28215 |

**Shipp To:**
Name_____
Address_____
City_____State_____Zip_____
Phone_____Fax_____
Email_____@_____

**Bill To:** We can bill a third party on your behalf.
Name_____
Address_____
City_____State_____Zip_____
Phone___(_____)_____Fax_____
Email_____@_____

| Pamphlet Number ($15.00 Each) | Qty | Total Cost |
|---|---|---|
| _____ | _____ | _____ |
| _____ | _____ | _____ |
| _____ | _____ | _____ |
| _____ | _____ | _____ |
| _____ | _____ | _____ |
| _____ | _____ | _____ |
| _____ | _____ | _____ |
| <u>Full Volume Set 1-92</u> | <u>92 Pamphlets</u> | <u>1,380.00</u> |

Free Shipping Shipping & Handling on Full Volume Orders
Add $1.00 Shipping & Handling per pamphlet          $_____

Total Cost                                           $_____

Thank you for your order. Management!

DID YOU ENJOY THIS BOOK?

Vision Books, LLC would like to hear from you! If you or someone you know has been fasely imprisoned, we would like to hear your story. If the 'North Carolina Criminal Law and Procedure' has had an effect in your life or if you have suggestions, we would like to hear from you. Send your letters to:

Vision Books, LLC
Attn: Staff Writers
P.O. Box 42406
Charlotte, NC 28215
Email: staff@visionbooks.org

Order Additional Copies:

| | |
|---|---|
| Fax Orders: | 1-980-299-5965 |
| Phone Orders: | 1-704-898-0770 |
| E-mail Orders: | www.visionbooks.org |
| Mail Orders: | Vision Books, LLC<br>P.O. Box 42406<br>Charlotte, NC 28215 |

www.ingramcontent.com/pod-product-compliance
Lightning Source LLC
Chambersburg PA
CBHW051631170526
45167CB00001B/150